Jerusalem Past and Present
in the Purposes of God

Other Tyndale House Studies *available*

ONE GOD, ONE LORD:
Christianity in a World of Religious Pluralism
 edited by Andrew D. Clarke and Bruce W. Winter

HE SWORE AN OATH:
Biblical Themes from Genesis 12–50
 *edited by Richard S. Hess, Gordon J. Wenham,
 and Philip E. Satterthwaite*

Jerusalem Past and Present in the Purposes of God

Second Edition

Edited by

Peter W. L. Walker

THE PATERNOSTER PRESS
Carlisle UK

Copyright © 1994 by Deo Gloria Trust, Croydon

First edition published 1992

This second edition published 1994 jointly
by The Paternoster Press, P.O. Box 300, Carlisle,
Cumbria CA3 0QS, U.K., and Baker Book House,
Box 6287, Grand Rapids, MI 49516–6287, U.S.A.

*All Rights Reserved. No part of this publication may be
reproduced, stored in a retrieval system, or transmitted,
in any form or by any means, electronic, mechanical,
photocopying, recording or otherwise, without the prior
permission of the publisher or a licence permitting
restricted copying.*

British Library Cataloguing in Publication Data

Jerusalem Past and Present in the
Purposes of God. – 2Rev.ed. – (Tyndale
House Studies)
I. Walker, P. W. L. II. Series
263.042569442
ISBN 0–85364–616–3

Library of Congress Cataloging-in-Publication Data

Jerusalem: past and present in the purposes of God / edited by P.W.L.
Walker
    p.   cm.
Includes bibliographical references and indexes.
ISBN 0–8010–9735–5
1. Jerusalem in the Bible. 2. Jerusalem in Judaism. 3. Jerusalem
in Christianity. 4. Jerusalem in Islam. 5. Zionism. 6. Jewish
–Arab relations—1917–   I. Walker, P. W. L. (Peter W. L.)
Bs680.J37J47   1994
263'.042569442—dc20   94–13598
                                                                 CIP

Typeset by Tyndale House, Cambridge
and Printed by
The Guernsey Press Co. Ltd., Guernsey, Channel Islands
for the publishers

FOREWORD

Rt Revd Kenneth Cragg
(formerly Assistant Anglican Bishop in Jerusalem)

What can a Foreword say when 'Jerusalem' is what follows? What foreword does Jerusalem need, unless it be an echo of Jeremiah's cry, 'O Jerusalem, who will turn aside to ask about your welfare?' (Jer. 15:5)? The conferences documented here proposed to do this, to consider the state of Jerusalem today and to ask important questions about its religious significance and 'holiness'.

The Note at the end of the Preface, stating that 'the land of Israel/Palestine is referred to by the name which would have been given in the particular period under discussion', gives us a point of departure. 'Israel/Palestine', Palestine/Israel'—which way should they go? Can they merge into one another, with 'Jerusalem' the unifying symbol?

Whatever we may say about continuing presences, historical right or divine mandate, we have to acknowledge a land that was, and is, competitively possessed. No sanctities can 'dis-locate' this fact, despite any pretensions to the contrary. The late Golda Meir is reported to have said:

> It was not as though there was a Palestinian people in Palestine considering itself as a Palestinian people and we came and threw them out and took their country away from them. They did not exist.[1]

whilst Menachem Begin said, 'if this is Palestine and there are Palestinians, then we are invaders'.[2] Yet the very Talmud itself has been entitled 'Palestinian'.

Readers in our contemporary world of 'peace processes' and the frustration of peace are no doubt already accusing this Foreword of *parti-pris*. Not so. The intention is to ask the moral question at the heart of all 'holiness': how ethical does the 'holy' need to be? Or does the 'holy' somehow transcend the ethical, so that divine association exempts from

---

[1] *Sunday Times* (June 15, 1969).
[2] In *Yediot Aharanot* (Oct. 17, 1969) and in Arie Bober, ed., *The Other Israel: The Radical Case against Zionism* (New York, 1972) 77.

human liability? Can the legitimacy of Zion—inwardly perceived and warranted by virtue of divine 'covenant' and 'election'—come to terms with the impossibility of human innocence? Blessedly there are many Israelis who are struggling to do so in concrete ways of co-existence. There is for them, certainly since 1988, a reciprocal Palestinian response, struggling in a comparable way with a bitter legacy of grief, anger and suspicion. That Jerusalem should be the focus of these papers is therefore timely and important.

Given the partisan emotion that quickly darkens counsel there may be point in a remote parallel. The New England poet, Robert Frost, writing in *The Gift Outright* about the sense of a land answering to the sense of a destiny and together fashioning the sense of a people, uses language which has heavy biblical overtones:

> The land was ours before we were the land's...
> Possessing what we still were unpossessed by...
> The deed of gift was many deeds of war...
> To the land we gave ourselves outright
> But still unstoried, artless, unenhanced,
> Such as she was, such as she would become.

Writing recently, an American Indian, however, sees it differently:

The obvious characters for Native Americans to identify with are the Canaanites, the people who already lived in the promised land...I read the Exodus stories with Canaanite eyes.[3]

Frost's conviction that 'the land was ours' might fit the thoughts of Abraham, still more the nomads coming out from Pharoah's Egypt. If 'there is one family' (Eph. 3:15), must not all conviction of explicit 'right' and 'destiny' consort morally with every other consciousness of ethnic and territorial belonging? The distinctive Judaic triangles of God-land-people and of kin-place-memory (the double triangle of the Israeli flag) belong diversely to all peoples insofar as who, where and whence are denominators of all identities? When R. Abraham Heschel wrote lyrically about Jerusalem in the thrill of 1967, he hailed 'an unbelievable event in which the presence of the holy burst forth'; in the deeds of the settlers 'God was at home in

---

[3]In R.S. Sugirtharajah, ed., *Voices from the Margin: Interpreting the Bible in the Third World* (London, SPCK 1991) 289.

Foreword

the world', and 'the city was radiant with holiness'. Yet, when he thought of that 'exclusivity in the intention of God', he insisted that the sacred could never be guaranteed by politics, but only in the secret places of the heart. Territory could neither ensure holiness, nor imprison it; the very *Shekinah* could go into exile.[4]

So the question of Jerusalem and its 'holiness' raises many questions. Is it right to call any city 'holy' unless all can be? How much 'conscience' does there need to be in the quest for sanctity? The 'holy' may indeed be *more* than the merely 'ethical' and 'just', being numinous, inherent and sublimely 'tremendous', yet surely holiness is never arbitrary or exonerated from righteousness? If we wish to say with Jewish wonder, 'God has an address on this earth'[5] and with Martin Buber that 'God is the God of history because he became the God of Israel',[6] the holiness of which we speak cannot be an intrinsic, unconditional privilege that can never be corrupted. How Jeremiah, who attacked those 'deceptive words—"the Temple of the Lord, the Temple of the Lord"' (Jer. 7:4), would cry out against such an approach to Jerusalem!—as if wrong could ever be merely superficial and external, leaving the identity of the 'chosen people' immaculate and inviolate.

Israel/Palestine—Palestine/Israel—such, if not the 'divine address on earth' is the land where any final 'promise' must be mutual and not exclusive, not the 'promise' which fosters 'holy prejudice'. The holiness that focuses dramatically, passionately and exclusively on Jerusalem must somehow be simultaneously centrifugal in its effect, reaching out to all in its embrace, especially to that diaspora which is still tragically contingent on its sense of Palestine as home.

The economic, political and physical issues are oppressively heavy, charged with passion and distrust. Land, water, mobility are all in the equation and difficult to resolve. Any solution for Jerusalem will therefore depend on the willingness of those who live there not only to 'mark her bulwarks' (Psa. 48:13, BCP), but also to visualise her without walls, bringing things now divided into unity and peace.

---

[4]A. Heschel, *Israel, an Echo of Eternity* (New York, Farrar, Straus and Giroux 1969) 209.
[5]*Ibid.*, 223.
[6]From *The Prophetic Faith* (Eng. transl., New York, 1949).

That Israel is a very divided nation few will doubt. Palestinians too have long been divided as to how they should reconcile their own legitimacy with the Zionists' determination to find in politicization and nationhood the one 'solution' to the meaning of Judaism. 'Politics', a Zionist realist wrote, 'has its own exigencies against which it is useless to rebel'. Hence the reciprocal terrorism, the mutual recrimination. On the contrary, rebel we must, seeing that the means of politics are for the ends of holiness. In this way once more the 'Word of the Lord may come forth from Jerusalem' (Isa. 2:3)?

CONTENTS

Foreword, by the Rt Revd Kenneth Cragg		v
List of Contributors		x
Editor's Preface		xii

Biblical and Historical Perspectives

1	A Christian Approach to Old Testament Prophecy concerning Israel *Chris Wright*	1
2	Jerusalem in the Old Testament *Gordon McConville*	21
3	Jerusalem in the New Testament *Tom Wright*	53
4	Jerusalem in the Early Christian Centuries *Peter Walker*	79

Contemporary Perspectives

5	Jerusalem in Judaism and for Christian Zionists *Margaret Brearley*	99
6	Jerusalem in Islam and for Palestinian Christians *Na'im Ateek* (with postscript)	125
7	Jerusalem and Justice: A Messianic Jewish Perspective *Baruch Maoz* (with postscript)	155
8	Jerusalem and the Church's Challenge *Peter Walker*	183
Epilogue, by Colin Chapman		213
Indices		220

LIST OF CONTRIBUTORS

The Revd Canon **Naim Ateek** is a Palestinian. He did his doctoral research in Berkeley, California, and is now a residentiary Canon of St George's Cathedral, Jerusalem, where he is the pastor of the Arab Anglican congregation. He is the author of *Justice and Only Justice: A Palestinian Theology of Liberation* (New York, Orbis 1989) and an editor of *Faith and the Intifada: Palestinian Christian Voices* (New York, Orbis 1992).

Dr **Margaret Brearley** is an Anglican, who was a Lecturer in Birmingham University and then until recently a Fellow of the Centre for the Study of Judaism and Jewish-Christian Relations at the Selly Oak Colleges, Birmingham. A former Medievalist, she is now researching nineteenth and twentieth century anti-Judaism, and the New Age movement.

The Revd **Colin Chapman** worked for over 10 years for the Church Missionary Society in the Middle East (first in Egypt and then in Beirut). After teaching at Trinity College, Bristol, he is now Principal of Crowther Hall, the CMS training college in Birmingham. He is the author of *Whose Promised Land?* (Tring, Lion 1983; revd. ed., 1989).

Baruch Maoz is a Jewish Christian, who, after emigrating to Israel as a child became a Christian in his twenties. He is now Pastor to Grace and Truth Christian Assembly in Rishon Letsion, Israel; he is also Field Director for Christian Witness to Israel and the Israel Coordinator for the Lausanne Consultation on Jewish Evangelism. He is a founder-editor of *Mishkan*, an international theological journal on Jewish evangelism and helped to form the Israel National Evangelistic Committee. He is editor and chief translator of HaGefen Publications.

Dr **Gordon McConville** lectures in the Old Testament at Wycliffe Hall, Oxford. His published works include: *Law and Theology in Deuteronomy* (Sheffield, JSOT 1984); *Judgment and Promise: Interpreting the Book of Jeremiah* (Leicester, IVP 1993), *Grace in the End: A Study of Deuteronomic Theology*

(Grand Rapids, Zondervan 1992) and volumes in the *Daily Study Bible* (Edinburgh, St Andrew Press) on 1 and 2 Chronicles (1984) and Ezra, Nehemiah and Esther (1985); he is also editor of the *European Journal of Theology*.

The Revd Dr **Peter Walker** has been on the staff of St. George's College, Jerusalem and a lecturer at Christ Church, Jerusalem; his Cambridge doctoral thesis was later published as *Holy City, Holy Places? Christian Attitudes to Jerusalem and the Holy Land in the Fourth Century* (Oxford, OUP 1990). After serving a curacy in Tonbridge, Kent, he is now a post-doctoral Research Fellow at Tyndale House, Cambridge, investigating New Testament attitudes to Jerusalem.

The Revd Dr **Chris Wright** worked for 5 years at the Union Biblical Seminary in India, and has recently been appointed as Principal of All Nations Christian College, Ware, where he lectures in Old Testament. He is the author of *Living as the People of God* (American title: *An Eye for an Eye*, Leicester and Downers Grove, IVP 1983), *God's People in God's Land* (Grand Rapids, Eerdmans; Exeter, Paternoster 1990) and *Knowing Jesus through the Old Testament* (London, Marshall Pickering 1992).

The Revd Dr **Tom Wright**, after teaching New Testament in both McGill University, Montreal, and Oxford University, is now Dean of Lichfield Cathedral. He is also Canon Theologian of Coventry Cathedral and on the Doctrine Commission of the Church of England. His recent publications include *The Climax of the Covenant: Christ and the Law in Pauline Theology* (Edinburgh, T & T Clark 1991); *The Crown and the Fire* (London, SPCK 1992), *The New Testament and the People of God* (London, SPCK 1992), *New Tasks for a Renewed Church* (London, Hodder and Stoughton 1992) and the forthcoming *Jesus and the Victory of God* (London, SPCK 1994).

EDITOR'S PREFACE

Few cities have so continuously exerted such influence upon the religious conscience of mankind as has the city of Jerusalem. In a few years this fascinating city will celebrate not only the 2,000th anniversary of the birth of Christ in nearby Bethlehem, but also the 3,000th anniversary of its foundation by King David, and throughout that time it has been a focus for people's prayers, an object of pilgrimage and a subject for written reflection. Our present period is no exception with Jerusalem receiving countless visitors each year and continuing to be a central issue in the settling of the Israeli/Palestinian problem.

Yet Jerusalem calls forth yet deeper reactions. In each of the three great monotheistic religions (Judaism, Christianity and Islam) there are traditions which see this city as 'holy', or in some sense special to God and unique within his purposes. Part of the tension which the city experiences is caused precisely by such religious convictions as they clash and frequently contradict one another.

In such a situation it is timely for Christians to reflect more deeply on their own attitudes towards Jerusalem. In doing so, they soon discover that there are several possible 'Christian' approaches to Jerusalem which need to be compared and evaluated. Some would find the notion of Jerusalem's 'holiness' an obvious category in the light of the unique events associated there with the life of Christ; others would find 'holiness' an uncomfortable notion, but be adamant that Jerusalem is special in God's sight on the grounds of the Old Testament revelation; whilst a third group would have questions about both of these.

The tensions between these different Christian attitudes towards Jerusalem are today that much greater, in the light of the return to the land of the Jewish people and the 'restoration' of Jerusalem in recent years; for some these are clear fulfillments of biblical prophecy, for others such ideas would be anathema. This latter issue is obviously of particular importance to Evangelical Christians who seek in their theology to acknowledge the authority of the Scriptures.

The papers in this volume all seek, in their different ways, to address this question of the theological significance of Jerusalem (though the first chapter relates more generally to the important, foundational question of the Christian use of the Old Testament today). Whilst some of the papers (particularly in the first section) reach similar conclusions, no single consensus has emerged, nor was this ever intended. On the contrary, the purpose of this volume is to illustrate the variety of theological approaches to this subject. Of necessity, therefore, opinions expressed in these pages cannot be attributed to any one institution associated with the project, only to their respective authors. In this process, however, it is hoped that some of the key issues in this debate will become identifiable to our readers, allowing them to draw their own conclusions. The debate must still continue.

Since 1989 there has been a series of Christian conferences in and around London focusing on issues relating to the Middle East. Each of the contributors to this volume has spoken to their subject at one of these, though the written paper in some instances is substantially different from the original address.[1] These conferences were held under the joint auspices of Christian Impact and the Deo Gloria Trust, with support in different ways from All Nations Christian College, the Tyndale Fellowship, the Church Missionary Society and the Church's Ministry amongst the Jews; the organising committee would like to thank all of these bodies for their timely help.

Personally I would like to add a word of thanks to: the Doe Gloria Trust, Tyndale House, Colin Chapman, Walter

---

[1] This is particularly the case with ch. 5 (substantially new) and ch. 6. (much abbreviated); ch. 8 appears here fore the first time. The following scholars also gave lectures, whose viewpoints (though not included here for reasons of space) we trust to be represented, at least in part, in this volume: Gervais Angel (on Rom. 9-11), John Edwards (on the Crusades), Michael Prior (Director of 'Living Stones'), Salim Munayer (a Christian Arab), Ruth Snow (a Messianic Jew), Richard Harvey (CMJ) and Walter Riggans. We were grateful too to John Levy and Taysir Kamleh for introducing us respectively to the Jewish and Islamic perspectives on Jerusalem. Because of the Kurdish refugee problem, Gabi Habib (General Secretary of the Middle East Council of Churches) had to withdraw at the last moment, though he was represented by David Goodenough.

Riggans, Bill Broughton, David Pileggi, David Goodenough, Richard Massey, Stephen Walley, Andrew Clarke, Bruce Winter, Ian and Margaret Keiller, my secretary, Anne Mills, and my wife, Georgie.

Finally, this volume may cause Christians to be better informed as they pray for all those who live and work in Jerusalem, not only for all political leaders in the important peace negotiations currently under way, but also for the leaders of the differing churches in their frequently stressful situations. The coming years will no doubt present them with many challenges or opportunities (including how best to celebrate the important anniversaries mentioned above). For British readers the issues of this Middle Eastern city may initially seem remote ('there is a green hill *far away*'). On closer inspection, however, the issues raised by Jerusalem prove to be of quite central significance within our Christian theology, while for those who actually live there they are naturally their daily concern. This volume is presented in the hope that Christians will be more aware of the issues at stake, and thereby better equipped to be agents of peace and increased understanding in a situation where these qualities are so often sorely needed.

Peter Walker
St Saviour's, Tonbridge

PREFACE to the 2nd EDITION

Since the appearance of the first edition two years ago there have been significant and welcome developments in the peace negotiations between Israel and the Palestinians. Although the issue of Jerusalem has been deferred to a later date, it seemed right to add some material which would take account of these events. The two authors who live in the Holy Land have therefore each appended a postscript to their chapters, and there is an additional epilogue by Colin Chapman. The remainder of the book remains unchanged.

Peter Walker
Tyndale House, Cambridge

IMPORTANT NOTE: To avoid confusion or suggestion of modern political affinities, the Land of Israel/Palestine is normally referred to in this volume by the name which it would have been given in the particular period under discussion.

CHAPTER 1

A CHRISTIAN APPROACH TO OLD TESTAMENT PROPHECY CONCERNING ISRAEL

Chris Wright

I. The Universal Context of God's Promises to Israel

The issue of Old Testament prophecy needs to be examined in the light of the total perspective which pervades the Old Testament, namely God's purpose for the whole of humanity and for the whole earth. Genesis 1-11 sets the agenda for the rest of the Bible, presenting us with the basic triangle of relationships within which the whole of the rest of the Bible's story lies: the relationship between God, humanity and the earth. The climax comes in Genesis 11 where the story of the tower of Babel reveals a world of nations, cursed, divided and scattered over the earth. It is into this dismal context that God then declares in Genesis 12 his universal intention: there is still to be a 'blessing for all nations', but it will now come through his covenant with a single individual, Abraham. This covenant reflects exactly the creation triangle, only now on a smaller scale: God, Israel and the land. The election of Israel and the promise of land are thus to be set in the context of God's ultimate purpose for the salvation of humanity and the re-creation of all the earth; they were not ends in themselves, but means to a greater end. God's commitment to Israel therefore needs to be seen as derivative from his commitment to humanity, not prior to it or separable from it.[1] Election indeed involves use of particular means, but for a universal goal.

---

[1] Von Rad made this point in commenting on the Table of Nations in Gen. 10, which significantly does not include Israel. The climax of God's work of creation in the primal history is the spread of the nations of humanity. Israel's arrival and history therefore take place within God's redemptive work on behalf of the nations: see G. von Rad, *Old Testament Theology* I (Edinburgh, Oliver and Boyd 1962), 162f. H.H. Rowley, *The Faith of Israel* (London, SCM 1956) 180 comments on Old Testament eschatology: 'it is to be observed that the pictures of the Golden Age are always of a universal character. . .There could be no Golden Age for Israel until all men shared it'. This universal dimens-

II. The Universal Thrust of Old Testament Eschatology

Secondly, Old Testament prophecies which specify Israel and/or the land need to be seen in light of the universal thrust of Old Testament eschatology, an emphasis which develops strongly in the Prophets (and Psalms). The Old Testament has a vision of the people of God which will include, but not be confined, to ethnic Israelites: 'many nations will be joined with the Lord in that day and will become my people' (Zech. 2:11).[2] This was not just an idea developed by the early church to legitimate the inclusion of Gentiles in response to Jewish rejection of Jesus. On the contrary, it was built in to the 'genetic code' of Israel from the outset, as the New Testament's scriptural quotation and argumentation on this point show clearly. Just as the patriarchal family was only a stage in the development of the people of God, so national and territorial Israel in the Old Testament period was a stage toward the development of an international and global people of God. This is not just a 'Christian idea' but intrinsic to the Old Testament itself.

Even in Old Testament times, to make a straight identification between Israel as the 'people of God' and the then nation state in any of its stages was questionable: the idea of a faithful 'remnant' is found as early as the time of Elijah (1 Kings 19:18). In the New Testament the idea that membership of the national community was enough in itself truly to belong to the people of God is denied, by John the Baptist (Lk. 3:8), by

---

ion of Israel's election and significance has long been expounded by theologians of mission; *cf.* J.H. Bavinck, *An Introduction the Science of Missions* (Philadelphia, Presbyterian and Reformed 1956) 11ff.; J. Blauw, *The Missionary Nature of the Church* (New York, McGraw Hill 1962) 18ff., R.R. Ridder, *Discipling the Nations* (Grand Rapids, Baker 1971) ch. 1. The growth of a more holistic canonical reading of the text has also lead to a revision of the tendency to read Genesis in the light of Exodus (on the grounds that the Israel who reflect on God as creator already knew him through their history of redemption). See *e.g.* T. Fretheim, 'The Reclamation of Creation: Redemption and Law in Exodus', *Interpretation* 45 (1991) 354-65. A similar point with regard to the Zion tradition is made by J.G. McConville below.

[2] This is discussed more fully in my *Knowing Jesus through the Old Testament* (London, Marshall-Pickering 1992), 34-54. Among the important texts are Isa. 11:1-9, 10, 12; 19:19-25; 25; 42:6; 44:5; 45:22ff.; 49:6; Amos 9:12; Jer. 16:19; Hag. 2:6ff.; Zech. 2:10-13; 8:20-23; Mal. 1:11; Psa. 22:27; 47:8ff.; 72:17; 86:9; 87; 102:13-22.

Jesus (Jn. 8:33-44) and by Paul (Rom. 2:28, 9:6ff.).[3] Thus those who today make such a direct identification (either in terms of the whole Jewish ethnic community, or that part of it living in territorial Israel) are open to the charge that they are misunderstanding the Old Testament and short-circuiting the New.

III. The Historically Contingent Nature of Prophetic Language when describing the Future.

When prophets spoke about the future, they could only do so meaningfully by using terms and realities that existed in their past or present experience. The realities associated with being Israel in their day included their specific history and such things as the land, the law, Jerusalem, the temple, sacrifices and priesthood. All of these had substantial significance in Israel's relationship with God, and also in Israel's ultimate role in relation to the nations and their relationship with God. Thus, for prophets to speak about God's future dealings with Israel and the nations, they had to speak in terms of these contemporary realities. How else could their hearers have grasped the point?[4] Thus, for example, Jeremiah's 'Book of Consolation' (Jer. 30-33) looks forward to a total restoration of Israel after the exile, and it does so in terms of restored people, return to the land, covenant renewal, the perfection of monarchy, priesthood and sacrifices—because all these things were the *realia* of Israel's faith and experience. To speak of restoration without recourse to such concrete features of being Israel would have been meaningless, even if it had been possible.

IV. The Transcendent Nature of Prophetic Use of Familiar Concepts.

Moreover, even in the Old Testament itself, there was an awareness that the fulfilment of prophecies that were made in

---

[3]This last reference (Rom. 9:6 ff.) is particularly significant in relation to the view of some scholars that, in Rom. 9-11, when Paul writes of 'Israel' he means nothing more nor less than the Jewish nation. Paul is more subtle than that and does make a distinction between the ethnic community and a true Israel. See further below, section XI.
[4]This feature of prophecy, and the need to take it into account in proper interpretation of the text, is discussed in most serious books on biblical hermeneutics.

terms of the concrete realities of Israel's life and faith would actually go beyond them. The familiar dimensions of Israel's national life are transcended in various ways. For example: the restoration of the exiles would be a reunification of ancient Judah and Israel into one renewed and repentant people, an event which never happened historically (Jer. 50:4f., 33; Ezek. 37:15ff.); the people of God would be restored to the full, perfect and eternal experience of their covenant relationship with Yahweh (Jer. 50:5, Ezek. 36, 39:25-39); the law would not only be perfectly obeyed by Israel, but also be sought out by all the nations of the earth (Jer. 31:33; 32:39-41; Isa. 2:3; 51:4f.); the new Davidic kingdom would be worldwide, and the new king would be perfect in all those respects where the historical kings had failed (Isa. 9:6f., 11:1-5, Jer. 23:1-6, Ezek. 34:1-24, 37:15-28); the new temple would be miraculously filled with the glory of God and the river of life (Ezek. 43:1-5, 47:1-12). In other words, there seems to be an awareness that although the future has to be described in concepts drawn from Israel's historical nationhood, it will in fact ultimately transcend them.[5]

Thus to claim that Old Testament prophecy can have a deeper spiritual meaning than its literal form is not some kind of Christian 'trick'. The dispensationalist's accusation that those who interpret prophecy in terms of a spiritual rather than a literalistic fulfilment are not taking the Old Testament seriously is false. For the Old Testament itself sometimes sees beyond the literal forms of its own eschatology.[6]

V. The Distinction between Promise and Prediction

As a result, it is not always appropriate to handle this prophetic material simply in the category of 'prediction'. Even at the time of their origin, prophecies would probably not have been seen as flat predictions. Rather they have to be handled as part of the 'promise'. Though there are indeed predictions within the Old Testament which have been or will be fulfilled, the Old Testament is not just a box of predictions: it is fundamentally a

---

[5] *Cf.* ch. 2 below, concerning the Jerusalem/Zion tradition. *Cf.* also the detailed treatment of the symbolic, theological and ethical functioning of the tradition in B.C. Ollenburger, *Zion the City of the Great King*, (Sheffield, JSOT 1987).
[6] Failure to recognize this can lead to seriously distorted exegesis of both Old and New Testament texts and theology: see ch. 3 below.

declaration of promise. That is, it declares God's committed purpose to act in history for the salvation of humanity and creation through the agency of his people Israel.[7]

There is an immense difference between prediction and promise. Promise presupposes, initiates or sustains personal relationship and involves personal commitment (prediction need not). Thus the fulfilment of a promise may, in the event, take a quite different form from the material terms in which it was made, yet still be a true fulfilment inasmuch as its purpose was bound up with the relationship, not the objective form of words used. Thus it must be asked of any prophecy not only, 'what was actually said at the time?' but also 'what was the promise for?' Later circumstances may enable the point and motivation of the promise to be fulfilled quite beyond the terms or expectations of the original words. To illustrate, imagine in the last century a father promises his young son a horse of his own when he 'comes of age'. In the meantime cars are invented. On his twenty-first birthday, his father therefore gives him a car instead. The promise is fulfilled, because the substantive meaning of the promise was a personally owned means of transport. It would be pointless to say that it would only be fulfilled if the son gets a horse as well, or later. That would be to take the original promise as a mere prediction which will have 'failed' unless it is literally honoured. This surely is what literalistic and dispensationalist treatments of Old Testament prophecy do when they argue that Old Testament prophecies still await a literal fulfilment to match their original predictive form, when the New Testament actually declares such prophecies to have been fulfilled in the coming of Jesus Christ, even though in surprising ways.

This is relevant to the contention that the land was promised to Israel 'for ever'. If this were a simple, historically linear, prediction, then the return of Jews to Palestine in our own day could be fitted into it, though the gap of eighteen hundred years would still look very suspicious. However, what is forgotten is that other features of God's many promises to Old Testament Israel were also explicitly 'for ever', and yet manifestly temporal in duration. The Aaronic Levites as priests (1 Chron. 23:13) and the descendants of David as kings (2 Sam.

---

[7]For a fuller discussion, see my *Knowing Jesus*, ch. 2 ('Jesus and the Old Testament Promise').

7:12-16) were likewise 'for ever', yet both have come to an end and are unambiguously seen as fulfilled in Christ in the New Testament. The expression 'for ever' (לְעוֹלָם) needs to be seen, not so much in terms of 'everlastingness' in linear time, but rather as an intensive expression within the terms, con-ditions and context of the promise concerned. 'For ever' is not, in Hebrew, as infinite as it sounds in English. God promised the Rechabites (the obscure and reactionary followers of Jonadab) that they would have descendants 'for ever' (Jer. 35:19). Where are the Rechabites now? If this had been a straight prediction, it has failed. If it is seen as a limited promise within its own historical context in support of the prophetic ministry of Jeremiah, it makes sense. Significantly, exactly the same form of words is used concerning the house of David and the levitical priests in Jeremiah 33:17f. This is not, of course, to suggest that Jeremiah put David and the priests on the same level as the Rechabites, but rather to point out that the expression 'for ever' varies in its significance according to its context, and that it can be limited in its scope when circumstances change or God's historical purposes move forward to new stages.[8] When the land, the kings and the priests were declared to be 'for ever', it meant that these dimensions were permanent and guaranteed while Israel as a nation was the limit of God's redemptive work and covenant relationship. Once this national and territorial basis was transcended through the coming of the Messiah and the extension of the gospel of redemption to Gentiles and Jews through him, then the 'for-ever-ness' of these things resides in Christ himself, the embodiment of Israel. Since, as we saw above at the outset, the whole point of God's promise to Israel was that 'there should be a people of God for the sake of humanity and the earth', and since that promise is now being fulfilled through a multi-national people, Jew and Gentile in Christ, then the 'forever' aspects of nation-state, land, king and priests have likewise been transcended, taken up, and fulfilled.[9]

---

[8]*Cf.* ch. 2 below, on the historical conditionality of covenant declaration.
[9]The language of fulfilment, a properly biblical language, should not be misunderstood and decried as 'replacement' or 'supersession'. To say that the church, as the messianic community of believing Jews and Gentiles, is the fulfilment of God's intention for Old Testament Israel,

VI. The Future of Israel and the Nations.

Old Testament prophecies concerning the future of Israel are inextricably bound up with the future of the nations also. There is even a comparable 'ambiguity' of judgement and hope. Israel is to be sifted in judgment virtually to extinction; yet Israel will be redeemed and restored. The nations are to be judged and destroyed as enemies of God; yet the nations are to be gathered in to share in the salvation and inheritance of the people of God.[10] In other words, the dividing line between judgement and salvation, between the doomed and the saved, is not a line that runs simply between the nations and Israel, but through both of them. Just as there will be a 'remnant of Israel', so there will be 'survivors of the nations' (Isa. 45:20ff., 66:19ff., Zech. 14:16ff.). It is both of these together (both the purified and obedient remnant of Israel and those of the nations who identify with Yahweh and his people) that the Old Testament sees as the eschatological people of God.

Examination of various prophetic texts about the future of Israel and the nations shows that they did not think in terms of a future two-tiered arrangement, but rather of the nations coming to share in the experiences, the privileges and the hope of Israel. It is a unified vision, including various great Old Testament themes, such as the kingship of God, the law of God, the salvation of God and the name of God.[11] This unified

---

should not be taken to mean that God simply rejected the Jews and transferred his affections to Christians, even if regrettably this is a common enough misconception. It is certainly true that in Christ the meaning of Israel has been redefined and extended from its national territorial meaning of the Old Testament. Yet this does not imply a replacement that devalues or rejects the vital importance of that stage of God's historical work of redemption, any more than one could say that the growth of the twelve tribes 'replaced' the family of Abraham in that derogatory sense. It needs to be remembered that the existence and blessing of the one 'great nation' and the existence and blessing of people from 'all nations', while chronologically distinct in the sense that one follows the other, are both intrinsic and explicit in the Abrahamic covenant.

[10]On Israel, *e.g.* Isa. 26:9; Amos 9; Mic. 2-3; Isa. 35; Jer. 16; 25:ff.; 30-33. On the nations, *e.g.* Isa. 24; 34; Mic. 4; Joel 3. In Zephaniah, the punishment of the nations is set in parallel to the judgement on Jerusalem and the restoration of Jerusalem also has universal implications (Zeph. 3:9ff.).
[11]*Cf.* also my *Knowing Jesus*, 49-54.

vision is then precisely what Paul calls the 'mystery' hidden for ages (Eph. 3:4-6), the mystery being as to how this vision could ever be accomplished; but now he rejoices to see it being brought into tangible reality in the inclusion of the Gentiles, through Christ, into a status from which they had hitherto been excluded, namely membership of the very 'household of God' (a common Old Testament metaphor for the people of Israel). His argument in Ephesians 2:11-22 is saturated with Old Testament imagery and could not be more clear in its portrayal of a unitary people of God in the Messiah, Jesus. This was not some remote future hope, nor merely an ideal by-product of the gospel. It was, he claims, the very content of his gospel and a present reality. He even coins words to describe it, in one emphatic verse (Eph. 3:6): the Gentiles are 'co-heirs, a co-body, and co-sharers' with Israel. Once again it is hard to avoid the conclusion that dispensational schemes of a two-tier covenant and of a continuing duality in God's purpose for Jew and Gentile are frankly unbiblical.

VII. Jewish Hopes at the Time of Jesus.

At the time of Jesus there was, within the variety of inter-testamental Jewish hopes, a strong strand of expectation that looked forward to a restoration of Israel that would include the ingathering of the nations.[12] The coming of the king to Jerusalem would mean peace and universal rule for the nations (Zech. 9:9ff.); when God acted to restore Zion and reveal his glory, then the nations would also gather to worship him (Psa. 102:13-22; *cf.* also Isa. 49:5f., 56:1-8, 60:10-14, 66:18-24). As these hopes continued into the inter-testamental period, 'the hope that seems to have been most often repeated was that of the restoration of Israel', within a complex that included also

---

[12] A seminal study of this theme which is enormously helpful in grasping Jesus' own sense of mission and purpose in his historical context is B.F. Meyer, *The Aims of Jesus* (London, SCM 1979). More recent studies have confirmed and expanded this understanding: see E.P. Sanders, *Jesus and Judaism* (Philadelphia, Fortress 1985); C. Rowland, *Christian Origins* (London, SPCK 1985) 87ff.; I.M. Zeitlin, *Jesus and the Judaism of His Time* (Oxford, Polity 1988) ch. 3; J.D.G. Dunn, *The Partings of the Ways* (London, SCM 1991); G. Theissen, *The Shadow of the Galilean* (London, SCM 1987).

the rebuilding of the temple and the entry of the Gentiles.[13] Restoration and ingathering were seen in eschatological terms as the final great act of God, the Day of the Lord. The two things would be part of the same final event that would usher in the new age, but the restoration of Israel was logically and in a sense chronologically expected first.

New Testament scholars set the ministry of John the Baptist within this eschatological framework. His was a winnowing ministry, sifting the nation by his call to repentance, in preparation for their restoration.

The mission of the Baptist belonged to a scenario of fulfilment. His role was to assemble by baptism the remnant of Israel destined for cleansing and acquittal and so, climactically, for restoration.[14]

Likewise, Jesus publicly identified himself with the goal of John's ministry and operated within the same eschatological framework. His note of fulfilment in relation to the kingdom of God included the fulfilment of the expectations regarding Israel. He too challenged his contemporaries to respond to what he clearly portrayed as their last chance.

VIII. Jesus' Understanding of his own Mission

Jesus clearly understood his own mission in terms of the fulfilment of the prophetic hope of the restoration of Israel.[15] This was no longer something future, but a present reality through the arrival of the kingdom of God in his own person. Indications of this self-understanding of his mission include:

a) His submission to baptism by John.

Jesus' acceptance of the ministry of John the Baptist is highly significant for understanding his own aims. If John was the one who had come to prepare Israel for its eschatological restoration by God himself, then Jesus had been sent to accomplish it.

---

[13]Sanders, *Jesus and Judaism*, 87; the material is presented in detail in his chs. 2 and 3.
[14]Meyer, *Aims*, 128. *Cf.* also Rowland, *Origins*, 131ff.
[15]In addition to the more recent work cited in footnotes below, three earlier works are still profitable: J. Jeremias, *Jesus' Promise to the Nations*, SBT 24 (London, SCM 1958); G.B. Caird, *Jesus and the Jewish Nation* (London, Athlone 1965); F. Hahn, *Mission in the New Testament*, SBT 47 (London, SCM 1965).

Like the Baptist, he understood his own role in terms of the age-old scriptural promise of the restoration of Israel; and, like the Baptist, he understood this restoration not as a divine act exclusively reserved for post-historical realization (located, that is, on the far side of a still future judgement) but as called for now and already begun![16]

b) His choice and use of scripture in relation to himself.

As is well known, Jesus affirmed that he was the fulfillment of Isaiah 61 (Luke 4:16-21). Yet this is only the 'tip of a very large iceberg': for the dominant motif of Jesus' usage of the scriptures is one of fulfilment, combined with a warning not to miss out on what God was doing in the here and now. R.T. France, who has studied this material exhaustively, observes:

The messianic figures which occur most prominently in the sayings of Jesus are among the least prominent in the Old Testament and those least emphasized in later Jewish thought, particularly the Suffering Servant of Isa. 53 and the mysterious figure who appears, sometimes in the roles of suffering and rejection, in Zech. 9-13. Strikingly absent from his selection is the traditional picture of the royal Messiah, son of David, the restorer of Jewish political sovereignty...[Evidently therefore]: a) Jesus saw in his own coming the age of fulfilment of the messianic hopes of the Old Testament, the emphasis being on present, not future, fulfilment; b) His conception of Messiahship had as little as possible to do with the political future of the Jewish nation.

Even where Old Testament prophecies are referred by Jesus to as yet future events (*e.g.* Dan. 7 and the Son of Man), Jesus himself is the central figure as judge and king. The Son of Man concept furthermore identified him as the corporate, representative figure who embodied the 'saints of the Most High'—*i.e.* Israel as the eschatological people of God. Thus his use of the Old Testament in his vision of the future was an extension or completion of his own eschatological ministry already begun on earth.

[There is] no instance where Jesus expects a fulfilment of Old Testament prophecy other than through his own ministry, and certainly no suggestion of a future restoration of the Jewish nation independent of himself. He himself is the fulfilment to which that prophecy points, the ultimate horizon of the prophetic vision.[17]

---

[16]Meyer, *loc. cit. Cf.* also B. Witherington III, *The Christology of Jesus* (Minneapolis, Fortress 1990) 34-56.

[17]R.T. France, 'Old Testament Prophecy and the Future of Israel', *Tyn Bull* 26 (1975) 56, 58. For the fullest treatment of all the material, see R.T. France, *Jesus and the Old Testament* (London, Tyndale 1971).

c) His choice of twelve disciples.
The number twelve is a stubborn element in the tradition, even though there is some fluidity over the precise names of the disciples: in other words, the intentional symbolism of the embryonic twelve tribes of a restored Israel was clearly remembered. This is strengthened by his reference to them as a 'little flock', which was a term from 'remnant theology' (Luke 12:32; *c.f.* the quotation of Ps. 37:11 in Matt. 5:5), and his saying about their judging the twelve tribes of Israel (Matt. 19:28).

d) His understanding of the Temple.
Jesus not only predicted its destruction, but symbolized it in his prophetic action, commonly called its 'cleansing'. E.P. Sanders uses this indisputably historical event in the ministry of Jesus as a major clue to discovering Jesus' own understanding of his significance and the reason for his crucifixion.[18] It was a powerful eschatological claim that the end of the old had come and the new temple of the restored Israel was imminent.

e) His 'triumphal entry' into Jerusalem.
For those who had eyes to see, his action was an unquestionable claim to be fulfilling the restorationist hope of Zech. 9:9ff. The crowds may have misunderstood the significance of what was happening, but they evidently did not miss the surface meaning of the action in relation to the prophecy (Matt. 21:5).

f) His 'new covenant' and his sacrificial interpretation of his own death.
In Mark 14:24 (and parallels) Jesus uses the familiar prophecies of a new covenant as the framework to explain his death. In the context of his own 'little flock' of twelve disciples, it meant that in them, the true, believing and obedient remnant of Israel, he had established the new covenant community itself.

g) His prediction and understanding of his resurrection.
In Luke 24 Jesus explained his resurrection to the Emmaus disciples. The significant point lies in verse 21—namely that their primary problem concerned the 'redemption of Israel': this is what they had hoped for from Jesus, but apparently in vain since he was now dead. Jesus leads them through the scriptures, not in order to dismiss their problem, but in order to direct their attention to the mode of its real solution—*i.e.* in the

---

[18]*Cf.* Sanders, *Jesus and Judaism*, chs. 1-2; Rowland, *Origins*, 162ff.; Dunn, *Partings*, ch. 3; Witherington, *Christology*, 107-116.

suffering, death and resurrection to glory of the Messiah. When they realized who he was and that he was alive, they saw the true answer to their problem: Israel had been redeemed, because Jesus was the Messiah after all. In the later scene of the chapter, back in Jerusalem, Jesus reinforces the point that his resurrection on the third day fulfils the scripture (v. 46); yet the only Old Testament reference to a third day resurrection is Hosea 6:1-2, which clearly refers to the restoration of Israel. If the resurrection of Jesus on the third day was thus declared scriptural, it must have been perceived not merely as relating to the few Old Testament references to resurrection in general, but specifically to the eschatological resurrection of Israel.[19]

h) His commissioning of his disciples as 'his witnesses'.
In Acts 1:1-8, the crucial hinge of Luke's two-volume work, Jesus deflected the disciples' question about restoring the kingdom to Israel into the matter of them being witnesses first to Jerusalem and then to the ends of the earth. Again, it is important to see that Jesus was not just dismissing their question (however clouded as yet may have been their grasp of the issue they were raising). Rather Jesus appears to move from the assumption that such matters are fully in the control of God to the practical matter of what the disciples must do next. 'You shall be my witnesses', he says. The phrase deliberately echoes Isaiah 43. There God promises to redeem, gather and restore Israel (vv. 1-7), and then declares, 'You are my witnesses' (vv. 10, 12), which in the context of this whole section of prophecy, especially ch. 45, means a universal witness to the ends of the earth. Jesus thus commissions his disciples to be witnesses to a restoration of Israel with worldwide effects, fully in line with the Isaianic eschatology.

---

[19]*Cf.* also Lk. 18:31-33, Mk. 8:31 and 1 Cor. 15:4—probably the earliest evidence of this tradition. On the redefining of Israel around Jesus, *cf.* ch. 2 below; also Dunn, *Partings*, ch. 6; C.F.D. Moule, 'Jesus, Judaism and Paul', in G.F. Hawthorne and O. Betz, edd., *Tradition and Interpretation in the New Testament* (Grand Rapids, Eerdmans 1987) 43-53.

IX. New Testament Interpretation of Fulfilment in Jesus

Moving from the sayings of Jesus himself to the New Testament authors, it is clear that they likewise interpreted his life, ministry, death and resurrection as being the fulfilment of Old Testament prophecies about the restoration of Israel.

a) Matthew.

The New Testament opens with a genealogy of Jesus in which Matthew is saying in effect: 'If you wish to understand Jesus, you must see him as the completion of this story'. He structures it schematically into three double sevens of generations—the implicit form thus supporting the explicit message of completeness and fulfilment. His name was to be Jesus, because he was to 'save his people' (1:21). He came from Bethlehem, the expected birthplace of the coming ruler of Israel, and his infancy is portrayed with a 'Moses-Egypt' typology that points towards a new exodus. These are only the opening shots in a continuous salvo on the same theme throughout Matthew.[20]

b) Luke.

The two-volume work of Luke is framed at key points with this theme. Luke 1 and 2 are saturated with the motif of fulfilment of Old Testament prophecies about Israel: John's mission is to bring Israel back to God (1:16f.); Jesus would possess the throne of David 'forever' (1:32f.); Israel's salvation is now being accomplished (1:68ff.); the arrival of Jesus fulfils the hope of Israel and the nations (2:29-32), and thus arouses thanksgiving among those who are 'looking for the redemption of Jerusalem' (2:36-38). Moreover, as noted just above, the Gospel ends with the apparent dashing of the same hope, but Jesus himself, no longer a babe in arms but the risen Messiah, restores and explains it; this is closely followed by the same theme at the beginning of volume two, in Acts 1. Finally, Luke ends his work with the same theme. He chooses to conclude with Paul in Rome, assuring his Jewish visitors that his whole ministry had been 'because of the hope of Israel', proving from the scriptures that that hope had been fulfilled by the coming of the Kingdom of God in the person of Jesus the Messiah, and

---

[20] An excellent survey of these themes is found in R.T. France, *Matthew: Evangelist and Teacher* (Exeter, Paternoster 1989). See esp. ch. 6 ('Matthew and Israel'); *cf.* also at a more popular level my *Knowing Jesus*, ch. 1.

that thereby, equally in accordance with the scriptures, 'salvation had been sent to the Gentiles' (Acts 28:20, 23, 28-31).

c) The apostolic preaching.
Since most of the recorded preaching of the apostles in the early part of Acts was to Jews, it is significant to see how they handled Old Testament prophecy. It proves to be entirely consistent with all that has been noted so far.

In his Pentecost sermon Peter identifies what is happening on that day with the prophecy of Joel which, in chapters 2 and 3 had included restoration for Israel in the climactic Day of the Lord (Acts 2:16-21); later he sees the promise to David of an eternal kingdom explicitly fulfilled in Jesus and his resurrection and exaltation (2:29-36). In his Temple sermon he stresses the fulfilment of prophecy and goes on to call for repentance so that the promised restoration may fully come, which he sees as now available to all nations in line with the promise to Abraham (3:18-26); he makes the same point more briefly before the Sanhedrin (5:29-32). Stephen, at the point of his death, claims to see the Son of Man presently at the right hand of God—*i.e.* in the position of vindication and glory that was to be the destiny of the saints of the Most High whom he represented (7:56, *cf.* Dan. 7:13f., 18, 27). Paul, preaching to the Jews of Pisidian Antioch, tells them that in Jesus and his resurrection God has fulfilled his promises to the patriarchs and prophets (13:32ff.). When some of the Jews reject his affirmation, he turns to the Gentiles, significantly using the servant theology of Isaiah as the scriptural justification for his missiology (v. 47). He applies to himself and his missionary band the mission of the servant in Isa. 49:6, which had been a mission first for the restoration of Israel and then for the extension of salvation to the ends of the earth.[21]

The message therefore seems unanimous. Both Jesus himself and his immediate interpreters tell us that in the events of his arrival, life, death, resurrection and exaltation, God had acted decisively for the redemption and restoration of his people Israel in fulfilment of the whole range of Old Testament prophecy that he would do so. To this they were called urgently

---

[21]*Cf.* F.F. Bruce, 'Paul's Use of the Old Testament in Acts', *Tradition and Interpretation*, 71-9. On the nature of the developing split between early Christians and other Jews over the new theological critique and construction reflected in Acts, see Dunn, *Partings*, ch. 4.

to respond there and then as a present reality, not as some still future hope. 'The time is fulfilled. . .'

X. The Significance of the Gentile Mission.

In the light of the three major sections above, the gentile mission of the church is especially significant. In fact, it is as important for an understanding of the meaning of Jesus' own ministry as was the work of John the Baptist. There is a strong linkage between the beginning of Jesus' ministry in the work of the Baptist for the restoration of Israel and its outcome in the birth of a movement committed (soon) to gentile mission. This convergence of what preceded and what followed him points to the eschatological decisiveness of Jesus himself as the initiator of the End, the expected Day of the Lord, with all it would mean for Israel and for the nations.[22]

There are definite indications in the ministry of Jesus that he had a universal vision of the gospel, in line with his scriptural understanding at other points.[23] Indeed, the surprising and presumably shocking fact is that he used texts that in their Old Testament context referred to the ingathering of Israel and applied them to the ingathering of the Gentiles instead. Thus, for example, Matthew. 8:11f. is an allusion to texts such as Isaiah 43:5f., 49:12 and Psalm 107:3, while Mark 13:27 picks up Deuteronomy 30:4 and Zechariah 2:6. In this way Jesus actually appears to redefine and extend the very meaning of the 'restoration of Israel' in terms of the Gentiles. Paul does the same thing in Romans 9:24f., when he takes Hosea 1:10 and 2:23, which clearly referred to Israel in context, and applies them to gentile believers.

It seems therefore, that, far from looking for some future regathering of the Jewish people to Palestine, Jesus actually took Old Testament passages which originally had that connotation and applied them to the gathering of the Christian community from all nations, even, in one case, to the exclusion of some Jews! [Matt. 8:12].[24]

---

[22]*Cf.* Sanders, *Jesus and Judaism*, ch. 3.
[23]*E.g.* Lk. 4:25-27; Mt. 8:11ff.; 22:1-4; 21:43; Mk. 11:17; 13:10, 27; *cf.* B. Witherington III, *Jesus, Paul and the End of the World* (Downers Grove, IVP; Exeter, Paternoster 1992), ch. 14; also F. Hahn, *Mission*, ch. 2 ('Jesus' Attitide to the Gentiles').
[24]France, 'O.T. Prophecy', 73.

Yet it remains true that, with a few exceptional cases which underline the general rule, he insisted that his own mission was first to the 'lost sheep of Israel' (Matt. 10:6); this was fully in line with the shape of the mission of the Servant (Isa. 49:5).[25]

After his resurrection the apostles did not immediately set about a gentile mission. However, this may be due, not to the fact that Jesus never taught it, but rather to the same kind of misunderstanding and surprise that surrounded his teaching about the Kingdom of God. It was 'already but not yet'. Likewise, according to Jewish expectation, if the ingathering of the Gentiles were to take place, Israel had first to be restored. Even after the resurrection and ascension, and the eager preaching of the apostles as witnesses, Israel had apparently not yet responded and experienced the 'times of refreshing' and redemption that were promised. So the ingathering of the nations could hardly happen yet, could it? God then surprised them through Cornelius: he did in fact 'grant repentance and life' to the Gentiles (Acts 11:15-18), and as events progressed, they began to flood into the new community. What could have happened? Nothing less than that in some sense the prophesied restoration of Israel must have happened already, and was being demonstrated precisely in the success of the gentile mission (as an eschatological act of God). This is precisely the point of James' interpretation of events in Acts 15. He sees in the success of the gentile mission the fulfilment of prophecy concerning Israel as well as the nations: the house of David is being restored and the nations are seeking the Lord (Acts 15:12-18, Amos 9:11f.). This is vitally important. At a council of the church convened to resolve this issue, the considered apostolic interpretation of events was that the inclusion of Gentiles into the new messianic community was the eschatological act of God in granting them repentance and salvation, and this was taken as proving the necessary fulfilment of the prophesied restoration of Israel and the Davidic kingdom.

---

[25]*Cf. Knowing Jesus*, ch. 4 ('Jesus and his Old Testament Mission').

XI. Paul's Eschatology for Jew and Gentile[26]

This is the most helpful framework into which to fit Paul's paradoxical teaching on the current relationship between believing Jews and Gentiles on the one hand, and the still unbelieving Jews on the other. It has to be put in the same kind of dual eschatological setting as the kingdom of God in the Gospels. The restoration of Israel both has taken place, and is yet to take place; and it is the ingathering of the Gentiles which fills the tension.

Romans 9-11 are obviously crucial to this issue, but are discussed more fully below in chapter 3.[27] Here it need simply be said that they must be interpreted in coherence first with Galatians 3 and 4, where Gentiles are included in the seed of Abraham through faith in the Messiah Jesus (and where unbelieving Jews are astonishingly likened to Ishmael, in the amazing reversal of types in his allegory in 4:21-31); then secondly, with Ephesians 2, where Paul insists on one new humanity in the Messiah, with no further distinction between Jew and Gentile in Christ. Certainly Paul does envisage a future salvation for 'all Israel' (Rom 11:25f.) but this cannot be understood in such a way as to concede to the whole ethnic Jewish community which remains unbelieving in Messiah Jesus more than Paul does here in Ephesians. It is not salvation for Jews as Jews, but for Israel in Christ. Paul has already made that distinction twice in his letter (Rom. 2:28f., 9:6-8).

Paul is adamant on God's faithfulness to Israel. But he argues that it is to be seen precisely in two facts: first, that there is a believing remnant among the Jews, to which he himself belongs and which fulfills scripture; secondly, the ingathering of Gentiles is taking place, which is eschatologically and scripturally significant because this was the

---

[26]In addition to the Pauline sections in works cited already, see A.J. Hultgren, *Paul's Gospel and Mission* (Philadelphia, Fortress 1985), ch. 5; J. Munck, *Paul and the Salvation of Mankind* (London, SCM 1959).
[27]In addition to the major commentaries on Rom. 9-11 and the outstanding recent exegesis of these chapters in N.T. Wright, *The Climax of the Covenant: Christ and the Law in Pauline Theology* (Edinburgh, T & T Clark 1991) ch. 13, see also B. Witherington III, *End of the World*, 99-128, and at a more popular level, S. Motyer, *Israel in the Plan of God* (Leicester, IVP 1989).

original divine purpose for the existence of Israel.[28] Paul wants to affirm two inseparable truths: the ingathering of Gentiles will not be at the expense of God's promises to Israel; nor will God's fulfilment of promise to Israel fail to extend his mercy to the Gentiles. In any case, nothing in the passages cited requires or supports a national or territorial restoration of the Jews as being necessary in order to fulfil prophecy which is explicitly seen as already fulfilled in Jesus the Messiah.

XII. Hebrews and what we already 'have' in Christ

The book of Hebrews is often sadly absent from discussion of this issue, but it has vital perspectives which complement the Gospel and Pauline material. Basic to its argument is that in Jesus Christ we have in reality all that was equally reality for Old Testament Israel. The reference to 'shadows' (8:5 *etc.*) does not imply that all the great phenomena of Israel's life (such as land, law, temple, priesthood, monarchy) were unreal or only a kind of pretence.[29] They were indeed real factors in the relationship which then obtained between God and his people. Moreover, they were filled, by the promise and the prophecies, with extended meaning in the light of what God would do in the future for and through Israel. Hence, to talk of what we have in Christ being 'better' (as Hebrews repeatedly does), is not just 'replacement theology', disparagingly so-called. It is more like 'extension theology'. In the same way the new humanity in the Messiah must be understood not as a radically new Israel, but rather as Israel redefined and expanded.

Hebrews' affirmations of what 'we have' are surprisingly comprehensive. We have the land, described as the 'rest' into which we have entered through Christ, in a way which even Joshua did not achieve for Israel (3:12-4:11); we have a High Priest (4:14, 8:1, 10:21) and an altar (13:10); we have a hope, which in the context refers to the reality of the covenant made with Abraham (6:13-20). We enter into the Holy Place, so we have the reality of tabernacle and temple (10:19). We have come to Mt. Zion (12:22) and we are receiving a kingdom, in line with Haggai 2:6 (12:28). Indeed, according to

---

[28] As argued above, section I.
[29] The 'Platonic' reading of these texts is inadequate; *cf.* N.T. Wright below.

Hebrews (13:14), the only thing which we do *not* have is an earthly, territorial city![30]

All this is consistent with other teaching within the New Testament: with Paul, who argues that we have the reality of the law by being released from legalism in the power of the Spirit, so that the true righteousness of the law is fulfilled in us (Rom. 8:1-4); with Peter, who affirms that we have the reality of the inheritance by being released from the material, territorial land with its vulnerability to robbery and destruction (1 Pet. 1:4); indeed with Jesus himself, who gives us the reality of the Davidic kingdom through our membership of the inaugurated kingdom of God which it had always represented.

In all of this, then, it is not a case of abolishing and 'replacing' the realities of Israel and the Old Testament, but of taking them up into a greater reality in the Messiah. Christ does not *deprive* the believing Jew of anything that belonged to Israel as God's people; nor does he give to the believing Gentile anything *less* than the full covenantal blessing and promise that was Israel's. On the contrary, we share together in all of it and more—in him, and for ever.[31]

---

[30] *Cf.* Dunn, *Partings*, 86-91.
[31] In addition to the works cited above, the following were consulted in preparation of this chapter: J. Green, *How to Read Prophecy* (Downers Grove, IVP 1984); F.F. Bruce, *This is That: New Testament Development of Old Testament Themes* (Exeter, Paternoster 1968); D.W. Torrance, *The Witness of the Jews to God* (Edinburgh, Handsel 1982); C. Chapman, *Whose Promised Land?* (Tring, Lion 1983); J. Goldingay, 'The Jews, the Land and the Kingdom', *Anvil* 4 (1987) 9-22; A. Kirk, 'The Middle East Dilemma: A Personal Reflection', *Anvil* 3 (1986) 231-258; O.C.M. Kvarme: 'The Theological Implications of the State of Israel' (unpublished paper, 1981); B.K. Waltke: 'An Evangelical Christian View of the Hebrew Scriptures', in Tannenbaum, Wilson and Rudin, edd., *Evangelicals and Jews in an Age of Pluralism* (Grand Rapids, Baker 1984); A.J. Rudin and M.R. Wilson, *A Time to Speak: The Evangelical-Jewish Encounter* (Grand Rapids, Eerdmans 1987); M. Hooker, *Continuity and Discontinuity: Early Christianity in its Jewish Setting* (London, Epworth 1986); R. Riches, *Jesus and the Transformation of Judaism* (New York, Seabury 1982).

CHAPTER 2

JERUSALEM IN THE OLD TESTAMENT

Gordon McConville

I. Introduction

The purpose of the present paper is to consider the topic of Jerusalem in the Old Testament both in its own terms and from the perspective of Christian interpretation. Such a task is somewhat daunting because of its huge importance in the lives of many people. For many, Christian as well as Jewish, the Old Testament promises about Jerusalem have been gloriously vindicated in events of the present century in modern Israel, while for others, the same events seem to threaten their very existence. Many of the latter are also Christians, and therefore also understand themselves in relation to the biblical revelation. These very different self-understandings imply, naturally, different interpretations of the Old Testament on the subject of the ancient 'promised land' in general, and on Jerusalem in particular. The topic well illustrates the close connection between interpretation and total personal commitment. The interpreter who meddles with these things must know that he deals with aspirations and emotions which are at the heart of people's sense of identity, and with issues which can literally have life and death implications.

For that very reason, however, it is imperative to attempt the task. Though interpretation inevitably begins and ends in some committed stance, and is quite properly passionate, there is a sense too in which it must be disciplined and detached, in order that the passion might not be blind. We shall therefore have to reckon with all the ordinary hermeneutical questions that are faced in the study of ancient texts in general, as well the special ones which arise when Christians read the Old Testament.[1]

The task is not a simple one. There can be no 'proof-texting' solution to this problem of interpretation, because disagreements originate at a more fundamental level. The

---

[1] See J. Goldingay, *Approaches to Old Testament Interpretation* (Leicester, Apollos 1990), and *Theological Diversity and the Authority of the Old Testament* (Grand Rapids, Eerdmans 1987).

reading of individual texts is only a part of a whole reading of Scripture, and for Christians it belongs within the wider endeavour of Christian biblical theology. This puts a question-mark against the idea that texts have an obvious, plain sense, an idea which can carry the implication that to opt for any sense other than the 'literal' is to undermine the authority of Scripture. There is a confusion in this line of thought, for we have in fact no choice but to understand the part, as best we can, in terms of the whole. The present paper is an attempt to do that. In it we will consider in turn the major sections of the Old Testament which are relevant to the topic; it proceeds in this way—rather than by looking at a series of potential proof-texts—for the reason (already given) that context must always be respected. Only at a later stage do we turn to the question of those texts which speak directly about a return of God's people to the 'promised land'.

Finally it needs to be said at the outset that there is no single Old Testament view of the significance of Jerusalem. In the long history of Israel and the diverse writings that emerge from it, Jerusalem is indeed one of the great, ever-present data of the story of her encounter with God. Yet it does not come to us in a coherent or univocal guise. On this topic, as on others, the Old Testament confronts us in its diversity, not to say its elusiveness. We are therefore compelled to sift and compare, and perhaps in the end to make choices—choices which are inevitably made in the context of our own interests.

II. Jerusalem in Israel's History.

The history of Jerusalem in ancient Israel may be sketched briefly.[2] As the Canaanite city of Jebus, it was one of those not taken by Joshua in the conquest (Josh. 15:63; Jdg. 1:21). It remained in Canaanite hands until it finally fell to David in the course of the victories which at last enabled Israel to enjoy that 'rest' from their enemies which had been entailed in the promise of land (2 Sam. 5:6-10; *cf.* Deut. 12:10; 2 Sam. 7:1). More than a mopping up operation, it is normally regarded by students of the Old Testament as a central plank in David's

---

[2]For a brief account see J. Rogerson, *The New Atlas of the Bible* (London, Macdonald 1985) 174-189; also D. Bahat, *Carta's Historical Atlas of the Bible* (Jerusalem, Carta 1976).

internal political platform.³ Israel, apparently, was never a naturally coherent entity which took readily to centralized power or institutions. The persistent disaffection of a Benjaminite-Saulide faction, after the deaths of Saul and Jonathan (see *e.g.* 2 Sam. 20:1f.), illustrates the strains within Israel which were only temporarily eclipsed by the brilliance of David's star within the oriental world. David not only captured Jerusalem, but made it his capital. The choice was intended to unite an Israel that might at any time be pulled apart by the Judean-Benjaminite rift. Jerusalem, on the borders of the two tribal territories, and without any significant patriarchal or ancient Israelite traditions which might have marked it as the real property of a faction, was perfect for the purpose. Jerusalem's symbolic power at its entry into Israelite history was not plucked from the past, but forged in the new event. The city was to be synonymous with Israelite unity.

David's coup, however, could not permanently overcome Israel's centrifugal tendency. When the nation divided into two kingdoms after Solomon's death , Jeroboam strove to legitimate his new northern kingdom by appealing to a more ancient tribal and patriarchal concept of Israel (1 Kgs. 12:16). This view of Israel limited David to his own 'house' (Judah). By the same token, Jerusalem was cast as a mere local sanctuary, and Jeroboam's own establishment of Dan and Bethel as the official worship-centres of his kingdom ensured that the point was not missed.⁴

Jerusalem continued as the capital of the southern kingdom until its fall in 587 BC. In the four centuries from David to Nebuchadnezzar it knew times of prosperity, if none to match that of Solomon, as well as straitened circumstances. Its prestige was particularly enhanced, however, by an event which arose out of one such moment of great distress, namely the siege laid to it by Sennacherib in 701 BC, as part of that king's subjugation of Judah, which, under Hezekiah, was involved in an anti-Assyrian coalition led by Egypt. The miraculous deliverance of Jerusalem from the besieging army (2 Kgs. 19:35-37) lent credence to the belief that God would

---

³D. Payne, *Kingdoms of the LORD* (Exeter, Paternoster 1981) 43; J. Bright, *A History of Israel* (London, SCM 1972) 195.
⁴For evidence of David's difficulty in keeping Israel united, see 1 Sam. 2-3; *cf.* Jdg. 20, Josh. 22.

defend it come what may. Having survived that siege, it continued as the capital of the vassal-state of Judah for a further century, subject first to Assyria and then to the new power Babylon. The submission to Babylon, however, was preceded by a temporary resurgence under King Josiah, in the years of transition between Assyria's decline and Babylon's rise.[5] The latter, under Nebuchadnezzar, finally found it expedient to raze the city and its Temple, and exile its people (2 Kgs. 25; Jer. 52).

The restoration of at least some of the next generation of exiled Jews by the Persian Cyrus after his accession in 539 BC is remarkable enough as a historical event, though quite in line, apparently, with that king's policy regarding subject peoples (see Ezra 1, and the so-called 'Cyrus Cylinder').[6] This return to Jerusalem is hailed as a fulfilment of prophecy in 2 Chronicles 36:22 (*cf.* Ezra 1:1), with a reference to Jeremiah's prediction of a seventy-year exile (see Jer. 25:12; 29:10). Its Temple was rebuilt by Zerubbabel (Ezra 6), and subsequently its walls by Nehemiah (Neh. 1-6). The city thus became the religious centre of Judaism—despite a growing and vigorous Diaspora—until its destruction by the Romans in 70 AD. Undoubtedly the rebuilding of the Temple, and the degree of security won for it by the successful completion of the walls, played a crucial role in the survival of the Jewish religion. Once again the symbolic power of Jerusalem cannot be over-estimated—as seen, for example, in the gloom of Nehemiah on learning of the dilapidation of the distant citadel (Neh. 1). The fulfilment of Jeremiah's prophecy, however, is not the last word in the story, and as we shall see, the status of the city as the centre of a small religious community in a large Empire, was capable of different theological constructions.

This sketch of Jerusalem's history suggests in itself its evocative power. Yet already something of its ambivalence emerges: at the inception of the kingdom, it was a force for

---

[5]For Hezekiah's tribute to Assyria, see 2 Kgs. 18:14f. Manasseh subsequently adopted a thoroughgoing Assyrian policy (2 Kgs. 21:1-9); see J. Bright, *op. cit.*, 309-12.
[6]For the text of the 'Cyrus Cylinder', see J.B. Pritchard, ed., *Ancient Near Eastern Texts* (Princeton, Princeton University Press 1969); for an account of its meaning and importance, D.J. Wiseman, ed., *Peoples of Old Testament Times* (Oxford, Clarendon Press 1973) 315-20.

unity, yet almost by the same token a catalyst of division; when God's power to deliver was in doubt, it could answer with a triumphant affirmative, yet also rephrase the question with a wholly new acuteness; when the Temple stood once more upon its Mount, it could speak of promises fulfilled, and yet point to a goal not yet reached (Neh. 9:32-36).

III. Jerusalem in Israel's Religion

As has been observed above, at the time of David, Jerusalem lacked a pedigree in Israel. While David could exploit this, it also posed a theological problem: how could Jerusalem be accepted as a centre of Yahwism? David's answer was to bring the Ark to Jerusalem (2 Sam. 6). The immediate effect of this was to claim for Jerusalem the centrality and primacy in Israel which had been enjoyed in the days of the Judges by Shiloh, by virtue of the resid-ence of the Ark in that place (*cf.* Josh. 18:1; Jdg. 18:31; 1 Sam. 1:3). The importance of Shiloh, however, was only intermediate, since the real significance of the Ark was its associations with Sinai.[7]

In the Sinai pericope (Exod. 19-34) we meet the Ark as the footstool of God, who is enthroned above it, and who from that place speaks to the people through Moses (Exod. 25:22). In Deuteronomy's account of the remaking of the Tables of the Law, we find the Ark as the place where these are kept (Deut. 10:5; *cf.* 31:9). The bearing of the Ark to Jerusalem, therefore, marked it as the place where the Sinai covenant was remembered and cultivated. Thus, Jerusalem succeeds Sinai as a symbol of Israel's status as the special people of God. It seems likely that the first procession of the Ark to Jerusalem was subsequently remembered in the Temple liturgy, in which it is depicted precisely as a march from Sinai to Zion (Ps. 68, esp. vv. 8, 17).[8] Furthermore, Psalm 50 pictures a theophany of God

---

[7]For the centralizing significance of the Ark, see J. Bright, *op. cit.*, 161f., 196; G.W. Anderson, 'Israel: Amphictyony: 'AM, KAHAL, EDAH', in H.T. Frank and W.L. Reed, edd., *Essays in Honor of H.G. May* (Nashville, Abingdon 1970) 135-51.

[8]The name 'Zion' probably originally referred to the hill located between the Tyropoeon and Kidron valleys which was the site first of the Jebusite stronghold and then of David's city. Jerusalem may have been the name for the city-state broadly understood. In time the former term came also to apply to the Temple-mount, perhaps because of the

in the Zion sanctuary (v. 2), in terms that are reminiscent of Sinai by virtue both of the imagery of fire and tempest (v. 3; *cf.* Exod. 19:6, 18) and of the allusion to a covenant made by sacrifice (v. 5; *cf.* Exod. 24:3-8). Perhaps most important in this connection, Psalm 132 pictures the arrival of the Ark in Jerusalem as God's election of Zion (v. 13—an extension of the idea formerly applied to the patriarchs and the whole people in Gen. 12:1-3 and Exod. 19:5f.), and as his own achievement of 'rest' (v. 14, *cf.* Deut. 12:10). In the Biblical story of God's election of a people for himself—a vital element in the history of salvation—it has a crucial place. Properly understood, the ark symbolizes nothing less than God's grace in his dealings with mankind.

With the forging of a link between Sinai and Zion, and the extension of the election idea to the latter, Jerusalem is assimilated to the ancient covenantal theology. The picture is then completed with the theology of the election of David. The narrative account of the origin of this election is that of the promise to David of a dynasty through Nathan the prophet (2 Sam. 7:4-17). However, the connection between the elections of king and Zion is most clearly established by certain Psalms, notably Psalms 2 (v.6) and 110 (1f.).

The election of Zion, therefore, becomes part of the Biblical story of election. That story, of course, is always moving forward, and there are frequent admonitions in the Bible against inferring permanence from election. The historic monarchy, after all, disappeared. The conditionality of the election of David is evident from 1 Kgs. 2:2-4 (more so here than in 2 Sam. 7). Indeed, election in the Old Testament cannot become self-serving; rather, it is purposeful, always pointing forward to something new (as with the promise to Abraham in Gen. 12:1-3, which would have as its ultimate outcome the 'blessing of all nations'), and imposing obligations (this is, for example, the basis of Amos' critique of Israel in Amos 3:2).

In this way, Jerusalem enters the very heart of Israel's self-understanding and piety. With all its colourful fabric and procedures it occupies a far more prominent place in Israelite religion than the pages of our Old Testaments, read through modern European eyes, reveal at first glance. In Israel, piety

---

transfer of the ark thither; indeed in many Biblical writings there is virtual synonymity between 'Zion' and 'Jerusalem'.

can hardly be separated from the material side of worship.[9] The Temple is the place where God is met; it is awe-inspiring, because he is holy, yet it is also a place of rejoicing, because it is good to be near God.[10] Something of its place in the Israelite psyche may be gleaned from the so-called 'pilgrimage Psalms' (such as 84, 122) with their expressions of longing to be in Jerusalem; others have simply been called 'Zion Psalms', because they celebrate the presence of God there with his people (*e.g.* 46, 48, 76, 78:68ff.). This divine presence proves to be the most important factor, and not the place itself: this is the crucial point that was adumbrated in 2 Sam. 7:5-7, and it will become evident again as we continue to examine the texts of the Old Testament.

IV. A 'Zion-Tradition'?

On the basis of material of this sort, it has become customary to speak of a distinct 'Zion-tradition' within the Old Testament, that is, a particular theological tradition which gives special prominence to Jerusalem in its understanding of the relationship between God and Israel. The elements in such a tradition, according to G. von Rad, are:
i) Yahweh takes up his abode on Mt. Zion;
ii) Zion thus becomes the throne of Yahweh and his chosen king;
iii) Yahweh wins a victory over an alliance of nations opposed to him and his king, with the battle and victory being couched in mythological terms.[11]

The main evidence for such a theological stream is found in the Psalms and in the Book of Isaiah. Its crucial assertion is that *Yahweh protects Zion, his dwelling-place, permanently and unreservedly*. At issue, therefore, is the nature of God's self-

---

[9]Hence, for example, the difficulty of deciding between 'thanksgiving' and 'thank-offering' as a translation of the Hebrew תּוֹדָה: compare RSV and NIV on the heading of Ps. 100).
[10]Notice the stress on 'rejoicing' in Deut. 12; *cf.* Neh. 12:43.
[11]G. von Rad, *Old Testament Theology* I (Oliver & Boyd, London & Edinburgh, 1962) 46f. The three elements mentioned can all be found in Ps. 2; note also Jerusalem in the 'far north' (Ps. 48:2) and the 'river' flowing through it (Ps. 46:7). For other treatments of the Zion—or Jerusalem—cult-tradition, see R.E. Clements, 'Deuteronomy and the Jerusalem Cult Tradition', *Vetus Testamentum* 15 (1965) 300-12; E.W. Nicholson, 'The Centralization of the Cult in Deuteronomy', *Vetus Testamentum* 13 (1963) 380-9.

revelation; in what sense can he be said to be interested in places?

If such a view of the relationship between Yahweh and his people really were advocated by any book or block of material in the Old Testament, it would be a major ingredient in an argument for the permanence of Jerusalem in God's purposes and therefore into the present day. Hence we must investigate this in some detail. Our conclusion, however, will be that, if a 'Zion-tradition' (as thus defined) ever actually existed, it was never in fact openly propounded or advocated either in the Psalms or in Isaiah, or indeed anywhere in the Old Testament.

The association of Zion with Sinai (noted earlier) already sets a question-mark against it; for if Zion embraces the theology of the covenant made at Sinai (with its ethical and conditional character), then by definition it will be understood that God's dwelling there is contingent upon Israel's faithfulness to the covenant.[12] But other considerations tell against it also. This will emerge best from a consideration of the major literary-theological blocks in the Old Testament in which Jerusalem/Zion plays a role (Psalms, Isaiah and the other major prophets). One of our central concerns, therefore, in the following, will be to see how the Old Testament interacts with this alleged 'Zion-tradition'.

V. An Old Testament Theology of Zion/Jerusalem: Initial Hesitations?

Before considering the reflection on Zion in the Psalms and prophets, it is important to notice a certain hesitation, in the traditions concerning the election of Jerusalem itself, about the building of a Temple there. This hesitation is registered in Nathan's oracle to David in which the king is promised a

---

[12]In taking the view that Zion takes over from Sinai a conditional covenantal theology I leave aside the contentious question of the historical development of covenantal theology in Israel; see E.W. Nicholson, *God and His People* (Oxford, Clarendon 1986) for a recent defence of the view that covenant is a relatively late arrival, the first scent of which may be detected only with Hosea. For a contrary understanding see J. Day, 'Pre-Deuteronomistic Allusions to the Covenant in Hosea and Psalm lxxviii', *Vetus Testamentum* 36 (1986) 1-12. A number of Psalms clearly bring together the language of covenant and of law (*e.g.* 50; 78; 81).

lasting dynasty: in response to David's declared intention to build a 'house' for Yahweh, Yahweh deters him from this, saying that, on the contrary, he will build David a 'house' (now understood as a dynasty); David's project is deprecated on the grounds that Yahweh has never lived in a permanent construction (2 Sam. 7:5-7). It is true, of course, that in the end a Temple is indeed built, by Solomon, with Yahweh's express permission and guidance (*cf.* 2 Sam. 24). Yet there is a certain parallel between the reluctance that yields to permission in this case and that reluctance, also yielding to permission, in the case of the institution of kingship itself. The debate on that subject is found in 1 Sam. 8-12; its ultimate outcome was the exalted king who reigned on Yahweh's holy hill.[13] The debate had begun, however, with the clear implication that the demand for such a ruler impugned the kingship of Yahweh in Israel, and that the thing demanded was not properly Israelite, but Canaanite.

There are reasons for thinking that a similar concern underlies the hesitation about a Temple expressed in 2 Sam. 7:5-7. The idea of a god who dwells on a holy hill, and thus guarantees the security of the people who worship him there within their borders, is entirely at home in Canaan, and a religious system at whose heart stands a manipulative cult. The Canaanite view of the world, like the Mesopotamian, has frequently been contrasted with that historical understanding of God and creation which is expressed in Biblical covenant theology. The contrast can be too crudely drawn. Yet it is salutary, at the beginning of a discussion of the 'Zion-tradition', to notice the hint of its conflict in principle with the idea of Yahweh's kingship (1 Sam. 8:7; *cf.* Deut. 33:5).

The hesitations about Jerusalem and its Temple in the passages quoted find their theoretical basis in Deuteronomy. Deuteronomy is, in my view, cool in its attitude to dynastic kingship (17:14-20), and conspicuously reticent about the identity of the place of worship which it directs the conquering tribes to establish (12:5, 14 etc.). While some treatments of Deuteronomy have seen in the altar-law a veiled promotion of the primacy of Jerusalem in Israel's worship, it seems to me

---

[13]For the unity of that narrative (in contrast to the older critical idea of contrary accounts woven together) see R.P. Gordon, *1 and 2 Samuel* (Exeter, Paternoster 1986) 105-30.

that the concern of Deuteronomy lies elsewhere: on the one hand in its insistence on the exclusive rights of Yahweh as opposed to other gods; on the other in its so-called 'name-theology', by which it expresses the 'real presence' of God on earth while guarding against any attempt to encapsulate him there (*cf.* 1 Kgs. 8:27). Indeed, though the altar-law clearly came at a certain point to be interpreted of Jerusalem (*e.g.* 2 Kgs. 21:7), it was, in my view, not always so (see Jer. 7:12). Deuteronomy, therefore, has a theology of Zion/Jerusalem only in the sense that it carries warnings against the attachment of undue importance to any place of worship in itself. This is also true of the Deuteronomistic History (Joshua to Kings).[14]

VI. Zion/Jerusalem in the Psalms

It is time to ask whether the observations we have already made about Zion in the Psalms are a sufficient guide to its understanding there. We have seen how on the one hand it becomes the successor of Sinai, and on the other how the ancient election theology is extended to embrace Zion and David together. If, however, a selection of Zion-Psalms celebrate the dwelling of Yahweh there, the Book of Psalms as a whole does not present us with that perspective in an unqualified way. One question-mark, for example, against von Rad's understanding of Zion in the Psalms comes from within the Zion-tradition itself, namely from Ps. 87, with its roll-call of nations 'who know me' (v.4); here is a clear hint that the

---

[14]The view that Deut. 12 has little interest in the 'place' of worship as such is argued in detail in my *Law and Theology in Deuteronomy* (Sheffield, JSOT 1984) 21-38; *cf.* G.J. Wenham, 'Deuteronomy and the Central Sanctuary', *Tyndale Bulletin* 22 (1971) 103-18. For the contrary view, see M. Weinfeld, *Deuteronomy and the Deuteronomic School* (Oxford, Clarendon 1972) and R.E. Clements, *Deuteronomy* (Sheffield, JSOT 1989) 27-30, who think that Deuteronomy promotes Jerusalem. I have also argued elsewhere against the idea of a first pro-Zion/David edition of the Deuteronomistic History in the reign of King Josiah, as advocated by F.M. Cross, *Canaanite Myth and Hebrew Epic* (Cambridge MA, Harvard University Press 1973) 274-89, in 'Narrative and Meaning in the Books of Kings', *Biblica* 70 (1989) 31-49. For a discussion of the influence of Canaanite Temple imagery on the Old Testament, see R.E. Clements, *God and Temple* (Oxford, Blackwells 1965).

theology of Zion will not finally be exclusive. Yet there is an even more important consideration.

If we put the Psalms' message about Zion in a 'canonical' light (in the sense advocated by Brevard Childs), the Zion tradition appears quite differently.[15] This is because the locus of the Psalter's formation is not the cult of the First Temple, but a setting after the exile, an event which the Zion-tradition could not pass through and emerge in anything like the form in which von Rad found it. For the exile witnessed the destruction of the Temple, and indeed was defined by this (1 Kgs. 25; Ezra 1), while the monarchy was destroyed permanently.

There are signs, indeed, that the Zion-tradition is actually experienced as a problem in the Psalms. Most significantly, Psalm 89 first portrays it in an eloquent hymn on the faithfulness of Yahweh, in which the permanence and security of Jerusalem and its king are celebrated at length. The extravagant, unqualified terms of vv. 1-37, however, become highly uncomfortable in the light of the closing sections of the Psalm (vv. 38-52), in which the familiar tones of the Psalm of Lament arise specifically from the anguish not only because of the loss of the city, but because the event has laid a certain understanding of God's promise about Jerusalem in ruins.

Psalm 89 stands in a crucial position in the Psalter, at the end of Book 3. Book 2 of the Psalms had ended with the editorial comment: 'The Prayers of David the son of Jesse are ended' (72:20). Davidic superscriptions do not exactly disappear from the Psalter at this point (see 101, 103, 108-110, 124, 131, 138-145). However, they do not appear anywhere in Book 3. Indeed, the contents of Book 3 (Pss. 73-89) make it look like a kind of response to the role of David which had been implied in Books 1 and 2 (partly by means of the editorial arrangement of superscriptions there, and partly by content, for example the prominence of Psalm 2). Book 3 opens with Psalm 73, that searching examination of Yahweh's justice; it contains at least one, probably two, Psalms (other than 89) which reflect directly on the destruction of Jerusalem (74, 79); and it closes with the Psalm in question, with its sustained and terrible protest at the dismantling of a way of looking at the

---

[15] B.S. Childs, *Introduction to the Old Testament as Scripture* (London, SCM 1979) 14.

nature of covenantal faithfulness which had become axiomatic. If the Psalms furnish evidence of a Zion-tradition in something like von Rad's terms, a tradition which provided the axioms of Psalm 89:1-37, the Psalter itself questions it in a devastating way.[16]

Nor does it do so only with the bewildered petitions of that Psalm. It is surely no accident that Book 4 switches the perspective at the outset from David and Zion. Psalm 90 is 'A Prayer of Moses'. Its opening verses lead the thoughts to the whole scope of Israel's history with God, and to an affirmation of God's endurance that is grounded, not in the covenant with David and Zion, but in creation-theology. The meditation on the brevity of human life (a Wisdom theme) sets the expression of faith in God on a broad canvas, that no longer seems to depend on a restoration of Zion. Indeed, the language of 'dwelling' and 'refuge', both here and in Psalm 91 (90:1; 91:1, 2, 4, 9), are reminiscent of Psalm 46 (one of the great 'Zion Psalms')—yet here without any allusion to Zion. Furthermore, Psalms 93, 96-99, emphasise the kingship of God, again grounded in creation, and again responding apparently to the deep doubts raised by the question posed in Psalm 89. Here too, the affirmations of Yahweh's kingship are removed from a context in Zion-theology.[17]

---

[16]Notice also A. Weiser's belief that Ps. 76 (a classic 'Zion Psalm') may be eschatological in character: *The Psalms* (London, SCM 1962) 526-528. On the present form of the Book of Psalms as indicating a coming to terms with the loss of the Temple, see G.H. Wilson, *The Editing of the Hebrew Psalter* (Chicago, Scholars' Press 1985).

[17]Oddly enough, it is these very Psalms which led Mowinckel to his idea of an Enthronement festival in which the kingship of Yahweh was represented by a dramatized enthronement of the Davidic king: S. Mowinckel, *The Psalms in Israel's Worship* I (Oxford, Blackwell 1962). His general theory, however, and his reading of these Psalms, is generally not followed now. For criticism of his views, and pointers to recent research on the Psalms, see P.C. Craigie, *Psalms 1-50* (Waco, Texas, Word 1983) 43-48. Incidentally, Ps. 110 may appear to spoil the picture offered above of the retreat of David from 'kingship Psalms' following Book 2. It may, however, be the exception that proves the rule, because of the comparison of the Davidic king with Melchizedek, the 'priest for ever'. With the allusion to the priest-king of Canaanite Salem (Gen. 14:17-24), the Zion-tradition is lifted out of the history of the Israelite monarchy and may strike an eschatological note (*cf.* the use of Melchizedek in Heb. 7).

The Book of Psalms as a whole reflects the movement in Judaism from a religion of Temple and cult to one of synagogue and Torah.[18] That movement is not simple, and of course Temple worship continued in Judaism until AD 70. Nevertheless, the Psalter confirms that the concept of Yahweh's dwelling with his people could not be the same after the exile as before. If there was a Zion-tradition in Israel, it cannot be said that the Psalms teach it. Paradoxically, the Book of Psalms, though perhaps more intimately associated with Jerusalem and its Temple than any other book, ultimately shows that their significance is only relative.

VII. Zion/Jerusalem in the Book of Isaiah

The prophet Isaiah is often held to be the other great exponent of the Zion-tradition. He is familiar with both court and Temple: his decisive experience of vocation comes in the context of a vision in the former (Isa. 6); and much of his ministry seems to unfold in the environs of the latter, in which he evidently has ready access to the king (Ahaz, Isa. 7; Hezekiah, Isa. 37:21-39:8, *cf.* 2 Kgs. 19:20). His language, furthermore, owes much to that set of concepts which we found in the 'Zion Psalms': Zion is Yahweh's holy hill, the place where he dwells (4:5f.; 8:18; 10:12; 12:5f.; 14:32; 24:23; 30:19; 31:4f., 9), and specific oracles promise that he will defend the city (31:4f.). One of the book's great climaxes, indeed, is the discomfiture of the army of Sennacherib in its siege of the city (37:33-38). This account might be seen as the vindication of the book's theme of the inviolability of Zion because of Yahweh's dwelling there.[19]

Just as with the Psalms, however, the individual statements have to be interpreted within the framework of the whole book. As is well known, a distinction is normally made between the words of Isaiah of Jerusalem and the book as a whole, which is said to represent the deposit of several

---

[18] The marks of Torah are indelible on the Psalter: Ps 1 is a superscription to the whole; the arrangement is in five Books; the longest Psalm (119) is a meditation on the Torah.
[19] See R. E. Clements, *Isaiah and the Deliverance of Jerusalem* (Sheffield, JSOT 1980) for his argument for a Josianic edition of the book of Isaiah, which emphasised the inviolability of the city; *cf. idem*, *Isaiah 1-39* (London, Marshall, Morgan and Scott 1982) 5f.

generations' additions and theologizing. In particular, Isaiah 40-55 and 56-66 are normally regarded as having quite separate origins, in Babylon and after the restoration to Palestine respectively. The question of authorship need not trouble us unduly. It is plain that the Book of Isaiah is at least intended for consumption in and beyond the exile, and one of our key texts (Isa. 2:1-4) is often attributed to Isaiah of Jerusalem (*cf.* Mic. 4:1-4).

However, the parts of the Book of Isaiah are not meaninglessly juxtaposed. As with the Psalms, there are signs of careful composition. Once again, the book should be interpreted 'canonically'. This means that the oracles suggesting Jerusalem's inviolability are qualified by the thrust of the whole. And that, patently, allows little quarter to the idea that Jerusalem would enjoy unlimited and unqualified protection. The call-narrative itself prepares prophet and reader for a hardness of the people to the message, and consequent judgment (Isa. 6:9-13). Isaiah, in his exhortation to King Ahaz not to put his trust in an alliance with Assyria, but rather in Yahweh (Isa. 7), requires him to believe in order that he might 'be established' (7:9b). On a broader canvas, the deliverance of Jerusalem from the Assyrian threat (37) turns out to be only a secondary climax in the composition of the book; for its sequel in chapters 38f. is of crucial importance. Hezekiah, having become ill, is told first that he will die (38:1), then in response to his prayer for healing, that his life will be spared for a further fifteen years (vv. 2-6). This temporary reprieve for Hezekiah is an echo of the temporariness of the reprieve for Judah following its deliverance from Assyria.[20] Isaiah 39 relates the embassy from Babylon, which, to Isaiah, is so clear a harbinger of the coming fall of the city to that power (39:5-7). At the beginning of Isaiah 40, the fall of the city is already history.

This is not to say that the Book of Isaiah thus finishes with Jerusalem. On the contrary, the new beginning at Isaiah 40 declares precisely that her 'warfare is ended' (40:1), and the deliverance from Babylon becomes a dominant theme of the lyrics that ensue (eg 43-6; 46:1f.; 47:1-4). The message of deliverance is addressed to 'Jerusalem' (40:1); it is

---

[20]The link between Hezekiah's lengthened span and the term put upon Judah's existence as a nation is made in v. 8.

Jerusalem/Zion that shakes itself free from captivity, and in which Yahweh shall again dwell with his people (52:1f.; *cf.* 59:20; 62:1, 6f., 11; 66:13). Nevertheless, the new thing that is thus envisaged is not a mere 'turning back of the clock'. As in the Psalms, the events of 587 BC have altered things irreversibly; there can be no such thing as an inviolable Jerusalem, capital of the kingdom of Judah, with its Davidic dynasty intact.

The language of Isaiah 40-66 makes this clear. The deliverance from Babylon is a real historical event indeed; yet it is depicted in highly symbolic terms. It is a New Exodus, recalling the first deliverance of Israel, namely from Egypt (43:16f.), and at the same time a New Creation (43:15; *cf.* 43:1f.). Yahweh is doing a completely new thing (43:18f.). Furthermore, although the prophecy undoubtedly expects a return to Jerusalem, the city in Palestine (44:26-28), the names 'Jerusalem' and 'Zion' can have a certain ambiguity about them. 'Jerusalem' often stands for the people themselves (40:2; 41:27; 49:14; 51:17). Sometimes, indeed, there is a fine line between literal and metaphorical uses of the name, as in 52:7-10: the return to 'Zion' is a token before the world that the God of Israel reigns.

In parallel to this extended understanding of Zion is a reinterpretation of the dynastic oracle to David, that covenant with him which promised him royal descendants 'for ever' (2 Sam. 7:12-17). The terms of this promise are plainly adopted in Isaiah 55:3, in which it is now addressed to all those (the verb is plural) who will hear the message of deliverance. The Davidic covenant is 'democratized'; the union of David and Zion which was essential to the Zion-tradition can no longer be understood in its original sense. This fits entirely with Isaiah 2:1-4, an oracle situated in a significantly prominent place in the book. Here the Zion-tradition has been drastically revised: Jerusalem is indeed the divine dwelling-place, but the Holy War imagery of Psalm 2 has disappeared, as has the Davidic king.

All this raises the question, what kind of Israel is being created as a new thing in the earth? Who are the real addressees of the oracles in Isaiah 40-55? In the previous paragraph a definition was offered, namely 'all those who will hear the message of deliverance' (a definition gleaned from Isa. 55:1, 6); the Zion that is restored, then, is presumed to be a faithful Zion. This emerges from certain passages which are reminiscent of the classical prophets (*e.g.* 43:22-24; 48:3-5). This note is struck rather more strongly in parts of Isaiah 56-66 (*e.g.* ch. 58). Furthermore, the theology of 'servanthood' is relevant to the discussion. For Israel, in its truest fulfilment of its mission, is a servant (note the identification of the servant with Israel, 49:3), and supremely a suffering servant (52:12-53:12). The theology of Zion in Isaiah 40-55 in particular is thus no mere declaration of imminent events, but much more a vocation to the people who are redeemed.

The dénouement of the Book of Isaiah in chapters 56-66 confirms this interpretation. Parts of this section are simply reminiscent of the tone of 40-55 (*e.g.* 60-62). Other parts strike the sombre note which we find in chapter 58, apparently in recognition that the restored community would not yet achieve that final ending of her 'warfare', in spite of the oracle of Isaiah 40:2. The righteous and the poor suffer at others' hands (57:1; 58:6f.); there is division and alienation in the community (63:16-19); Zion is again a 'wilderness' (64:10); and the ideal of 'servanthood' is embodied only in a minority (64:13f.). Correspondingly, the image of Zion begins to take on the tones of apocalyptic and eschatology. In other words, its redemption is now put on a plane which seems less in imminent history than in a great culmination of it. Yahweh is not now merely doing a new thing, but creating new heavens and a new earth (65:17), a new creation which is in parallel with a creation of Jerusalem. Moreover, 'heaven [and not the city in Palestine] is my throne, and the earth is my footstool' (66:1; contrast Ps. 132:7, 13). Notice also the apocalyptic tendencies in 60:17-20, and in the development of 2:2-4 in 66:18-21. By the end of Isaiah, Zion is understood as God's glorified people in a new creation which is at the end of time and on a cosmic scale.[21]

In regard to the Book of Isaiah, therefore, as with the Psalms, the impression that there is an unquestioning promotion of the historical Jerusalem as the place of God's special favour is superficial. More important is the idea of

---

[21]For accounts of the theology of Isa. 40-55, see B.S. Childs, *op. cit.*, 316-38 (in the context of his treatment of the whole book); G. von Rad, *Old Testament Theology* II (London, SCM 1975) 238-62; C. Westermann, *Isaiah 40-66* (London, SCM 1969) 8-21.

God's presence with his people, albeit depicted in 'Jerusalem' language.

VIII. Zion/Jerusalem in the Book of Jeremiah

Regarding the place of Jerusalem and its Temple in Israel's life, Jeremiah is in a sense at the other end of the spectrum from Isaiah. The burden of his message, far from promising Yahweh's defence of the city, is its forthcoming destruction, because of the persistent sin of the people. As in Isaiah, the Zion terminology is capable of both literal and extended usage (notice the address to the 'daughter of Zion', 4:31; 6:2, 23). The context of such terminology, however, is the portrayal of desolation and grief that will accompany the fall of the city. That the Zion-tradition itself forms the backcloth of such preaching is clearest in 8:19, where the prophet echoes, rhetorically, a cry of the people:

'Is the LORD not in Zion?
Is her King not in her?'

The perplexity of this anguished utterance is explicable only in terms of the Zion-tradition with the assumption of Yahweh's dwelling on his holy hill, and the idea of his kingship there.[22]

Jeremiah's consistent burden, indeed, could be called the insecurity of Zion. The point is made with great force in one of the most famous incidents in the book, the so-called Temple-sermon, which occurs twice, in longer and shorter versions, at 7:1-15 and 26:1-6. Its message is that, contrary to the people's evident expectation, Yahweh's commitment to Jerusalem and its people is not a blind guarantee, nor can it be cultivated by an attention, however fastidious, to ritual worship alone. The mere intoning 'This is the Temple of the LORD, the Temple of the LORD, the Temple of the LORD' (v. 4) avails nothing if the weightier matters of the law are neglected. Jeremiah insists on the point in terms reminiscent of Deuteronomy's conditional understanding of covenant (vv. 5-7; *cf.* Deut. 4-5). The example of Shiloh, formerly the place which enjoyed the privileges now Jerusalem's, but which had disappeared from history, is appealed to as sombre evidence of the truth of Jeremiah's words (vv. 12-15).

---

[22] As defined above, n. 11.

Jeremiah's announcement of Jerusalem's doom is the hallmark of his prophetic work. His inversion of the Zion-tradition is so complete that he can even use the language of 'holy war'—typical of that tradition—in reverse: far from his fighting for Jerusalem to defend it (recall Isa. 31:4f.), God is now its resolute enemy, ready to bring destruction on his own heritage because of its treachery (21:4-7). His chosen instrument would be Babylon, and Jeremiah's charge was to show that the way of faithfulness was acceptance of the chastisement: there was a future for those who bowed to the yoke, but not for those who resisted (Jer. 24). The writing was on the wall not only for the city and population but also for the Davidic dynasty. Jeremiah has little but scorn for its last representatives before the fall of Judah (ch. 22), with the exception of Josiah, though even for him his praise is fainter than one might have expected from the Deuteronomic portrayal of him in 2 Kings 22f. (*cf.* Jer. 22:15f.). Of King Jehoiachin (Coniah), borne off to Babylon in 597 BC, Jeremiah says:

> 'Write this man down as childless
> for none of his offspring shall succeed
> in sitting on the throne of David,
> and ruling again in Judah' (22:30).

His message, therefore, can be regarded as a sustained attack on the Zion-tradition. It is hardly surprising that, for his adherence to that message, he could be regarded as a traitor (37:11-15).

Hitherto, however, we have considered only the main theme of the 'prophet of doom'. Contained in it, however, was a pointer to the future salvation of the people, precisely through the purging of exile (ch. 24). The exile would last just seventy years, after which Babylon in turn would fall (25:12-14) and the exiles would return to their land (29:10). Jeremiah too had a Gospel to proclaim, most celebrated in his announcement of Yahweh's New Covenant with Israel and Judah (31:31-34). That well-known passage is embedded, in fact, in a more sustained collection of sayings on the theme of salvation, known as the 'Book of Consolation' (chs. 30-33). Briefly, this section looks beyond the judgment of exile to a marvellous restoration. And most interestingly for our present purposes, it seems to revive those very things which the main thrust of

Jeremiah's preaching appeared to have laid firmly in the dust of the Babylonian depredations. The immediate implication of the New Covenant is that Jerusalem will again be inhabited; concrete topographical parameters are indicated (31:38-40). Furthermore, old, false conceptions of permanency are replaced with new promises which proclaim, in the most emphatic terms, a new and permanent Davidic covenant (33:12-26), in which Jerusalem shall again be for Yahweh 'a praise and a glory before all the nations' (33:9).[23]

Paradoxically, therefore, the prophet who was undoubtedly, for the greater part of his ministry, the most hard-bitten opponent of the Zion-tradition, leaves us a book which, taken as a whole, holds out a far more specific hope for the restoration of the city than the Book of Isaiah had done— though superficially the latter appeared more sympathetic to the tradition.

In this connection the promises of re-possession of land in Jer. 30-33 should be noticed. This indeed is the central focus of these chapters: Jeremiah's purchase of a field from his cousin (told at length in 32:6-15) serves as a guarantee that 'houses and fields and vineyards shall again be bought in this land' (*i.e.* that the exile would end and the people would return). A passage like 32:36-41 has therefore been an important text for those who consider that certain biblical prophecies either have been fulfilled in events of the present century, or still await fulfilment.[24]

Two brief points need to be made in response to this approach. First, the logical and theological movement within the book of Jeremiah is rather complex. It is true of this great block of material, as it was of the Psalms and Isaiah, that the exile has altered things irrevocably. The hopeful statements in the book are not simply promises of a return to the former *status quo*. Rather, they occur in the context of the New Covenant theology, at whose heart is the affirmation that Yahweh's future relationship with his people will be precisely

---

[23]Jer. 33:14-26 is absent from the LXX. The essence of its thought, however, is present elsewhere in the Book of Consolation; *cf. e.g.* Jer. 32:37.
[24]For a defence of the view that Biblical prophecy is still being fulfilled in events in the Middle East today, see *e.g.* D. Prince, *The Last Word on the Middle East* (Eastbourne, Kingsway 1982). Contrast C. Chapman, *Whose Promised Land?* (Tring, Lion 1983).

not as it was hitherto. The promises of restored, and permanent, institutions are in the context of a new kind of covenant, in which Israel's faithfulness will, in some mysterious new way, be possible, where in the past her hardness of heart had frustrated it (31:33; 32:40-41). In Jeremiah, therefore, the future of Jerusalem is inseparable from its possession by a faithful people.[25] This consideration must always be a crucial qualification of the promises of return to the land.

The second parting comment about Jeremiah is that, on the broader canvas of the Old Testament, the book cannot be taken in isolation. This is because his prophecy of a seventy-year exile followed by a return is taken up in subsequent literature, namely in Chronicles, Ezra and Nehemiah, which will put a distinct slant upon it, to which we must shortly turn.

IX. Zion/Jerusalem in the Book of Ezekiel

Though the name 'Zion' does not occur in the Book of Ezekiel, the Zion-tradition is central to its message. The opening vision, as is well known, depicts Yahweh enthroned over Babylon, using symbolism (the Ark's chariot-wheels, cherubim) drawn from Tabernacle and Temple;[26] the inference is often drawn that Ezekiel breaks away from traditional concepts to an understanding of the universal reign of God. However, this conclusion can be too hastily drawn. For the whole structure of the prophecy is built on the idea of a temporary withdrawal of Yahweh from Jerusalem, in expression of his wrath over a corrupt people, to be followed in due course by his triumphant return: chapters 8-11 relate the departure of the Glory of Yahweh from the Temple (10:18; 11:2), whilst the return of his Glory is described in 43:1-5. In the meantime, Yahweh himself has been 'a sanctuary to them [the exiles] for a little while in the countries where they have gone' (11:16). Thus, the subject of the whole book may be said to be the presence of Yahweh with his people, conceived in terms of the Temple. The great closing vision of Yahweh dwelling among his people in a new Temple

---

[25]The theology of the Book of Jeremiah is examined in greater detail in my *Judgment and Promise: Interpreting the book of Jeremiah* (Leicester, Apollos 1993).
[26]*Cf.* 1 Sam. 6:7f. (for evidence of the ark being borne on a wheeled vehicle) and Exod. 25:21f.

(chs. 41-48) is the climax of this theme. The rationale of such a restoration is not dissimilar to that in the Book of Jeremiah; the language of New Covenant (without the term itself) reappears as the basis of the expectation that the future relationship between Yahweh and his people will be viable, while it had not been so hitherto (11:19f.).

On the face of it, therefore, the Zion-tradition receives strong affirmation from Ezekiel. The impression gains strength from closer scrutiny. The promise of the exiles' return to the 'high mountain of Israel' (Ezekiel's typical way of referring to Jerusalem) is associated with the expectation of a renewed Davidic monarchy. In 17:22-24, such a scenario follows upon the fall of Babylon. In 20:40, it is seen as Yahweh's measure to preserve the people from falling into idolatry among the nations (cf. 20:32), and thus to vindicate himself both in their eyes and in those of the nations (20:41b, 42). The Davidic Messianic promise gains its own elaboration; David will be Yahweh's 'shepherd' (under Yahweh himself, the Shepherd, 34:23f.); he will rule over a unified nation, a 'prince for ever', Yahweh's sanctuary being in the midst of the people (37:22-26). The echoes of the dynastic promise to David (2 Sam. 7) are unmistakable. The message of Ezekiel seems clear: Yahweh will vindicate himself among the nations by delivering the exiles from Babylon, and by dwelling among them in Jerusalem, with a Davidic king on the throne (see also Ezk. 36:24, 33-38). Like that of Jeremiah, therefore, Ezekiel's prophecy has an important place for the literal restoration of God's people to the historic land, and therefore to Jerusalem.

However, this picture requires some qualification. The manner of allusion to Jerusalem throughout is worthy of comment. As already noted, the term 'Zion' is never used. The language which is typically used, furthermore, has certain mythological overtones. The phrase 'the high mountain of Israel', especially because it appears to be co-extensive with the whole land (20:40a), calls to mind the Canaanite conception whereby Temple-mount and land are one and the same.[27] This mythological language is easily adapted to the rather eschatologized hope with which the Book of Ezekiel ends. The

---

[27]The plural form of the phrase also appears in Ezk. 34:14, perhaps heightening the identification of a mythic mount and the whole land (cf. 6:2; 37:22; 39:2, 4).

war of Yahweh on behalf of his people in chapters 38f. is based on their deliverance from Babylon (39:28a), yet also suggests, anticipating aspects of apocalyptic literature, a grander and final conflict (see *e.g.* 38:5f., 15f., 20). In this context, the imagery of cultic feasting is appropriated to a vision of eschatologized Holy War, in which the sacrificial flesh and blood is that of the enemies of Yahweh and his people (39:17-20). The conflict takes place, indeed, on the 'mountains of Israel' (38:8); yet the Zion-tradition (which of course incorporates the Holy War) has been expanded to depict something that transcends it.[28]

There is also a distinctive development of the tradition, furthermore, in chapters 40-48. There too the Davidic promise, though not absent, is muted (the 'prince' apparently playing 'second fiddle' to the Zadokite priests).[29] More interestingly, the vision of the new Temple is highly stylized, and located in a land with stylized boundaries. The extravagant vision of life and fruitfulness in the land (47:1-12) involves a highly poetic portrayal of the Temple as the source of it. The water issuing from beneath the threshold belongs (like the Holy War of 38f.) to the Zion-tradition (*cf.* Ps. 46:4), but the motif is derived in turn from mythological ideas, according to which the mountain of the gods was a place from which rivers flowed (*cf.* also Gen. 2:10-14). The life-giving properties of the Temple revitalize even the Dead Sea, in a bold portrayal of creative power. The image is a prelude to the stylized fixing of tribal boundaries, according to its traditional ultimate limits (47:15-20). Jerusalem is to be a separate territory in the midst of the tribal allotments, 'a portion set apart for the LORD' (48:9). The tribal allotments are a succession, from north to south, of equally proportioned bands of land running across the country. The city is itself a thirteenth such territory (eighth in the series that begins in the north, vv. 8-22), and is conceived, in a twist on the traditional allocation of cities within the tribal lands to the Levites, as a תְּרוּמָה an offering to Yahweh (v. 10). Finally, the city is named 'The LORD is There' (48:35); the ordinary name of Jerusalem is replaced by an expression which conveys the essential character and destiny of the city, but which, in Hebrew, hints at

---

[28]Note, incidentally, that the Davidic aspect of that tradition finds no place here.
[29]Notice also the criticism of kings in Ezk. 43:7-9.

the literal name, by virtue of its sound (Yahweh Shammah; *cf.* Yerushelaim).

The interpretation of Ezekiel's use of the Zion-tradition is complicated. On the one hand, it can be seen as a ringing affirmation of the main elements in that tradition (so Zimmerli).[30] The poetic use of the mythological language which had already found a home there can be regarded as a free re-statement of it; the idealized picture of a new Temple, if it is not a literal blueprint, at least depends for its force on the actual re-building of a Temple in the ancient city; moreover, the explicit hope of a new Davidic dynasty (in 34:23f.) is in keeping with this view.

Against it, on the other hand, stands the fact that Ezekiel nowhere uses the name 'Zion'. Similarly, the eschatological note struck in chapters 38f. may be thought to set the context for the picture in chapters 40-48, which, with its own poetic imagery and stylized re-presentation of the traditions of election and settlement, avoids promising a mere return to conditions that prevailed before the exile. In chapters 40-48, moreover, 'David' is reduced to a 'prince', who plays a minor role (44:3). The essence of the final vision is simply that Yahweh will again dwell among his people. Bringing the wider context of the book to bear, that people is one which can be expected to be faithful because of the theology of New Covenant.[31]

In favour of the second of these approaches to Ezekiel is our point that the Jerusalem of the final vision is portrayed according to its true character and destiny. Ezekiel no doubt holds out the hope of an imminent return of the exiles to the land, and probably the task of reconstructing the Temple. But, like Jeremiah, he knows that the idea of a mere restoration is misguided. He looks for a decisive and new act of God in the history not only of Judah but of the nations.

X. Hope for Zion/Jerusalem after the Exile

Our study of some of the major blocks of Old Testament literature has shown that Jerusalem's fall in 587 BC and the exile that ensued had a massive impact upon Israel's thinking about itself and its destiny. In each of them, in different ways,

---

[30]W. Zimmerli, *Ezekiel* I (Philadelphia, Fortress 1979) 41.
[31]See above on Jeremiah; *cf.* also Ezk. 11:16-21.

the Zion-tradition is in the centre of the theological reflection; the loss of Jerusalem, in the light of the promise made to David, compelled new ways of conceptualizing the nation's hope in its God. What more may be said about Old Testament views of Jerusalem after the exile?

The Book of Jeremiah, it will be recalled, held out specific hopes of a return, even giving a timetable. In seventy years Babylon would lie in ruins and Jerusalem and the cities of Judah would be repopulated.[32] Jeremiah's prediction is specifically taken up in the largest single block of Old Testament post-exilic literature, namely Chronicles-Ezra-Nehemiah. The Books of Chronicles date from c. 400 BC;[33] they re-tell the story of Israel from the beginning (actually from the beginning of the world) to the restoration of the exiles at the hand of Cyrus. This restoration is seen as the fulfilment of the prophecy of Jeremiah (2 Chr. 36:21). An almost verbatim repetition of the last two verses of Chronicles in Ezra 1:1f. shows that Ezra-Nehemiah (which continue the story from the point at which Chronicles left it, into the restoration period) proceed from the same starting-point.[34] Does it follow that Chronicles-Ezra-Nehemiah see the restoration under Cyrus as the definitive fulfilment of the prophets' promises of a redemption that will follow the judgment of exile? If so, it would raise questions about any simple application of those promises to present-day events.

---

[32]The 'seventy years' can be reckoned in either of two different ways: as from c. 605 BC (the time of Nebuchadnezzar's first raids on Jerusalem, when, according to Dan. 1:1-7, the first deportations of Jewish people to Babylon took place) to c. 535 BC (shortly after the decree of the Persian King Cyrus permitting the exiles to return to their own land, Ezra 1:1ff.); or from 587 BC (the date of the destruction of the Temple) to its rebuilding in 516 BC. In each case the figure is approximate. The latter is to be favoured because of the significance attached to the loss of the Temple and its furnishings in 2 Chr. 36:18f. and Ezra 1.
[33]H.G.M. Williamson, *1 and 2 Chronicles* (London, Marshall, Morgan and Scott 1982) 15f. dates Chronicles in the mid-fourth century BC, though allowing that precise dating is speculative.
[34]There are other evidences of Ezra-Nehemiah's dependence on Jeremiah, especially in its use of the term גּוֹלָה ('exiles'. This word is found several times in Jer. 29 (vv. 1, 4, 16, 20, 31), in the same context as the prediction of the seventy-year exile (v. 10). It then appears, for example, in Ezra 1:11, 2:1, 4:1 etc.; *cf.* Ezk. 1:1; 3:11, 15 etc.

The answer is complicated, first of all, by the question whether Chronicles-Ezra-Nehemiah is a literary and theological unity (which we cannot discuss in detail here).[35] On the face of it, it would seem that Chronicles takes a highly positive view of the return to Jerusalem and the rebuilding of the Temple there, since that is where the book ends. Its theological message (briefly, that God is always ready to turn again in favour to those who return humbly to him, *e.g.* 2 Chr. 7:14) makes such a view of its final position quite plausible. The likelihood that 2 Chr. 36 is in some sense a finishing point is suggested by the nature of the linkage between it and Ezra 1, which looks editorial. It is necessary, therefore, to ask whether Ezra-Nehemiah take the view of the return to Jerusalem which seems to be present in Chronicles.

In my view, Ezra-Nehemiah are somewhat guarded in their praise of the restoration and its aftermath.[36] There are definite indications that both books express dissatisfaction with the circumstances in which they find themselves. First, the returned exiles still toil under foreign domination;[37] secondly, the laying of the foundations of the new Temple has a decidedly mixed reception from those who had seen that of Solomon (Ezra 3:10-13); thirdly, the sin in the community (*i.e.* the mixed marriages) directly throws the fulfilment of prophetic promise into question.[38] It is no accident that both Ezra and Nehemiah finish with the story of mixed marriages, and therefore the apparently irresolvable problem of recurring sin, and hence ongoing slavery.

---

[35]The contention that Chronicles-Ezra-Nehemiah form a theological and compositional unity is a commonplace of Old Testament criticism, represented, for example, by M. Noth, *The Chronicler's History* (Sheffield, JSOT 1987). The recent challenge by H.G.M. Williamson, *Israel in the Books of Chronicles* (Cambridge, CUP 1977), has been influential, but the case for unity has been defended again by D.J.A. Clines, *Ezra, Nehemiah, Esther* (London, Marshall, Morgan and Scott 1984) 9-14.

[36]For fuller argument, see my 'Ezra-Nehemiah and the Fulfilment of Prophecy', *Vetus Testamentum* 36 (1986) 205-24.

[37]Notice the allusion to the Persian overlord as the King of Assyria (6:22) and the prayers of Ezra (Ezra 9, Neh. 9, esp. vv. 32-6) where the inhabitants of Jerusalem are spoken of as 'slaves'.

[38]Note Isa. 40:2: 'your warfare (עָוֹן) is ended'; but it is precisely the exiles' עָוֹן, still alive and well in the community, that causes Ezra's horrified reaction in Ezra 9: see v. 13.

This does not mean that Ezra-Nehemiah do not think that prophecy has been fulfilled by the return from Babylon. On the contrary, they incorporate a highly sophisticated reading of certain prophecies (especially Jer. 31 and Isa. 40), such that Ezra's act of repentance actually functions as a prerequisite of the realization of the New Covenant.[39] It does mean, however, that in their view what has happened in their time is only a beginning.

This consideration of Chronicles-Ezra-Nehemiah poses a question: if there are actually two views here (*i.e.* in Chronicles: prophecy fulfilled; in Ezra-Nehemiah: prophecy only *begun* to to be fulfilled), which does the Old Testament affirm? We return to this question in a moment.

A word is necessary first, however, about other post-exilic literature. The period has been the subject of considerable speculation about the shape of its theological development, because of large gaps in our knowledge of its history, and because the texts often tell us less than we would wish. It has become common, however, to suppose that the post-exilic community became sharply divided. On one side stood a group that supported the official religion, centred on Jerusalem, and believed that in all essentials prophecy was fulfilled in the restoration and the reconstituted cult (Chronicles represents this view; Haggai and Zechariah 1-8 could also be counted here). On the other was a group that was critical of the cultic establishment, and looked for the salvation of the faithful elsewhere. This group found its voice in apocalyptic literature in particular.[40]

The polarization of these reconstructed groups is probably exaggerated; there is an obvious danger of reading back into the restoration period some of the tensions known to have existed around the turn of the eras. Nevertheless, it is true that there is literature in which Jerusalem forms at best a small part of the hope that is expressed. This includes Daniel, which in general builds but little on covenantal theology, and therefore on the Zion-tradition, though Daniel 9 forms an important exception. In Esther, the fate of the people of God

---

[39]J. G. McConville, *op. cit.*, 213-223.
[40]See P.D. Hanson, *The Dawn of Apocalyptic* (Philadelphia, Fortress 1979); O. Plöger, *Theocracy and Eschatology* (Richmond, John Knox 1968).

seems to be played out at the centre of the Persian Empire; here the 'exile' continues, and the obligation laid upon the faithful to return to the holy city in Ezra-Nehemiah is unknown.[41] For completeness, mention should be made of the whole Wisdom stream in the Old Testament, in which covenantal theology plays, at most, a very minor role. The fictitious setting of Ecclesiastes in the mouth of a king in Jerusalem is far from an affirmation of the Zion-tradition, but rather a device which serves the theme of the futility of all things.[42]

There is, therefore, no unified view of the significance of Jerusalem in the post-exilic literature. Rather, the watershed of 587 BC produced different responses. Where 'Zion' imagery is retained in expressions of hope for the future, it is rarely (if ever) in the form of a simple return to the *status quo ante*. The shared prophetic vision of a restored Israel is of an entity that is qualitatively different; in the terms of the New Covenant, this is based in turn on an act of God that is qualitatively different. It is not easy to turn such prophecies into a vision for the historical city of Jerusalem. This is the more true of that literature in which hopes for Jerusalem introduce an eschatological element, removing it from the ordinary historical plane. Jerusalem becomes, in the prophetic vision, a symbol of God's final work of salvation for all the nations, who unite in their knowledge and worship of him. In all this Jerusalem—the historical city—recedes into the background. Just as it was not in evidence at the beginning of the Old Testament story (not even in tribal Israel—according to some, the 'truest' manifestation of the people of God in the Old Testament), so it is not essentially (or at least uniformly) there at the end.

---

[41] See S.B. Berg, 'After the Exile: God and History in the Books of Chronicles and Esther', in J.L. Crenshaw and S. Sandmel, edd., *The Divine Helmsman* (New York, KTAV 1980).
[42] The Wisdom literature is not, of course, all post-exilic. It is important, however, to notice this whole dimension of the Old Testament. Ecclesiastes shows that it was still flourishing in the late Old Testament period, in a form which was posing sharp questions to covenantal theology. See G. von Rad, *Wisdom in the Old Testament* (London, SCM 1972); and for a statement of sharp contrast between the wisdom and covenantal strains in Old Testament theology, J.L. Crenshaw, *Old Testament Wisdom: an Introduction* (London, SCM 1982).

Nevertheless, a problem of interpretation remains. At the outset we noted that the story of Jerusalem in the Old Testament inevitably presents the interpreter with choices, the nature of which by now should be clearer. Christian interpreters already stand in a tradition of choice-making on the subject that goes back as far as the form of the Old Testament canon which we find in the Christian Bible. The contrast between the order of the books there and in the Hebrew Bible is interesting in regard to this issue. In the Christian Bible (based on the LXX), Chronicles-Ezra-Nehemiah immediately follow the other historical books, with which they have much content in common (namely Samuel-Kings). This is so in spite of the fact that they come from a later and wholly different period in Israel's history, and have a quite different message. The effect of placing them after Samuel-Kings is to make them a kind of repository of additional information about the history of Israel (as actually implied by the LXX's name for Chronicles—Παραλειπόμενα or 'Things Left Out'). Consequently, Chronicles has not, by and large, occupied a prominent place in Christian biblical interpretation. The Christian form of the Old Testament closes rather with the prophets. This is in accordance with the emphasis on promise and fulfilment in an approach to the Old Testament which takes its starting-point in the New Testament. There is, therefore, in the arrangement of the Christian Old Testament, an interpretative bias towards an open, expectant Old Testament. The nature of that expectation, for Christian interpretation, is controlled by the New Testament.

The Hebrew Bible makes an equally revealing choice. In it, Chronicles is in the final position, aligned not with other history-books (the Former Prophets in Jewish understanding), but with the Writings, in the third division of the Hebrew canon. That this is not a relegation of Chronicles to a low position appears from the fact that the natural order of Chronicles-Ezra-Nehemiah (*i.e.* the chronological order retained in the Christian Bible) has been reversed. In this way, Chronicles, rather than the somewhat pessimistic Ezra-Nehemiah, occupies what is in fact the climactic final position. The last word in the Hebrew Bible is about the restoration to Jerusalem and the rebuilding of the Temple there. Future development of the relationship between God and his people, in Jewish interpretation, should happen within that framework; the interpretative choice made in the order of books chosen by the canonizers of the Hebrew Bible prescribes it.[43]

We have seen above that the diversity of usage regarding Jerusalem in the Old Testament, particularly in post-exilic literature, allows for diverse evaluations of its significance. It should also be clear that strikingly different evaluations have actually occurred and entered the traditions of the two main religions that have an interest in the Old Testament. By laying its accent on the prophets, Christian expectation regarding Jerusalem is governed by the sorts of considerations we outlined in our treatment of the main prophetic corpora. The language of the Zion-tradition was used, but as the vehicle of a hope for something qualitatively new. The Old Testament does not promise mere repossession of land and restoration of institutions.

It is in the light of this conclusion that one must, in the end, evaluate those passages which seem so unequivocally to speak of a return to the land and to the city of Jerusalem (*e.g.* Ezk. 36:22-38; 40-48), and which have been taken by many to find their fulfilment in the modern immigrations of Jews to Israel. I have argued from a study of the Old Testament books themselves that passages like these cannot be interpreted 'literally', as fixed promises concerning a remote future. On a symbolic level, of course, they remain to be fulfilled at the end of the Old Testament period, as is suggested by the conviction in Ezra-Nehemiah that they were incompletely fulfilled in their time.

There is, however, a further reason why it is difficult for Christians to read them thus. This has to do with Christian theology more broadly understood, and the re-focussing of Christian hope upon Christ himself, who has rendered hope in the institutions of the 'Old Covenant' obsolete.[44] This happens most explicitly in the Letter to the Hebrews, but also in the

---

[43]W.J. Dumbrell, *The Faith of Israel* (Leicester, Apollos 1989), is an interesting treatment of the books of the Old Testament, by a Christian writer, according to the order of the Hebrew canon.
[44]We have observed above in Section III that talk of Jerusalem in the Old Testament is impossible apart from talk of the cultic institutions of the Mosaic covenant.

Gospels and in Paul.⁴⁵ Such a recognition releases us from the need to try to interpret literally a passage like Ezekiel 40-48, which in my view was never meant to be taken so (its use of figurative language seems clear in ch. 47), but whose essence is a promise of God's presence (Ezk. 48:35b). For Christians, this translates very well into the presence of God with his people the Church in Christ.

XI. The Old Testament and Modern Jerusalem

As noted at the beginning, the interpretation of biblical texts about Jerusalem inevitably inspires great passions. If the foregoing seems to suggest that the Old Testament has little or nothing to say to us about the living, historical city of Jerusalem, this is hardly a satisfying conclusion of our study in itself. It is true that the Old Testament attaches no importance to Jerusalem in the simple sense of a geographical location; there is no basis in a Christian reading of the Old Testament for a continuing idea of 'sacred space'. The idea of some necessary, special significance of a place leans more towards Canaan than biblical theology (which, as we have now seen, nowhere simply adopts what we have called the 'Zion-tradition'). Yet Jerusalem remains symbolically very powerful in the Old Testament, even if the so-called Zion-tradition is criticized and finally transformed there. Moreover, as this whole volume makes abundantly clear, the city of Jerusalem remains powerful for those who live there (or who would like to live there!) and who still require to bring their theological traditions to bear upon it.

Jerusalem evokes a number of ideas in the Old Testament. David saw its potential as a unifying force; it is associated with the kingship of God over all the earth; it is the place of true worship. From the perspective of the New Testament, none of these things need—or can—any longer be posited of Jerusalem alone. Nevertheless, they may be helpful as we try to think what Jerusalem, that modern meeting-point of the faiths, and branches of them, might be. We saw in our study how an understanding of Jerusalem (the 'Zion-tradition') came gradually to be transformed. A key text was Isaiah 2:2-4, in which the rather inward-looking focus of election was

---

⁴⁵Such a position is outlined in greater detail in ch. 3 below.

turned outward, so that Jerusalem became the place to which the nations made pilgrimage, and from which the law (Torah, or knowledge of God) went forth. This might become our text for a view of modern Jerusalem—a city rejoicing in its international and inter-denominational character and in which (and from which) the Church bears a clear witness to the God who Christians believe dwells uniquely in Christ.

Such a view can be no more than sentimental wishful thinking, however, without the recognition that this demands a certain kind of attitude on the part of the various interested groups, especially, for our present purposes, Christian groups. Two points need to be made in closing.

First, those who desire 'reconciliation' should not be content to spiritualize it, as if our belonging together in Christ automatically did away with our practical difficulties. This is patently not the case. On the contrary, different groups of Christians can be strongly committed to courses of action which inevitably lead to collision. Reconciliation of the legitimate interests of different groups is inescapably political, and requires action, especially to alleviate the suffering of the weak. This is where the Old Testament prophets most directly confront those interested in Jerusalem and Israel today.

Secondly, there is in Christianity (and even in certain Old Testament laws, *e.g.* Deut. 24:19-22) an imperative to be ready to relinquish that to which one appears to have a perfect right. The situation in modern Jerusalem, and in the land of which it is part, is one of those in which different groups seem to have clear rights, yet these rights exactly contradict each other. In such a situation it is strictly speaking impossible to think of a 'solution'. Kenneth Cragg has spoken in this connection of a need to 'relativize our legitimate particularities'— though he acknowledges the enormity of such a demand. This 'relativizing' is not spoken of allegiance to Christ in itself; it evokes, rather, the vision of a Church which, though diverse, proclaims the reality of love, self-sacrifice and reconciliation. This is the essential condition of witness to Christ in Jerusalem and a truly Christian contribution to the peace of that city.

CHAPTER 3

JERUSALEM IN THE NEW TESTAMENT

Tom Wright

I. Introduction

This chapter is inevitably written with mixed feelings. Having lived in Jerusalem recently for a period of three months one is painfully aware of the way in which almost anything that one says on this whole subject is bound to hurt or offend someone: a case could therefore be made for remaining silent. That is not, however, a Christian option: for there is currently a good deal of misinformation on the subject of the New Testament and its attitudes towards the Jewish people in general and to Jerusalem in particular. This needs to be countered squarely. The following is therefore offered in the hope that it will at least dispel some current false readings of the text, and perhaps raise useful questions and possibilities in doing so.

II. Jerusalem in the First Century

The exiles had returned, but the exile was not over. That paradox dominated the self-perception of many first-century Jews. As we see clearly in the Scrolls, but equally in various other writings of the period, there was a common sense that the destruction of Babylon had not, after all, been the end of exile, the fulfilment of the great promises of what Israel's God would do for his people in the end.[1] New 'Babylons' had arisen:

---

[1] See *e.g.* Neh. 9.36f.; Baruch 1:15-3:8; 1 Enoch 85-90; 2 Macc. 1:24-9; *Damascus Document* 1:2-2:1; and many other primary sources. These are discussed, and this point made, in *e.g.* O.H. Steck, *Israel und das gewaltsame Geschick der Propheten. Untersuchungen zur überlieferung des deuteronomistischen Geschichtsbildes im Alten Testament, Spätjudentum und Urchristentum* (WMANT 23: Neukirchen-Vluyn: Neukirchener Verlag 1967); D.E. Gowan, 'The Exile in Jewish Apocalyptic', in *Scripture in History and Theology: Essays in Honor of J. Coert Rylaarsdam* (ed. A.L. Merrill and T.W. Overholt: Pittsburgh Theological Monograph Series 17, 1977) 205-23; M.A. Knibb, 'Exile in the Damascus Document', *JSOT* 25 (1983) 99-117; N.T. Wright, *The Climax of the Covenant: Christ and the Law in Pauline Theology* (Edinburgh and Minneapolis, T & T Clark and Fortress 1991) 141 and elsewhere; idem, *The New Testament and the People of God* (London and Minneapolis, SPCK and Fortress 1992), ch. 10; J.M. Scott, '"For as

Persia, Egypt, Syria. Another false dawn had come and gone in the Maccabean uprising, the Hasmonean dynasty (the last independent Jewish state before 1948). Now, since Pompey in 63 BC, the Romans had taken the place of the traditional enemy. And, at a local level, the Herodian dynasty simply projected the ambiguity of Israel's situation on to a monarchical screen. The would-be 'kings of the Jews' were disliked, distrusted, and disobeyed when possible. National uprisings came and went, their scale difficult to assess but their zeal for God, the Torah and the Kingdom indisputable.[2]

Meanwhile, in the middle of it all, Jerusalem remained the focal point of everything that the Jews were and did. It is a measure of how far modern Western Christianity has forgotten its roots that most church people can read the psalms and the prophets and blithely spiritualize their meaning without feeling the resonances of geography and local culture throbbing through them. However far away from the Land a Jew might be, the regular reading of the psalms and prophets as part of the Diaspora synagogue liturgy (not to mention the regular prayers and benedictions) could not fail to remind him or her that Jewish identity was bound up with, and focussed upon, a single city, and within that city a single shrine. What enormous implications there are, both theological and practical, from the repeated emphasis in the Psalms that the Creator of the Universe had decided to take up residence on the little hill called 'Zion'. However much, as a Christian, one may be well advised to read them in a new light, one cannot avoid

---

many as are of works of the Law are under a curse" (Galatians 3:10)', in *Paul and the Scriptures of Israel*, ed. J.A. Sanders and C.A. Evans (Sheffield, JSNT Supp 1993).
[2]For differing views see M. Hengel, *The Zealots: Investigations into the Jewish Freedom Movement in the period from Herod 1 until 70 AD* (Eng. transl., Edinburgh, T & T Clark 1989). and R.A. Horsley, 'Josephus and the Bandits', *Journal for the Study of Judaism* 10 (1979) 37-63; 'The Sicarii: Ancient Jewish "terrorists"?', *Journal of Religion* 59 (1979) 435-58; 'Popular Messianic Movements around the time of Jesus', *Catholic Biblical Quarterly* 46 (1984) 471-95; 'The Zealots: their origin, relationships and importance in the Jewish revolt', *Novum Testamentum* 28 (1986) 159-92; R.A. Horsley and J.S. Hanson, *Bandits, Prophets and Messiahs: Popular Movements at the time of Jesus*, (Minneapolis, Winston Press 1985); M. Goodman, *The Ruling Class of Judaea: the Origins of the Jewish Revolt against Rome AD.66-70* (Cambridge, CUP 1987).

their literal meaning as the original basis from which such reinterpretation must start.

The importance of all this would certainly not have been missed by first-century Jews, as can be seen by noting what they habitually did.[3] The great majority of Jews went up to Jerusalem for the festivals singing the psalms *en route*; the great majority of Jews heard scripture read regularly in their synagogues. In these ways they acted out, and thereby demonstrated to themselves, their belief that Jerusalem, and its Temple, were the centre of the created order, the place where the creator of the world, who had entered into special covenant with them as a nation, had chosen to place his 'name'.

However, Jerusalem remained ambiguous. Herod had beautified it beyond description: it was 'a structure more noteworthy than any under the sun'.[4] Yet this was the work of Herod!—a work inspired no doubt by political motives, in order to legitimate himself and his heirs as the real Kings of the Jews, the real temple-builders in the line of Solomon; yet most Jews knew that Herod could not be the true King that would come, the genuine Davidic article. Jerusalem remained a beautiful puzzle. Then again, people at large resented rather than respected the ruling class who dominated public life through the period between Herod the Great and AD 70; yet they continued to come to the Temple with their sacrifices, and to keep the festivals in all circumstances. One of the startling things in Josephus' account of the War is his relating that the daily sacrifices were eventually stopped; for it alerts us to the astonishing fact that, despite the horrendous factional fighting in and around the temple for a long time before this, worshippers had still come in daily with their offerings, and that, even more amazingly, the revolutionary and counter-revolutionary fighters clearly let them past! During this

---

[3] Many studies of the period base themselves too closely upon the written texts that have happened to come down to us from the period, such as the Pseudepigrapha or the Scrolls. Vital though these are, we cannot tell how many Jews of this period read (say) 1 Enoch privately, or how many would have secret copies of (say) 1QM hidden away in a cupboard; the answer is probably not many.
[4] Josephus: *Antiquities*, 15. 412.

internecine war pilgrims also still came for the festivals.[5] Seemingly only a total disaster would stop them coming, as indeed eventually it did.

There were, however, some groups at least who refused to join in the pilgrimages. The Essenes are the best example of this, who, as we know from the Scrolls, established a counter-temple movement, regarding their own community as the new temple and rejecting the other one as hopelessly corrupt; like Ezekiel, they cherished a vision of a rebuilt temple, purified, holy, and fit for the living God to dwell in once more; for the moment they themselves were the interim temple, awaiting the great day when God would act to fulfil all his promises.[6] At the same time, temple-ideology informed other movements that flourished away from the holy city: for example, the Pharisees seem to have attempted to reproduce in their own table-fellowship the state of purity required for priests in the temple, thus producing a religious system logically derivative from, and not intended to replace, the central cult.[7] In all these ways Jerusalem played a central, if ambiguous, role in the Judaism of Jesus' day.

III. Jerusalem in the Ministry of Jesus

It was in this world that Jesus grew up, and to this world that he addressed his preaching. If we are to understand the thrust of Jesus' ministry, we must project ourselves as far as possible into the worldview and mindset of a first-century Jew.[8]

Thus, for example, Jesus' summons to Israel simply cannot have looked like something that we would recognise as a 'preaching mission'. People did not leave their workplace and go out to the Galilean hills to be told about a heavenly future

---

[5]This is evidenced, for example in the fact that John of Gischala was able to smuggle his men in to the inner court during such an occasion: see Josephus,*War*, 5. 98-105.
[6]*E.g.* 1QS. 8:5-11; see the discussion in E.P. Sanders, *Judaism: Practice and Belief, 63 BCE - 66 CE* (Philadelphia and London, TPI & SCM 1992) 357 ff.
[7]See the discussion in Sanders, *op. cit.*, chs. 18, 19; N.T. Wright, *The New Testament and the People of God*, ch. 7.
[8]On recent studies of Jesus, see S.C. Neill and N.T. Wright, *The Interpretation of the New Testament, 1861-1986* (2nd ed., Oxford, OUP 1988) 379-403; on this whole section see my forthcoming *Jesus and the Victory of God* (London, SPCK, 1994).

awaiting them after death. Jesus' challenge must have sounded far more like the founding of a political movement. When Jesus called twelve men, took them up into the hills, and told them that they were his special close followers through whom he wished to operate, anyone hearing about such an event would surely have interpreted it, not as a foretaste of what the church thinks of as 'ordination', but on the model of other groups that collected up in the hills of Galilee to plan their strategy: the λῄσται, whom we know from Josephus, the holy brigands bent on assisting God in the bringing of his kingdom.

Thus when Jesus took these twelve to Caesarea Philippi, elicited from them the recognition that he was Messiah, and told them that they were to go up to Jerusalem on a dangerous mission through which 'the Son of Man' would be glorified, they cannot have heard him talking about himself as a divine being whose intention was to act out an abstract atonement-theology, dying for the sins of the world. They must have heard him speak in terms such as these:

If you recognise me as the rightful King, it is time for us to march on to the capital and displace the present usurping crew who are in power there. We will win: you and I together are the new temple, and the present city cannot stand against us. But it's time for resolution: some of us may get hurt, some may die, but God will give us the victory.

Translated back into first-century imagery, this reads more or less as follows:

Blessed are you, Simon, for your confession of me as Messiah: and I tell you, you are the foundation-stone of the new temple, and the gates of hell will not prevail against it.[9] Now, if anyone will follow me, let him take up his cross; anyone who is ashamed of me and my words [i.e. my agenda, my programme] will find that the Son of Man is ashamed of him when he comes in the glory of the Father with the holy angels. But remember this: there are some standing here who will not taste death until they see the kingdom of God come with power.

This reading of Jesus' summons and challenge to his followers, in the context (from their point of view) of a Galilee-based revolutionary movement with intentions to replace the present corrupt Jerusalem system, is reinforced importantly by

---

[9] I owe this reading of the 'gates of hell' to Dr Colin Brown of Fuller Seminary. The recognition that the 'stone' imagery belongs with the 'new temple' theme is made by B.F. Meyer, *The Aims of Jesus* (London, SCM 1979).

a consideration of the significance of the habitual actions which (uncontroversially within the present climate of scholarship) characterized Jesus' ministry.

For example, the table-fellowship he celebrated could not have been offensive to anyone if he had been simply acting as a private individual; the reason it caused a stir was that his whole ministry, just as John the Baptist's had done before, presented itself as a national movement of renewal. His table-fellowship looked, therefore, like a bizarre parody of the Pharisaic model: instead of eating in strict ritual purity, he implied that purity came as a result of eating with him. 'Who are my mother and my brothers?. . .Anyone who does the will of God' (Mark 3:33, 35) Israel was being redefined around him. Moreover, if the Pharisaic model was derivative from the Jerusalem/temple ideology, his could only be seen as a replacement for it. If one was with Jesus, one did not need the restoration into covenant membership which was normally attained by going to Jerusalem and offering sacrifices in the temple: 'Today salvation has come to this house; this man too is a Son of Abraham!' (Luke 19:9)

The force of such sentences is lost unless it is realised that, in making such pronouncements, Jesus was implicitly claiming to do and be what the temple was and did. It is not enough to say, within a normal western-Christian mode of thought, that he was 'claiming to be God'. What he was claiming to do was to act as the replacement of the temple, which was of course the dwelling-place of the Shekinah, the tabernacling of Israel's God with his people. His offering of forgiveness and restoration undercut the normal system; in modern terms, it had the force of a private individual offering to issue a passport or a driving licence, thus bypassing the accredited office. Jesus was offering just such a 'bypass'.

It is in this context that Jesus' warnings about the imminent disaster that was hanging over the head of Jerusalem and the temple can be seen in their proper light. Such warnings were not exceptional in the first century. It was almost predictable that a leader of a new movement would announce the coming downfall of the city that personified (for the Galilean) the southern domination of Judaism and (for the poor) the arrogance and impiety of the aristocratic rich. It was nothing unusual to predict that Jerusalem would be destroyed by enemy action—Josephus claims that he, acting prophetically, did so himself.[10] Such statements were by no means abnormal in the years prior to AD 70.[11] The Essenes themselves waited in the desert, confident that their day would come, and with it the end of the present Jerusalem and the building of the new.

The threat-tradition in the synoptic gospels must therefore be taken very seriously indeed.[12] Jesus' stance was based on old prophetic traditions according to which Jerusalem would be destroyed for her rebellion against her God; not for nothing did some in the crowds say he was Jeremiah (Matt. 16:14). Jesus was announcing the way of peace, of loving one's enemies, of marching an extra mile with the Roman soldier; and the announcement was reinforced by the warning, which at one level is straightforward *Realpolitik*, that, if Israel and particularly Jerusalem refuse this path, the alternative will be destruction at the hands of Rome. Where Jesus differed was in his insistence that when this happened it would have to be seen as the wrath of Israel's God against his wayward people.

This line of thought is developed until it reaches its climax in the 'Apocalyptic Discourse' (Luke 21 and parallels). For example, back in Luke 13, the Galileans whose blood Pilate mingled with their sacrifices would become typical of all inhabitants of Jerusalem who refused to turn from their present way: in other words, Roman aggression would engulf those who insisted on revolt and rebellion. The tree which refuses to bear fruit is given one more year, and then it will be cut down. Then, at the end of that same chapter, Jesus declares, in words reminiscent of Ezekiel's vision of the departing *Shekinah*:

Jerusalem, Jerusalem, the city that kills the prophets and stones those who are sent to her! How often have I desired to gather your children together as a hen gathers her brood under her wings, and you were not willing! See, your house is left desolate to you. And I tell you, you will not see me until the time comes when you say, 'Blessed in the name of the Lord is the one who comes'. (Luke 13:34-5)

---

[10] *War*, 361-420.
[11] Hence, for example, Josephus (*War*, 6. 300-309) speaks of another Jesus, son of Ananias, who during the war went about Jerusalem announcing its imminent fall, and who was scourged for his pains.
[12] See M.J. Borg, *Conflict, Holiness and Politics in the teachings of Jesus* (New York, Toronto, Edwin Mellen Press 1984), though this present paper will go beyond Borg in some significant ways.

The problem with Jerusalem, and the Temple, is that, though outwardly cleansed, they have not been re-occupied by the living presence of God. The unclean spirit that has been cast out returns to its house, bringing others with it, and 'so will it be with this generation' (Matt. 12:43-45): in other words, the Maccabean cleansing,[13] had resulted in a clean but empty temple, and the demons would return with catastrophic results. Drawing on the rich resources of prophetic and apocalyptic language, so often misunderstood, Jesus predicted a coming cataclysm which would have to be seen as the outworking of the judgment of God. In one telling phrase he said that, 'where the body is, there the eagles will be gathered together' (Luke 17:37), an image that no-one familiar with Roman standards could fail to interpret as predicting the legionary vultures swooping down over the carcass of Jerusalem.

Such a reading of Luke 13-21 produces, in passage after passage, a sustained climactic effect which it is impossible to describe here in detail. For example, the controversies in chapter 20 take on new force: the vineyard will be taken away and given to others; the hierarchy have already (quite literally) bought into the Roman system, and whether or not they are giving God his due they will shortly be giving Caesar his. The Apocalyptic Discourse then needs to be read in this light.[14] Jesus is not speaking in this discourse about a supernatural figure floating downwards on a cloud to bring the space-time world to an end; rather he is speaking, as his use of Danielic imagery should have made clear, about the 'beasts' that make war on the 'people of the saints of the most high', and about the 'son of man' who will be exalted and vindicated over them. The 'coming' of the Son of Man, is emphatically not, therefore, his 'coming' from heaven to earth, but his coming from earth to heaven, in vindication and exaltation over his enemies. Moreover, just as no interpreter imagines that Daniel, or Jesus (or the author of Revelation) envisaged real 'beasts' emerging

---

[13]This was still powerfully present to the minds and imaginations of first-century Jews; see W.R. Farmer, *Maccabees, Zealots and Josephus: an inquiry into Jewish nationalism in the Greco-Roman period* (New York, Columbia University Press 1956). The word 'house' would automatically mean 'temple' to a Jew of this period.
[14]For this understanding of apocalyptic (especially Mark 13), see G.B. Caird's brilliant short work (often overlooked): *Jesus and the Jewish Nation* (London, Athlone Press 1965).

from the Mediterranean, so no interpreter ought to imagine that the 'Son of Man' can be interpreted 'literally' as a human figure floating on a cloud. The image speaks clearly, to anyone with ears attuned to the first century, of the vindication of the true Israel over her enemies.

But who is the true Israel? Just as the Essenes would have answered 'we are', so Jesus by implication announced, throughout his ministry, that he was. Just as some of Josephus' contemporaries had reinterpreted Daniel to fit their own situation (making the fourth beast into the Romans instead of Antiochus Epiphanes),[15] so Jesus reinterpreted the book of Daniel (chs. 2 and 7) so that he was the Son of Man, the true representative of the true Israel, and that the present Jerusalem hierarchy were the 'fourth beast': he would build his true temple, and the gates of hell would not prevail against it.

This explains why the Old Testament imagery in the Apocalyptic Discourse is drawn not only from the predictions of the destruction of Jerusalem or Israel[16] but also from the predictions of the destruction of Babylon. There are unmistakeable echoes of Isaiah 13 and 52 (and of Jeremiah 50-51) throughout the chapter. Significantly, Isaiah had commanded the people in these passages to flee from Babylon, lest they partake in the great destruction that would come upon the enemies of the people of God; for the destruction of Babylon is to be seen as the coming of the Kingdom of God:

How beautiful upon the mountains are the feet of the messenger who announces peace, who brings good news, who announces salvation, who says to Zion 'Your God reigns.'. . .Break forth together into singing, you ruins of Jerusalem; for the Lord has comforted his people, he has redeemed Jerusalem. The Lord has bared his holy arm before the eyes of all the nations; and all the ends of the earth shall see the salvation of our God (Isaiah 52:7-11).

The proclamation, 'your God reigns', is indeed a theological truth; but the historical referent of the same sentence (that which has happened within space-time history which enables the announcement to be made) is the destruction of Babylon. Babylon, the enslaver of God's people, has fallen; Israel may now be sure that her God is sovereign over the whole world.

---

[15]Josephus, *War*, 6. 312-15; see N.T. Wright, *The New Testament and the People of God*, 312-14.
[16]E.g. Jer. 21:7, *cf.* Luke 21:23f.

Jesus now boldly applied all this to himself and his cause (seen together as Zion) and to Jerusalem (seen as Babylon). It is from Jerusalem that the true Israel must now flee, lest they partake in her destruction. It is Jerusalem whose destruction will be the sign that the God whom Jesus has proclaimed is now indeed manifestly the king of the whole earth.[17] According to Jesus, therefore, the real referent of Daniel 7 is the destruction of Jerusalem: the Son of Man will be vindicated but the fourth beast (Jerusalem) will be destroyed. Jerusalem and its hierarchy have taken on the role of Babylon, Edom and Antiochus Epiphanes. They are the city whose fall spells the vindication of the true people of Israel's God. The prophecies of rescue from the tyrant have come true in and for Jesus and in his people. When this city falls they must leave quickly; this is their moment of salvation and vindication.[18]

So when Jesus came to Jerusalem he came embodying a counter-system. He and the city were both making claims to be the place where the living God, Israel's God, was at work to heal, restore and regroup his people. Though many people still say that Israel had no idea of incarnation, this is clearly a mistake: the temple itself, and by extension Jerusalem, was seen as the dwelling-place of the living God. Thus it was the temple that Jesus took as his model, and against whose claim he advanced his own.

The action in the temple was therefore inevitable; it forms the exact parallel, within the context of Jerusalem, to Jesus' flouting of kosher and sabbath laws in the context of Galilee. Moreover, seen in this light, the saying about telling 'this mountain' to be 'cast into the sea' (Mark 11:23) must surely be read as referring to Mount Zion; anyone using this language while standing in the vicinity of the Mount of Olives and looking towards the city could only mean one thing, especially in the first century. Jesus' 'trial' then drew together the themes of controversy throughout the ministry, with Caiaphas' most probably hearing Jesus' reference to Daniel 7 as casting him, Caiaphas, in the role of Chief Beast.

---

[17]This is perhaps the best way to interpret Mark 9:1.
[18]*Cf.* Jer. 51:26 with Mark 13:2; Isa. 13:10, 34:4 with Mark 13:24; Isa. 52:11f., Jer. 51:6, 45 with Mark 13:14-17; Jer. 51:46 with Mark 13:7f.; Zech. 2:6 (in context) with Mark 13:27; and Dan. 7:13f. with Mark 13:26.

So Jesus went to his death, convinced within his own first-century Jewish worldview that Israel's destiny had devolved upon him and that he represented the true Israel in the eyes of God. His death would therefore be the means of drawing to its climax the wrath of God against the nation, forging a way through that wrath and out the other side;[19] as a result, all who wanted to do so could follow his way, be joined to his people, and find rescue from the great and imminent disaster, while those who chose to stick to the path of nationalistic militarism would find that such a route led only one way: 'if they do this when the wood is green, what will they do when it is dry?' (Luke 23:31). He applies his last beatitude to the children who will be his age when the great war comes, a generation later:

Blessed are the wombs which never bore, and the breasts which never gave suck; then they will begin to say to the mountains 'fall on us' and to the hills 'cover us' (Luke 23:27-31, drawing upon Hosea 10:8.)

The above presentation of Jesus' message differs markedly from much present scholarship and also from many more popular approaches to the question of Jesus and Jerusalem. For example, the sayings about judgment are normally either read as *post facto* rationalizations or spiritualized into threats of *post mortem* hellfire. They are neither. They are the solemn historical warnings, based on Jesus' understanding of himself and his vocation, that the system which now operates in Jerusalem is playing out the role of Babylon, and is ripe for the destruction predicted in the prophets. The beautiful city has indeed become the 'harlot'.

Jesus' understanding of his own death and vindication must be seen in this light. He was drawing together the threads of Israel's destiny, and acting them out in pursuit of one of Israel's oldest goals and vocations, long forgotten in the dark years of foreign oppression: she was to be the 'light for the nations' (Isa. 42:6). God's house in Jerusalem was meant to be a 'place of prayer for all the nations'(Isa. 56:7; Mark 11:17); but God would now achieve this though the new temple, which was Jesus himself and his people. As stated fairly explicitly at the last supper, Jesus on the cross was to become the place of sacrifice; he also there acted out the destruction (the death of the rebel, at the hands of the occupying forces) which he had

---

[19]*Cf.* N.T. Wright, 'Jesus, Israel and the Cross', *SBL Seminar Papers*, ed., K.H. Richards (Chicago, Scholars Press 1985) 75-95.

predicted for Israel, so that his fellow-countrymen might have a way by which to avoid it. Then on Easter morning Jesus was raised to life as the beginning of the real return from exile, the real liberation of the people of God, from the exile which lay deeper than the exile of Egypt or Babylon. All along, to his disciples' shock, he had been fighting the real enemy (not the enemy they expected him to fight); and he had won. Meanwhile, the hanging on a tree of the 'King of the Jews', outside the walls of the capital city, and his burial in a cave with a large stone at its mouth, had strange resonances going back into the Old Testament and into early anthropological symbolism, which spoke of the ritual pollution of the land and its final expropriation. Never again could it be the same.[20]

IV. Jerusalem in the Early Church: Paul

This understanding of Jesus' message is confirmed as we turn to St. Paul and note his clear awareness that the days of Jerusalem, as he knew it, were strictly numbered. This is how his conviction must be interpreted that the 'day of the Lord' was imminent. Contrary to the thinking of both scholars and pietists of many backgrounds, Paul was not envisaging the 'Parousia' as an event which had to take place in his lifetime, and which would result in the ending of the space-time order. If that were so, how could he possibly write in 2 Thessalonians 2:1-2 that the church should not be alarmed if they received a letter saying that the 'day of the Lord had come'? If Paul meant by 'the day of the Lord' the end of the space-time universe, the Thessalonians would presumably not need to be informed of the fact *via* the Roman postal service! Instead, Paul here reflects the early Christian tradition, going back to Jesus himself, according to which Jerusalem was to be destroyed, and according to which that destruction was to be interpreted as the wrath of God against his sinful people. In the same Thessalonian correspondence, Paul asserted that the wrath of God had indeed come upon them 'to the uttermost' (εἰς τέλος, 1 Thess. 2:16.)

It is this awareness of an imminent end to the way the Jewish world had looked for so long, rather than an imminent end to the space-time universe, that drove Paul on his mission

---

[20]*Cf. e.g.*, Josh. 8:29, 10:26f. I do not know of anywhere where this theme has been explored further, though it would repay such study.

with such urgency. From his own point of view he lived in an odd interim period: judgment had been passed on Jerusalem, but not yet executed. There was a breathing space, a 'little time' in which people could repent, and in which the message of Jesus could spread to Gentiles as well as Jews (though it always remained, for Paul, 'to the Jew first'). When Jerusalem fell, Jews on the one hand would undoubtedly blame those who had reneged on their Jewish responsibilities, including those Jewish Christians who, like Paul, had been enjoying fellowship with pagans and regarding it as the kingdom of God and the true expression of the covenant God made with Abraham. On the other hand, Gentile Christians would probably respond by regarding Jews as an odd early stage in the purposes of God, allowed in at the beginning of the new worldwide movement but now destroyed or at least marginalised. It was in order to avoid this double danger, which would mean that the principalities and powers had won after all and that Christ had not after all created a new humanity, that Paul engaged on his mission, with the aim of creating Jew-plus-Gentile churches on Gentile soil before the fall of Jerusalem. This explains both the urgency of his mission and the language in which he expressed that urgency. It also explains the collection of money which he took to Jerusalem: this was not just an example of poor-relief, but a demonstration to Jewish Christians that Gentile Christians were in solidarity with them and a reminder to Gentile Christians that they were a junior part of the same olive tree.

For a more positive view towards Jerusalem in Paul some are tempted to turn to Romans 11. There, in verse 26, he quotes from Isaiah 59:20 ('the deliverer will come from Zion') in confirmation of his statement that 'all Israel will be saved'. Does this refer to a renewed physical Jerusalem and a large-scale last-minute salvation of all Jews (or nearly all)? [21] No, it does not. For in the crucial passage (Romans 11:25-28) Paul is clearly offering a deliberately polemical redefinition of 'Israel',

---

[21]Space forbids a full discussion of this vital question. Different traditions of interpretation have invested so much in this issue, and therefore the following may sadly cause frustration or pain; I myself took the opposite view for many years but now regard it as exegetically unfounded.

parallel to that in Galatians (6:16),[22] in which the people thus referred to are the whole company, Jew and Gentile alike, who are now (as in chapter 4 and 9:6ff.) inheriting the promises made to Abraham.

The composite scriptural quotation which follows in 11:26b-27 (including the reference to 'Zion') then points in a direction very different from that normally supposed.[23] The quotations used here come from Isaiah 2:3, 27:9, 59:20f. and Jeremiah 31:34. All have to do with God's action the other side of judgment. First Paul combines Isaiah 59:20 f. with Isaiah 2:3 to create the new prediction that the redeemer (not the Torah) will come out from (not 'on behalf of') Zion. These are both passages which speak of the final great renewal of the covenant, the overcoming of the exile, and the blessing which will then flow to the nations as a result of the vindication of Israel.[24] We are here very close to the thoughts in Romans 9:30 and 10:13, and this increases the probability that what Paul is here referring to is not the Parousia but the gentile mission; v.26b is explaining v.26a, with reference to covenantal promises of gentile inclusion in the blessings of the people of God.

Next Paul refers to Jeremiah 31, which invokes the whole concept of the 'new covenant'. This new covenant, which God makes with his people the other side of exile and death, is the real reaffirmation of the Abrahamic promises, and is therefore the final vindication of the righteousness of God. Moreover, the new covenant is emphatically not a covenant in which 'national righteousness' (which, as Paul has already demonstrated, was not envisaged even in the initial promises to Abraham) is suddenly reaffirmed. Instead it is the covenant in which sin is finally dealt with. This was always the purpose of the covenant: now at last, as in Jeremiah 31:34, it is realized.

---

[22] Those who insist on reading the Galatians passage as if it refers to an exclusively Jewish-Christian group should consider the way in which such an interpretation undoes at a stroke the entire argument of the rest of the letter.

[23] The rest of this discussion depends closely on ch. 13 in my book, *The Climax of the Covenant*.

[24] Within the Old Testament, this blessing could be thought of in terms of Torah going out to the nations (*e.g.* Mic. 4:2f.); for Paul, what the Torah could not do is now done in Christ and the Spirit. Hence the replacement of Torah's outgoing by that of 'the Redeemer'.

Finally Paul draws upon Isaiah 27:9, which in its context is not about the vindication of ethnic Israel as she stands but about forgiveness of sins the other side of cataclysmic judgment on the temple. Moreover, the ὅταν ἀφέλωμαι in 11:27b enables Paul to include the idea of a recurring action: 'whenever' God takes away their sins (i.e. whenever Jews come to believe in Christ and so enter the family of God), in that moment the promises God made long ago to the patriarchs are being reaffirmed. As a result, the Roman Gentile Christians must not stand in the way of this fulfillment, for in it there is at stake nothing other than the covenant faithfulness and justice of the one God. This is then celebrated in the paean of praise which concludes the chapter (11:33-6).

There is no justification, therefore, for taking Romans 11, as a whole or in its parts, as a prediction of a large-scale, last-minute salvation of Jews. In particular, the reference to 'Zion' has nothing to do with a renewed physical Jerusalem; rather, it picks up the Zion-tradition according to which Zion was to be the source of blessing for the world and claims that this has now come true in Jesus. The Gentile mission of the Jew-plus-Gentile Christian church is, for Paul, the fulfilment of what Israel's God always purposed to do with the place where he had made his Name and Presence to dwell.

In this light we can interpret two further passages which are of considerable significance for a Christian understanding of the Land in general and Jerusalem in particular. In Romans 4:13 Paul says, startlingly, 'The promise to Abraham and his seed, that they should inherit the world.' Surely the promises of inheritance were that Abraham's family would inherit the land of Israel, not the world? Paul's horizon, however, is bigger. The Land, like the Torah, was a temporary stage in the long purpose of the God of Abraham.[25] It was not a bad thing now done away with, but a good and necessary thing now fulfilled in Christ and the Spirit. It is as though, in fact, the Land were a great advance metaphor for the design of God that his people should eventually bring the whole world into submission to his healing reign. God's whole purpose now goes beyond Jerusalem and the Land to the whole world.

---

[25]For this meaning in Gal. 3, and Rom. 5-8: see my book, *The Climax of the Covenant*, chs. 2, 7, 8.

Incidentally, this then helps us to understand the famous question and answer in Acts 1:6-8. When the disciples ask Jesus, 'Lord, will you at this time restore the Kingdom to Israel' they are presumably thinking of the traditional Jewish expectation that the whole world would eventually be subject to Jewish rule.[26] Jesus' answer is usually taken as a 'not yet': 'it is not for you to know times or seasons.' Yet Luke surely intended us to read it as a 'yes, but not in that way': 'You will receive power, when the Holy Spirit comes upon you and you will be my witnesses. . .to the end of the world.'[27]

The second Pauline passage relating to Jerusalem comes in the middle of a difficult paragraph in Galatians:

for Sinai is a mountain in Arabia, and corresponds to the present Jerusalem, for she is in slavery with her children. But the Jerusalem above is free, which is our mother (Gal. 4:25-6).[28]

Whether explicitly or implicitly, much of Galatians has been about Jerusalem. Paul has been careful not to imply that he and the Jerusalem church disagree with one another (he and they have been misrepresented by first-century opponents as well as twentieth-century scholars); yet, on the other hand, he cannot but regard the present earthly Jerusalem as enslaved. For it is the place where the Torah keeps Israel firmly anchored to her racial and national identity, a situation which is opposed to the message of the Cross which now denies that these things are the inalienable and automatic marks of the people of God (2:19-21, 3:10-14). Such a situation is no better than slavery, even though Israel, the 'young son' in the illustration of 4:16, is 'heir of all things'; it is the junior version of the full humanity which God intended all along for his people. The implied critique of Jerusalem is thus closely tied in to Paul's critique of Israel's abuse of her status and her misuse of Torah. This is a

---

[26] Josephus (*War*, 6. 312-15) tells us that a prophecy to that effect was the most popular passage during the revolt; it is often assumed that he means Dan. 7.
[27] The attempt of D.R. Schwartz, in '"The End of the ΓΗ" (Acts 1:8): Beginning or End of the Christian Vision?', *JBL* 105 (1986) 669-76, to suggest that ἕως ἐσχάτου τῆς γῆς means 'to the end of the land' (i.e. the borders of Israel), is extremely tendentious.
[28] The well-supported reading (τὸ γὰρ Σινᾶ) best explains the other variants in v. 25, and makes best sense in the context. The word πάντων ('of us all') in v. 26 may be a later addition, but has certainly caught the sense Paul intends.

central theme in Galatians and provides us with the right context in which to understand 4:25ff. In these verses Paul sees the Land, and its focal point Jerusalem, as both in theory and in practice relativized by the death and resurrection of the Messiah. This is then confirmed by the fact that Jerusalem, as Paul knows well from his own experience, is a source of opposition and persecution for the church (4:29). The present Jerusalem regime is thus declaring itself by its deeds to be the descendents of Ishmael, not of Isaac.

At the same time, however, there is a 'Jerusalem above', a 'new Jerusalem'. Although there are only two other references to this theme in the New Testament (Heb. 12:22 and Rev. 21:2), the way Paul casually introduces it here implies that already in the early church there was a well-established idea of an alternative city, a city 'to come', which God would bring to birth at its proper time, and to which his true people would belong. Now this is not a Platonic 'idea' of Jerusalem; 'heaven' in both Old and New Testaments is not the place of non-material reality, but the place of God's present and future reality. Rather, it is where the coming things are stored up ('in the mind of God' as we say), so that the heavenly reality is the glimpse of God's intended future. Paul assumes in Galatians 4 the reality of a city which is God's city, for which the earthly city Jerusalem had been simply an advance metaphor. This is then a parallel thought to Paul's conviction that the Torah is an advance metaphor for the Spirit, and the Land for the World.[29] It also corresponds closely with his statement that 'our citizenship is in heaven' (Phil. 3:20). In other words, the church belongs to the renewed people of God in their corporate identity in a parallel way to the manner in which Israel, dispersed or not, belongs to Jerusalem or in which a Roman colony belongs to the mother city. As a result, if someone were to ask Paul, on the basis of Galatians, whether Jerusalem retained in his mind the status which it had had between David and Herod, his answer would surely be 'no'.

A final point, which confirms this Pauline understanding that the earthly Jerusalem was no longer of any spiritual significance, concerns the way in which, almost

---

[29] Paul makes it clear in 2 Cor. 3 that to see Torah, Land and Jerusalem in this light in no way disparages these entities but rather ennobles them.

casually, he refers to the church, and indeed to individual Christians, as the 'temple of the living God' (1 Cor. 3:16, 6:19).[30] To Western Christians, thinking anachronistically of the temple as simply the Jewish equivalent of a cathedral, the image is simply one metaphor among many and without much apparent significance. For a first-century Jew, however, the Temple had an enormous significance; as a result, when Paul uses such an image within twenty-five years of the crucifixion (with the actual temple still standing), it is a striking index of the immense change that has taken place in his thought. The Temple had been superseded by the Church. If this is so for the Temple, and in Romans 4 for the Land, then it must *a fortiori* be the case for Jerusalem, which formed the concentric circle in between those two in the normal Jewish worldview.

V. Jerusalem in the Early Church: Hebrews and Revelation

Although the letter to the Hebrews breathes such a very different air from Paul, a similar collocation of themes emerges in relation to Jerusalem. On the basis of Jeremiah's prediction of the new covenant in which sins will be dealt with once and for all, the author asserts that the temple is 'obsolete and growing old', and 'will soon disappear' (8:13), rendering redundant the regular sacrificial system. Not surprisingly, then, he portrays the heroes of faith from the Old Testament as seeking 'a better country, that is, a heavenly one'; 'therefore', he asserts, 'God is not ashamed to be called their God; indeed, he has prepared a city for them' (11:16). These ideas then prepare us for the thoughts of the final chapters:

You have not come to something that can be touched, a blazing fire, and darkness, . . .But you have come to Mount Zion and to the city of the living God, the heavenly Jerusalem, and to innumerable angels in festal gathering. . .We have an altar from which those who officiate in the tent have no right to eat. . .Therefore Jesus also suffered outside the city gate in order to sanctify the people by his own blood. Let us then go to him outside the camp and bear the abuse he endured. For here we have no lasting city, but we are looking for the city that is to come. (12:18, 22; 13:10, 12-14)

---

[30]Note too the similar theme of 'indwelling' (*e.g.* Rom. 8:9).

Once again, this is not Platonism; the perspective of the writer is thoroughly Jewish and eschatological. Thus the 'heavenly' is that which God intends to bring to birth on earth, and which therefore already exists in his intention; the 'city' which he has prepared for them is therefore not simply a 'mansion in the sky', but a human community of the redeemed in the coming Kingdom, when there will be new heavens and a new earth. Yet this city is by no means to be identified with the earthly Jerusalem. A contrast is developed (similar to that of Paul in Gal. 4) whereby the old covenant is seen in terms of Sinai and slavery, whilst the new is seen in terms of the Jerusalem that belongs to God's ultimate reality (i.e. 'heaven'). In order to belong to this city, one must be prepared to leave the earthly city behind, out of the reckoning, taking as one's model the suffering of Jesus outside the city wall. The present Jerusalem (and therefore the Temple and the Land) belong to the created things that will be shaken; the new community to which Christians belong is of the order of things that cannot be shaken, the Kingdom prepared for God's people (12:26-8).

Finally something must be said, despite its difficulties, concerning the book of Revelation. The above presentation adds some weight to the quite controversial thesis that the city which is to be destroyed (the 'great whore' that has become drunk with the blood of the saints) is to be identified, not with Rome, but with Jerusalem. As with any interpretation of Revelation there are problems with this, but there are also some strong arguments in favour.[31]

First, the whole symmetry of the picture of the whore and the bride (the city that symbolizes rebellion against God and the city that exemplifies salvation and obedience) suggests that, if the new city is the New Jerusalem, that with which this Bride is contrasted is likely to be the Old Jerusalem. Second, although it is popular in scholarly circles to see mentions of the persecution of the church as indications of Roman persecution, it remains the case that far and away the best evidence we possess for sustained and regular attacks on Christians in the first century is the evidence for the attacks carried out by Jews, not least by Jews in, or based in, Jerusalem. If the early church heeded Jesus' teaching in any way, and regarded the present

---

[31] See M. Barker, *The Gate of Heaven: The History and Symbolism of the Temple in Jerusalem* (London, SPCK 1991) 49 and elsewhere.

Jerusalem as at best ambiguous,[32] and at worst as the focal point of that national idolatry which was leading the nation into ruin, then it would be natural for them to share his attitude, according to which Jerusalem had come to symbolize all that was resistant to the gospel and violently opposing the very existence of a counter-Israel, a new people of God; moreover, insofar as the Christians represented one version of a peace movement within pre-war Judaism, they would come in for fierce persecution from the various more militant groups. This provides, not of course the only, but at least a plausible *Sitz im Leben* in which to locate the book. It also confirms again the overriding approach to the earthly Jerusalem in the New Testament, namely that with the coming of Christ it had lost its former significance: the 'new had come'.

VI. Jerusalem: The New Testament and Today

Finally, what does this mean for Jerusalem today? Such a question, involving as it does the application to the present century of these New Testament insights, is an enormous one, but still it must be asked. Moreover, there are certain key points that can and must be stated firmly in our reply.

In this regard, some helpful insights emerge from taking as our hermeneutical model[33] one in which the early church saw history as a five-act play, with creation, fall and the story of Israel as the first three acts, and the drama reaching its climax in the fourth act, the events concerning Jesus of Nazareth. The early church itself was living in the fifth act, where the actors are charged with the task and responsibility of improvising the final scenes of the play on the basis of all that has gone before.

Yet the very end of the play, the final goal to which it is all the time progressing, has also been adumbrated in advance. According to Romans 8 all creation will be renewed; according to the final chapters of Revelation, there will be a marriage of

---

[32]Christians continued to use it as a natural place of worship in Jerusalem (Acts 3:1, *etc*); we are not told whether they stopped offering sacrifices, but Eusebius (*EH*. 3.5.3) does suggest that the church evacuated the city as the war drew to its climax.

[33]This model is expounded and defended in my recent article, 'How Can the Bible be Authoritative?', *Vox Ev.* 21 (1991) 7-32; *cf.* also *The New Testament and the People of God*, 139-44.

heaven and earth, as God dwells with humankind; according to Hebrews 12 there will be a great celebratory gathering of the whole people of God. God's intention for the end of the play is clearly, not that certain humans should live in a disembodied state of bliss, but that the creation itself should be renewed, should be flooded with the love of God as the waters cover the sea. With this goal in view it is possible then to work backwards towards our present tasks, whilst at the same time working forwards to them from the New Testament. But what does this imply about Christian attitudes to Jerusalem?

This difficult question, on closer examination, proves to be quite close in some ways to the set of questions which Paul addresses in Romans 9-11. As indicated above,[34] this central text can easily be mis-read, and there are definite parallels between such misreadings and the ways in which those chapters are often read and the ways in which Christians often answer the question, 'what then about Jerusalem?'.

First (as an equivalent to Romans 9:6-10:21) it must be stated clearly beyond any shadow of doubt that there can be no basis in the New Testament for a vestigial remainder of 'holy-city-ness' lingering on from the period before Jesus. The New Testament is unequivocal in its interpretation of the fall of Jerusalem as being inextricably linked to the vindication of Jesus and his people. Jesus' whole claim is to do and be what the city and the temple were and did. As a result, both claims, the claim of Jesus and the claim of 'holy land', can never be sustained simultaneously. Any attempt to claim that they can (on the basis of a supposed 'literal' meaning of the many Old Testament promises of restoration, as yet supposedly unfulfilled) has failed to reckon with the total New Testament reading of those promises, according to which, as Paul says, they have all come true in the Messiah (2 Cor. 1:20). This is no simple 'spiritualisation'. Rather, these promises, seen now through the lens of cross and resurrection, have been in one sense narrowed down to a point and in another sense widened to include the whole created order.

Modern attempts to revive such a geographical nationalism, and to give it a 'Christian' colouring, provokes the following, most important, theological reflection: the attempt to 'carry over' some Old Testament promises about

---

[34]See n. 23-25 above.

Jerusalem, the Land or the Temple for fulfilment in our own day has the same theological shape as the attempt in pre-Reformation Catholicism to think of Christ as being re-crucified in every Mass.[35] If, as suggested above, Jesus was claiming to be, in effect, the new or true temple, and if his death is to be seen as the drawing together into one of the history of Israel in her desolation, dying her death outside the walls of the city, and rising again as the beginning of the real 'restoration', the real return from exile, then the attempt to say that there are some parts of the Old Testament (relating to Jerusalem, Land or Temple) which have not yet been 'fulfilled' and so need a historical and literal 'fulfilment' now, or at some other time, is an explicit attempt to take something away from the achievement of Christ in his death and resurrection, and to reserve it for the work of human beings in a different time and place. The work of Christ is once again 'incomplete'. The analogue for this in Paul's writings is perhaps best summed up in Galatians 2:21: 'if justification came by Torah, Christ died to no purpose'. Only when would-be 'Christian Zionists', or near equivalents, can show that they have taken Galatians fully into account (and for that matter Rom. 1-4 and 9-10, 2 Cor. 3, Phil. 3 and Hebrews) can their claim to be acting in accordance with scripture be taken seriously.

Moreover, if we grasp the nettle of the significance of AD 70 in this way, it is not only 'Christian Zionism' which is cut off at the root; it is also, most significantly, 'Christian anti-semitism'.[36] If the wrath of God spoken of by Jesus and Paul was truly *finished* with the awful events of AD 70, then the only appropriate attitude in subsequent generations towards Jews, the Temple, the Land or Jerusalem must be one of sorrow or pity.[37] Naturally, this has not stopped Christians from thinking and acting in ways totally at variance with the New Testament; nevertheless, to grasp the significance of the fall of Jerusalem in this way is to cut off all the spurious legitimation that can be offered for would-be 'Christian' anti-semitism.

---

[35]Even if not the view of many mediaeval theologians, it was certainly a popular view, and one to which the Reformers reacted vigorously.
[36]Both of those 'labels' are ultimately contradictions in terms.
[37]Indeed Paul insists in Rom. 9-11 that this always was the most appropriate attitude.

Beyond this important reflection, however, there are possibilities for some further exceedingly cautious moves. Some might prefer to stop with the argument thus far, but that would be somewhat like stopping at the end of Romans 10. Now, since, as argued earlier, it is my view that Paul in Romans 11 is expressing nothing other than the continual desire of God that some Jews in every generation should come to believe the gospel, the analogue to Romans 11 within my present argument would certainly not be any idea of the reconstitution of the land, or the city, as a 'holy land' or 'holy city' once more in virtue of some inalienable geographical right; but are there other options?

The responsibility of the church in the present age is to anticipate the age to come in acts of justice, mercy, beauty and truth; we are to live 'now' as it will be 'then'. We can only do this, of course, insofar as we have got quite clear in our minds that there is no going back to the old lines that demarcate human beings (race, colour, gender, geography, etc.). That is to say, among other things, that there can and must be no 'Christian' theology of 'holy places' (on the model or analogy of the 'holy places' of a religion that has an essentially geographical base), any more than there can be a 'Christian' theology of racial superiority on the model or analogy of a religion that has an essentially racial base. To that extent, 'Christian Zionism' is the geographical equivalent of a *soi-disant* 'Christian' apartheid, and ought to be rejected as such.

Once that is grasped, though, new possibilities emerge. There might be other ways of articulating a different call within the purposes of God, a call for some peoples to develop one type of culture, beauty and experience and others to develop differently. This might function as a corporate version of the body of Christ metaphor. There might also be a place for a different Christian theology of 'holy places' along the following lines: a double-edged theology of place, in which one both looks backwards with grief and gratitude, and yet also looks forward with hope.

First, it looks back. Inescapably, as Christians, we focus on one time and place as the temporal centre of world history, forming a chronological analogue to the old idea of Jerusalem being at the centre of the world. This is a non-negotiable part of a genuinely Christian worldview. In other words, it was no accident that Jesus lived and died when he did. This is not to say that first-century Jews were ideally prepared to appreciate his teaching (part of Paul's puzzle in Romans is that that was clearly not the case). Rather, it is to say that God's plan had always been to save the world through Israel; and in Christ it becomes clear that God, in making that plan, always intended that he would come himself to represent Israel in person. He called Israel to a task which he would eventually perform himself: Isaiah (59:15-20) says as much. Christians are right, then, to look to the geographical locations of this fulfillment as special, to be approached with gratitude.

At the same time, we must also approach them with grief. For, on the one hand, there is a proper Christian grief for the folly of the crusades and the sin of continuing to treat so-called 'holy places' as the private property of this or that denomination or tradition.[38] Yet, on the other hand, there is also a proper grief for something which has gone, never to return, a natural mourning for a beautiful earlier stage in God's purposes, which went on its course with ambiguity and ended with deepest tragedy. If, then, there are 'holy places' in the land for Christians to visit, they must be regarded, in some senses, as one might regard the grave of a dearly loved friend, perhaps even an older brother.

Yet, if we look back with gratitude and grief, we also look on with hope. If it is our experience that particular churches can become 'holy places', this does not require us to return to some quasi-Jewish theology of 'sacred turf'; rather, it is because one day the *whole creation* will be sacred, will throb and thrill with the presence of the living and loving God, and because at certain points 'where prayer has been valid' this can be seen as it were in anticipation.[39] To that extent, the church is called to worship the God revealed in Jesus and by the Spirit in every corner of the globe, and so to claim it for his wise and healing rule. In this process, moreover, there are clear

---

[38]Surely nothing else so damages Christian witness in Jerusalem and elsewhere as this persistent attitude. Quoting the Old Testament, Jesus said of the Temple, 'my house is a house of prayer for all the nations' (Mk. 11:17); how much more should churches be for all Christians!

[39]This alone seems to explain the phenomenon of entering a strange church for the first time and sensing that the living God is there already, loved and worshipped.

indications of God's ultimate purposes: he intends to establish his new city, new Jerusalem, as the place where he will live with his people for ever. If, then, we are called to anticipate what God is going to do in the future with our acts now (for example, we are called to implement already the justice which will be perfectly worked out in the age to come), we should surely also be seeking to create societies in the here and now, which will anticipate the nature of the renewed and healed Jerusalem. Not that we could ever ourselves build or bring about the New Jerusalem itself; such thinking leads to delusion and ruin. Rather, we are called, while forswearing all racial, cultural or geographical imperialism, to create communities of love and justice out of which healing can flow to others. What better place to do this than in the old city of peace, Jerusalem?

This may be a romantic dream. It may be that, if we are to imagine any sort of earthly locale for a renewed Jerusalem, it must be found somewhere so totally different from the present one that there will be no danger of confusion. Nevertheless, it must surely be God's will that those Christians, who find themselves in positions where they can influence what happens in the actual physical Jerusalem today, should use that opportunity in a thoroughly Christian way, working together without geographical pride or renewed emphasis on race, to create a community in which justice and *shalom* for all will flourish and spill over to the world.

In this way 'holy places' might be created anew, not so much by association as by anticipation, not so much by memory as by new meaning. If some of those newly-reborn holy places happened to coincide with those already hallowed by grief and gratitude, there would be a certain appropriateness. It might be a sign that the Easter which is celebrated in the church of the Holy Sepulchre is also good news for those who wait at the foot of the Western wall, and for that matter those, too, who worship on its Eastern side.

CHAPTER 4

JERUSALEM IN THE EARLY CHRISTIAN CENTURIES

Peter Walker

I. The questions before us

For the orthodox Christian in any age faith in Christ necessarily entails the further conviction that the eternal God has acted redemptively for the world in a unique way in a Middle Eastern city called Jerusalem. God has been involved with Jerusalem in a special way. Moreover the scriptures speak much about this city, seeing it sometimes as a place of God's special blessing, sometimes as the object of his judgement.[1] This raises several questions of a truly 'theological' nature (enquiring into the very will of God) which, though difficult to formulate exactly, are of great importance:

a) Did Jerusalem have some special 'status' in God's sight during some or all of the Old Testament period? Was this a status dependent on the existence within Jerusalem of the Temple?

b) How, if at all, has this status been changed by the events of the New Testament located in and around Jerusalem (the Incarnation, the Cross, the Resurrection, the Ascension, the beginnings of the Church, and the prophesied judgement upon the city realised in AD 70)?

c) Does Jerusalem have any such special status in God's purposes now or for the future, or is this all a thing of the past?

Clearly such an intriguing city will have many historical associations and memories relating to salvation-history, but such associations are strictly a different consideration from these theological questions as to the hard-to-fathom relationship between this city and God himself. Yet such questions cannot be escaped by any Christian who believes in the genuine involvement of the eternal God in his world, his self-consistency and his authoritative revelation of his will through the scriptures. How does God view Jerusalem? What is his will for that city in the here and now? It is these questions

---

[1]See above, chs. 2 and 3.

that are in mind whenever we refer below to the 'theological significance' of Jerusalem.

These questions are indeed those which underlie all the contributions in this volume. Here, however, our concern is this: When this matter was given consideration by the theologians of the Early Church, what were their conclusions? During this period was there but one view or were there several? If more than one, what were the reasons for these different opinions, and what were the methods which were used to justify them theologically? Moreover, since Christians today are engaged in the same enterprise and confronted with the same scriptures, a further question may be asked: is there anything which can be learnt from the methods and conclusions of these Early Church Fathers which, even in our own very different circumstances, will help us to formulate an authentic Christian 'theology' of Jerusalem for today?

II. Why Eusebius and Cyril?

Our attention will be given to the writings of just two people: Eusebius of Caesarea (c. 260 - 339) and Cyril of Jerusalem (c. 320 - ?386), important bishops in Palestine in the period close to the coming of Constantine to the East (in 324). There are two chief reasons for this apparently narrow selection.

First, there are very few references to this question of Jerusalem's theological significance in the previous three centuries. Christian writers naturally refer quite frequently to Jerusalem as known through the Bible, but seldom do they then pause to consider the consequences of those biblical events and statements on the surviving city of Jerusalem.[2] The very nature of the subject, despite its importance, means that it will chiefly be of concern only for those who are currently involved with the continuing city of Jerusalem; yet of those Christians who lived and taught in and around Jerusalem in those early

---

[2] The only possible exceptions occur in Tertullian (*Adv. Marc.* 3.25), Justin Martyr (*Dialogue with Trypho* 80-81) and Irenaeus (*Adv. Haer.* 5.32-6) when they consider Palestine as a probable scene for the Second Coming, but they do not in these passages evaluate the status of Jerusalem.

centuries few written works have survived.³ Moreover, in any age the theological significance of Jerusalem is a subject which is necessarily of secondary importance when compared to the primary questions of Christian doctrine and living. Given the comparative weakness of the Christian church in Palestine between AD 70 and 325 and the general shift in focus away from Palestine in the thought and mission of the Church, it is not surprising that the issue did not truly surface in Christian theology until this later date:⁴ it remained low on the theological agenda until the events in the fourth century brought it, quite suddenly, to the fore.

Secondly, it was precisely the emergence of Constantine and the 'Christian Empire' within the lifetime of both Eusebius and Cyril which brought the issue into the limelight: new possibilities, previously unthinkable, emerged for Jerusalem. For example, would it not be fitting to mark appropriately those sites associated with the life and work of Christ, now recognised as the true King by so many thousands throughout the world? Moreover, could not this powerful symbol, Jerusalem, be harnessed to bolster the new order?— could not a Christian Jerusalem be the flagship for the new Christian empire? The existence of a Christian emperor meant that the time had come at last when, if Christians so desired, they could develop a new 'Christian Jerusalem' in both word and deed. For this reason the year 324/5, on this matter as on others, is of pivotal importance. An entirely new approach to Jerusalem became possible, replacing any former notions: it is this clash between the old and the new that can be seen quite clearly in a study of Eusebius and Cyril.

---

³Eusebius' *Ecclesiastical History* is our chief source for extracts from Hegesippus (*EH.* 3:20, 32; 4:22) and Julius Africanus (*EH.* 1:6.2, 7.1ff.; 6:31), but in none of these is our question addressed.
⁴For the weakness of the Jerusalem church, see J. Wilkinson, *Jerusalem as Jesus knew it* (London, 1978) 176; for a general history of the Jerusalem church in this period, see *e.g.* W. Telfer, *Cyril of Jerusalem and Nemesius of Emesa* (London, 1955) 54-63. The universal outlook of the Church is seen clearly in Eusebius himself, though a native of Palestine, with his continual emphasis on the Gospel having gone out to the 'ends of the earth': see *e.g. Comm. in Psa.* [68.8], 677c; *Comm. in Is.* [42.10], 272.17 ff.; *Proph. Eclg.*, 2.10. Rome, Alexandria and Antioch were clearly more central within Christianity throughout this period.

III. Their contrasting views

Eusebius, probably the 'most learned man' and the 'greatest scholar' of his day,[5] a prolific writer both as a historian of the Church and as a apologist of the faith, and (from 313) the metropolitan ('presiding') bishop of Palestine, was already around the age of sixty-five when Constantine came to power in the East. The essential shape of his theology, reflecting the work of a lifetime, had therefore been established long before; in all his works prior to 325 we are hearing the mature reflection of the pre-Constantinian church.[6] As a native of Palestine, moreover, trained in the Christian school founded by Origen in Caesarea[7] and by temperament interested in Palestine's history, Eusebius not surprisingly presents us with our first extant reflection on this local issue, concerning Jerusalem. What were his conclusions in his writings before 325? Did Jerusalem continue to have some abiding 'theological significance'?[8]

Eusebius answered decisively in the negative. The days of Jerusalem's elevated status within God's purposes were over. If such a status had truly pertained in the Old Testament period (though he wondered if more truly this status should have been ascribed simply to the Temple),[9] then the events of the New Testament clearly changed all that: the rejection by Jerusalem of her true Messiah led inevitably on God's side to a divine rejection of Jerusalem which was apparently final: 'the

---

[5]For such descriptions of Eusebius, see *e.g.* F.J. Foakes-Jackson, *Eusebius Pamphili* (Cambridge, 1933) 44, 133; L.I. Levine, *Caesarea under Roman Rule* (Leiden, 1975) 126; G.F. Chesnut, *The First Christian Histories* (Paris, 1978) 245.

[6]This is the central thesis of T.D. Barnes in *Constantine and Eusebius* (Cambridge, MA, 1981); for his chronology of Eusebius' life and works, see pp. 277-9.

[7]Eusebius' personal admiration for Origen is seen throughout his works, especially in *EH*. 6; yet his historical interests will have introduced an inevitable tension with Origen's 'spiritualizing' approach: see *e.g.* T.D. Barnes, *op.cit.*, 94-105 and L.I. Levine, *op. cit.*

[8]The following summaries of Eusebius and Cyril are based on an examination of all their works: full primary references will be found in my work *Holy City, Holy Places? Christian Attitudes to Jerusalem and the Holy land in the fourth century* (OUP, 1990, hereafter *HCHP*), esp. chs. 2, 10, 11.

[9]See esp. *Theoph.* 4.19 and passages discussed in *HCHP*, 376-83.

Church of God has been raised up in place of Jerusalem that is fallen never to rise again';[10] 'when you shall see [the city] besieged by armies, know that which comes upon it to be the final and full desolation and destruction'.[11]

Moreover, the whole spirituality of the New Testament was one which was less concerned with physical realities and instead looked upwards to the 'heavenly Jerusalem'.[12] As an apologist Eusebius was concerned that Christianity should offer a distinctive spirituality from Judaism: it therefore needed to preserve such priorities and not suddenly manifest a more 'Jewish' interest in the earthly Jerusalem.[13] Indeed within the scriptures themselves there were warnings against a too simplistic adulation of Jerusalem and of using its powerful symbolic function for less than noble ends. No, the city of Jerusalem might be of great interest from a historical point of view (hence his references, for example, to the 'throne of James the Lord's brother),[14] but theologically its significance in the present and for the future was nil.

The adherent of such views (common as they were, no doubt, in the years up to the time of writing) would naturally need to examine the whole question afresh after the dramatic events of 324/5! Suddenly Christians emerged with potential power over Jerusalem and almost immediately the new emperor expressed a keen personal interest in the fate of Jerusalem.[15] Could such negative views survive in the new

---

[10]*D.E.* 6:18.26, as translated in W.J. Ferrar, *The Proof of the Gospel* II (London, 1920) 31.
[11]*Theoph.* 4.20, as translated in S. Lee, *Eusebius on the Theophaneia* (Cambridge, 1843) 251.
[12]Eusebius loved, for example, the story of the Egyptian martyrs who, when questioned by the governor of Caesarea as to their homeland, replied 'Jerusalem', referring to the 'heavenly Jerusalem' (*Mart. Pal.* 11.6-13). This exhibited for him the essential outlook of the pre-Constantinian Church.
[13]See below section IV (2).
[14]*EH.* 7.19.
[15]Constantine never succeeded in visiting the Holy Land; but such a visit was probably in his mind in 324/5 (see *VC.* 2:72.2) and later he expressed his unfulfilled wish of being baptized in the River Jordan (*VC.* 4:62.2). Instead he acceded quickly to the wishes of Macarius, bishop of Jerusalem, who most probably approached the emperor at the Council of Nicaea to obtain permission for the removal of the pagan temple over the traditional site of Christ's tomb; Constantine's

positive atmosphere? Would the detractors of Jerusalem be given a hearing in the sudden rush of Christian enthusiasm for Jerusalem and the Holy Land?[16] Not surprisingly, therefore, the last fourteen years of Eusebius' life were extremely busy; for, on this as on other issues, the essentials of his life's thought had to be re-examined and re-stated in ways appropriate to the new circumstances.[17] Charting these changes is regrettably beyond our present purpose but to do so makes for some truly fascinating discoveries.[18] Suffice it to say, however, that though there are clarifications and minor adjustments in his thought, the overall negative thrust in his approach to Jerusalem remains predominant. In a key passage, for example, which refers explicitly to the new church of the Holy Sepulchre (and which therefore needs to be read alongside the more oft-quoted chapters in the *Life of Constantine* relating to that church), Eusebius repeats his affirmation that the physical Jerusalem is not to be thought of as a 'holy city'.[19] Moreover, in his speech delivered at the opening ceremonies of the church of the Holy Sepulchre he deliberately focused attention away from the physical tomb to the powerful witness of the universal Church.[20] Despite the new, and no doubt welcome,

---

subsequent correspondence with Macarius is recorded in *VC*. 3:30-2; see *HCHP*, 275 ff.

[16]The 'travelogue' of the Bordeaux Pilgrim, dating to 333, can be taken as probable evidence of the new spate of pilgrimage in the years after 325. Before this time we know the names of only a few pilgrims (if Melito, Alexander and Pionius are to be seen as such) and, though the 'volume of devout tourism must have been much greater than these isolated examples suggest' (H. Chadwick, 'The Circle and the Ellipse' in *Variorum Reprints* (1982) 7) it seems not to have been a widespread phenomenon in this earlier period: see *HCHP*, 11-14 and J. Wilkinson, *op.cit.*, 33f.

[17]See *HCHP*, 94-99, where it is suggested that Eusebius' embarrassment after his fairly humiliating experience at the Council of Nicaea (almost being outlawed for 'heresy') will have given him an even greater incentive to prove the value of his life's work; the *Theophaneia* may have been written as a summary of his essential thought to ward off potential critics.

[18]See instead *HCHP*, 93-116.

[19]*Comm. in Psa.* [87.11-13], 1064b.

[20]In his book *In Praise of Constantine* (Berkeley, 1976) H.A. Drake has argued convincingly that this speech at the Dedication of the Holy Sepulchre can be found in *de Laudibus Constantini*, 11-18. For the

circumstances, Eusebius' thinking remained essentially the same.[21]

Cyril, by contrast, approaching the subject afresh, as a child of the new era, was able to come to quite different conclusions. In his *Catechetical Lectures*, delivered in 348, though the issue was never addressed directly as such, Cyril's new and wholeheartedly positive approach to Jerusalem and its theological significance is unmistakeably clear.[22]

Any divine judgement on Jerusalem, he asserts, was a thing of the past and was certainly not 'final'.[23] In any case such judgement had really been focused either on the Temple alone (the 'Temple of the *Jews*')[24] or on the Jewish Jerusalem which had rejected him, not on the Christian Jerusalem: *'that* Jerusalem crucified Christ, but that which now is worships him'.[25] Cyril's contemporary Jerusalem was therefore, on the one hand, quite a different entity from the Jewish Jerusalem of the first century. On the other hand, it could draw a line of continuity back to all that was true and best of the Jerusalem in the scriptures: hence, for example, several prophecies in Isaiah concerning Jerusalem (Isa.1:26-7, 60:1, 65:18) could be applied directly to Cyril's own baptismal candidates;[26] moreover, it

---

important insight this gives us into Eusebius' thinking concerning Jerusalem and 'holy places' in his final years, see *HCHP*, 114-16.

[21] His reference to the 'New Jerusalem' (*VC*. 3.33), which is often raised in this regard, is actually his description of the church of the Holy Sepulchre, not of Constantinian Jerusalem. As such it in fact only endorses our contention that Eusebius was reluctant to give any special status to the city as a whole (see *e.g. HCHP*, 281).

[22] Some scholars prefer a date of 350 (as discussed in *HCHP*, 410), but this little matters here. Since the *Mystagogical Lectures*, commonly attributed to Cyril, may well come from the generation after his death (see *HCHP*, 410-11), they have been excluded from this examination into Cyril's thinking; however, in Egeria's narrative of her stay in Jerusalem (*c*. 384-7) we have a clear witness of a different kind to the way in which Cyril's liturgical vision for Jerusalem had developed by the end of his episcopate.

[23] The following presentation of Cyril's thinking on Jerusalem is a summary of *HCHP*, ch. 8.

[24] *Catech*. 15.15 (italics mine).

[25] *Catech*. 13.7 (italics mine).

[26] *Catech*. 18.34.

was here that both Christ and the Holy Spirit had 'descended from heaven'.[27]

What, however, about Jerusalem's treatment of Jesus resulting in the crucifixion? Had that affected Jerusalem's status in God's sight? Cyril would have turned this argument on its head by developing the Johannine teaching concerning the Cross as truly the revelation of Christ's 'glory': the Cross was a 'crown, not a dishonour' and the 'glory of glories' for the world-wide Church.[28] Jesus may have been expelled from Jerusalem in the first century to be crucified outside its walls, but the site of Golgotha was now (providentially, no doubt) at the very heart of the Constantinian city and very much to the greater glory of Jerusalem.[29] No, the fact that this salvific event, combined with the other events of the Incarnation,[30] had occurred in Jerusalem and nowhere else could only mean one thing: Jerusalem had been, and still was, a city of special significance in God's sight.

Hence Cyril pointedly refers to his contemporary Jerusalem as a 'holy city'. Referring to the strange event in the Passion-narrative (unique to Matthew 27:53) when the 'saints who had fallen asleep were raised and. . .went into the holy city', Cyril takes exception to the view espoused by Eusebius and others before him that Matthew's 'holy city' is a reference to 'heaven', and asserts instead that Matthew was clearly speaking of 'this city in which we are now'.[31] Jerusalem was truly a 'holy city' in a theological sense, special to God and not simply to the faithful through its many historical associations.[32] As a result Cyril then felt able to claim for his city of Jerusalem that it should be given a natural 'pre-eminence' (ἀξίωμα) in the

---

[27]*Catech.* 16.4.
[28]*Catech.* 13.22, 13.1.
[29]See *HCHP*, 328.
[30]He draws attention to the fact that the Ascension (*Catech.* 14.23), the descent of the Spirit (*Catech.* 16.4, 17.13, 16.26) and the institution of the Eucharist (*Catech.* 18.33) all occurred in Jerusalem, and also notes that 'all Jerusalem' (Mark 1.5) went to the Jordan for John's baptism (*Catech.* 3.7).
[31]*Catech.* 14.16, in contrast to Eusebius (*Comm. in Psa.* [87:11-13], 1064b) and Origen (*Comm. in Matt.* [17:1-2], 12:43, 169:5-7).
[32]As argued in *HCHP*, 325-30.

life of faith, in the Church, in the Holy land, and indeed within the whole world.³³

The views of Eusebius and Cyril are therefore far removed from one another, if not in mutual contradiction. One denied Jerusalem the status of a 'holy city' in God's sight, the other categorically asserted it. As in our own very different times, the adherents of these two seemingly incompatible standpoints were both able to appeal to the Scriptures as the ultimate authority for their views. Hence it is necessary to enquire more deeply into their reasoning and into their methods. What drove them to these quite different conclusions and what hermeneutical framework did they use to justify their views from Scripture?

IV. Their Reasons

1. Contemporary circumstances

Theological thinking can rarely, if ever, be done in a vacuum; a theologian's context invariably results in certain theological truths receiving greater emphasis than others. If this is true today, as people respond variously to the realities of Israel/Palestine, it was no less true in the fourth century for Eusebius and Cyril.

For Eusebius, formulating his ideas at the end of the third century, the pitiable physical state of Jerusalem would inevitably influence his understanding of its possible theological status. After the devastation of the city by the Romans in both AD 70 and 135, the garrison-town that remained was called 'Aelia Capitolina', a pagan name which Christians used apparently without any qualms.³⁴ It was

---

³³Cyril uses the word ἀξίωμα on three separate occasions (*Catech.* 3.7, 16.4, 17.13); presumably it was no coincidence that this was the very word which had been used twenty years earlier by the Nicene fathers (Canon 7) in their attempt to preserve for Eusebius and subsequent bishops of Caesarea a 'distinctive pre-eminence' over the see of Jerusalem: see *A New Eusebius*, ed., J. Stevenson, London, 1957) 360. *C.f. HCHP*, 330-346 for the way Cyril develops this theme of 'pre-eminence'; note especially how in *Catech.* 13.28 he describes Golgotha as the 'very centre of the world' (based on an interpretation of Psa. 74:12).
³⁴'The Roman city changed its name and *is* called Aelia' (Eusebius, *EH*. 4:6.4, italics mine). For Eusebius' use of the name 'Aelia' see *HCHP*, 5,

indeed in a sorry state, with probably no defending walls, and the Temple area left in complete ruins.[35] An edict of Hadrian forbade any 'circumcized person' from even setting eyes on the town, thus leaving it devoid of any Jewish population;[36] meanwhile the Christians were a tiny minority, possibly meeting in a small church on Mount Zion and preserving in a small library a (not very reliable) record of the church's bishops since the time of James.[37] Any Christians who visited had the custom of going primarily to the Mount of Olives and viewing this sorry spectacle which only confirmed the truth of those prophetic words spoken by Jesus in that self-same place warning of the coming judgement:

believers in Christ. . .congregate, not as of old time because of the glory of Jerusalem, nor that they may worship in the ancient Temple at Jerusalem, but they rest there that they may learn about the city being taken and devastated as the prophets foretold.[38]

In such circumstances it would only be natural for Eusebius to approach Jerusalem in a negative light. In one sense, after all, there was now no such place as 'Jerusalem'! Instead its current forlorn state only gave emphasis to that strand in scripture of divine judgement, suggesting that God had acted in a full and final form to exert his judgement upon the city and all that 'Jerusalem' stood for.

Moreover, Eusebius was not only a resident of the flourishing and cosmopolitan city of Caesarea on the coast but also the Metropolitan bishop of the entire province of Palestine with jurisdiction over the bishop of Aelia. Relations between

---

n.9, and 394-6; 'Aelia' is also used in the seventh Canon of Nicaea (*loc. cit.*) but never by Cyril.

[35]For the geography and condition of Aelia in this period, see Y. Tsafrir, 'Jerusalem', in *RBK*, III, 543-51.

[36]M. Avi-Yonah in *The Jews of Palestine* (Oxford, 1976) reconstructs the wording of the edict as follows: 'It is forbidden for all circumcized persons to enter or stay within the territory of Aelia Capitolina; any person contravening this prohibition shall be put to death'. For the continuing discussion, suggesting that the edict was still on the statute-book, but not necessarily enforced, see *HCHP*, 8, n.12.

[37]For the Christian community worshipping on Mt Zion, see E.D. Hunt, *Holy Land Pilgrimage in the Later Roman Empire* (Oxford, 1982) 19, and *HCHP*, 287. Eusebius refers to the episcopal lists in *EH*. 4.5.3-5 and 5.12.1-2.

[38]*DE*. 6.18, translated by Ferrar.

the sees had generally been good through the previous century,[39] but there are some indications that even before 325 the Jerusalem church had begun to seek a greater standing in relation to the see of Caesarea.[40] This was certainly the case from 325 onwards as Constantine did business on occasions directly with Macarius, the bishop of Aelia[41] and as the new Constantinian churches attracted an increasing number of pilgrims. In such circumstances the one person who might suffer adversely from this new imperial interest in Jerusalem was ironically Eusebius himself, whose metropolitan status as the bishop of Caesarea would now come into question: surely the metropolitan should instead be the bishop of Jerusalem? In the course of history such arguments would eventually prevail,[42] but Eusebius evidently did his best to stem the tide: for example, despite his many references to the Jerusalem church in his writings before 325, he succeeded in referring to it only once in his writings after that date, thus drawing attention away from this 'rival' church.[43] Not surprisingly, therefore, when Eusebius came to consider the theological status of Jerusalem, he had every personal reason for playing down its significance.

Eusebius had made no secret of his negative attitude towards Jerusalem: it comes through as one of the recurrent themes in his *Proof of the Gospel* (written in the 310's). It would therefore be far from easy, if he so wished, publicly to alter his position once Constantine came to power and new possibilities emerged for Jerusalem; to do so with theological consistency would have been impossible, and there is ample evidence that one of Eusebius' prime concerns in the years of

---

[39] As evidenced in numerous passages in Eusebius' *Ecclesiastical History*.

[40] See Z. Rubin, 'The Church of the Holy Sepulchre and the conflict between the sees of Caesarea and Jerusalem' in L.I. Levine, ed., *Jerusalem Cathedra* II (Jerusalem and Detroit, 1982) 79-105.

[41] Constantine's letter to Macarius is preserved in Eus., *VC.* 3.30; see also *HCHP*, 276 ff.

[42] Jerusalem was eventually elevated to the status of a Patriarchate at the Council of Chalcedon in AD 451 during the episcopate of Bishop Juvenal.

[43] This one occasion was when introducing Constantine's letter to Macarius (*loc. cit.*), a letter of great importance which he could hardly omit from the emperor's biography.

flux after 325 was precisely to argue for the need for continuity in the Christian tradition and to avoid any rash abandonment of the old in favour of the new.[44] What was true for the thinking of the Church as a whole would be even more true for the thinking of Eusebius himself. As a result, though there would have been a natural temptation in the Constantinian climate to avow a more positive approach to Jerusalem, Eusebius had strong personal reasons, both theological and ecclesiastical, for resisting the temptation.

For Cyril, however, speaking thirty years later for the new generation in the new Christian empire, all the contemporary circumstances pointed in the opposite direction. He was himself the bishop of Jerusalem,[45] naturally anxious to increase his see's importance, and the new wave of pilgrims called forth a new understanding of this central city in salvation-history. Moreover, the emerging Christian empire needed powerful symbols of the new order, which Jerusalem could provide in a unique way.

The 'Jerusalem mystique' was present and powerful, the potential of the city inviting, the presence of the pilgrims demanding and the possible increased status of the Jerusalem Church compelling.[46]

Different circumstances thus called forth from Cyril a different theology, but one, of course, which he would claim to be equally biblical and authentically Christian.

Evidently, therefore, both Eusebius and Cyril were much affected by the situations in which they did their theology. In our own day, we must ask, what are the chief influences upon us from our own circumstances, and how can awareness of these help us to be more critical of our supposedly 'biblical' approaches to this subject?

---

[44] See *HCHP*, 94ff. for Eusebius' natural conservatism in these years, especially after his humiliating experience at the Council of Nicaea; if this position is correct, it confirms a central contention of T.D. Barnes in *Constantine and Eusebius* (Cambridge, MA, 1981) that the essential contours of Eusebius' theology had been established long before the emergence of the Christian empire.

[45] The death of Maximus, his predecessor, is normally dated to AD 348; if the *Catechetical Lectures* were delivered in that same year Cyril may have been asked to deliver them on Maximus' behalf as his probable successor.

[46] *HCHP*, 314.

2. Spirituality

Cyril's positive attitude towards Jerusalem was based in part on a new emphasis in his spirituality on the Incarnation. Cyril marvelled, in a way which Eusebius did not, at the mystery of this event, and the vision of Christ which he presented to his catechumens was very much that of Christ incarnate, not so much the exalted Christ in glory. Eusebius had focused on the concept of Christ as the Eternal *Logos* to such an extent that he has in modern times been accused of being 'unable to make the Incarnation central in his theology';[47] Cyril, by contrast, encouraged his hearers in many passages to take comfort from the divine identification with humanity shown in the Incarnation:

The perfect teacher of children became himself a child among children, that he might instruct the unwise. The bread of heaven came down to earth to feed the hungry.[48]

This emphasis on God's work in the Incarnation then gave legitimacy to a more 'sacramental' approach both to Jerusalem and to all the 'holy places' touched by the feet of God incarnate. 'Here' (ἐνταῦθα) and nowhere else had occurred the Incarnation and the Ascension.[49] As a result, Cyril's catechumens through being in Jerusalem had a privilege denied to others, a privilege similar to that bestowed on doubting Thomas: 'others merely hear but we see and touch'; 'it was for our sake that he touched so carefully'.[50] Being in Jerusalem enabled them to come into a closer contact with Christ than was possible elsewhere.

Such an emphasis fitted in well with the wider concerns of the fourth-century Church. Not only was the very truth of the Incarnation being contested in the Arian controversy, resulting in a necessary emphasis upon this doctrine, but part of the way in which the Church was increasing her sway over the formerly pagan majority was to relax from her previously more spiritual and other-worldly focus and to emphasize instead the importance of this physical realm: under such circumstances, the sacraments, 'holy places',

---

[47]G.H. Williams, 'Christology and Church-State Relations in the Fourth Century', *Church History* 20/3 (Sept. 1951) 17.
[48]*Catech.* 12.1.
[49]*Catech.* 14,23, 16.4, 17.13, 17.22.
[50]*Catech.* 13.22.

relics, pilgrimage and the like could all be given a new importance. In such a situation the Incarnation inevitably came to the fore as a central doctrine in the Church's life.

Eusebius' spirituality, however, belonged to the former era. Influenced no doubt by the fact that the Church was still at this earlier stage a minority, often persecuted, Christians in the first three centuries after Christ had tended to continue the emphasis found in the New Testament of focusing on the exalted Christ, not the Christ of the Incarnation:

since you have been raised with Christ, seek the things that are above, where Christ is, seated at the right hand of God' (Col. 3:1-2).[51]

This would then explain not only the comparative lack of spiritual interest in the actual Gospel sites of the Incarnation (noted above), but also the general emphasis on the 'heavenly Jerusalem' rather than on the earthly one:

the present Jerusalem. . .is in slavery with her children, but the Jerusalem above is free, and she is our mother (Gal. 4:26-7); you have not come to what may be touched. . .but you have come to Mount Zion and to the city of the living God, the heavenly Jerusalem (Heb. 12:22).

Such emphases, which focus on the spiritual world rather than the physical world, are to be found throughout Eusebius' writings.[52] As a result he would naturally come to quite different conclusions from Cyril, who emphasized instead the Incarnation and its sacramental consequences.

In our own day our spirituality will also affect our understanding of Jerusalem. Some will see Christianity as a religion which essentially transcends the physical realm and therefore will find little room in their thinking for the city of Jerusalem. The spirituality of others will incline them to accept that a physical entity such as Jerusalem can still have a significant role in God's purposes, but on the basis of which theological principles? Some today would use the Incarnation

---

[51]Origen, to whom Eusebius was greatly indebted, is perhaps the clearest example of this overriding 'spiritual' emphasis in the Early Church: see *e.g.* R.P.C. Hanson, *Allegory and Event: a Study of the Sources and Significance of Origen's Interpretation of Scripture* (London, 1959); T.D. Barnes, *op. cit.*, ch. 6.

[52]*E.g. DE.* 4:12.4; 10:8.64; *Comm. in Psa.* [87.11-13], 1064b; *Mart. Pal.* 11.9, 19.

and the sacramental principle in a manner similar to Cyril's; others, however, would appeal to the Hebraic emphasis on the physical city of Jerusalem found in the Old Testament scriptures. Jerusalem is thus not simply a place *of* spirituality, a place where religious faith is practised; it is also has a place *in* spirituality, acting as a touchstone of all that a Christian holds dear.

3) Christian definition over against Judaism

A third factor which affected Eusebius and Cyril, and which inevitably affects us today, is the whole question of the relation between Christianity and Judaism. This has never been an easy one for Christians to resolve, caught between the desire on the one hand to distinguish themselves quite strongly from Judaism in their central beliefs about Jesus of Nazareth, and yet on the other to acknowledge their enormous debt to Judaism as their 'parent religion'. Different Christian approaches to Jerusalem emerge as people come to different conclusions about how this balance of distinction and continuity is to be maintained.

For Eusebius the issues were reasonably clear-cut. For him it was axiomatic that spiritual interest in the physical Jerusalem was a characteristic feature of Judaism. Eusebius often labelled literal interpretations of scripture as 'physical and Jewish';[53] his Old Testament commentaries were full of references to the 'true Zion' and the 'true Jerusalem', implying a contrast with the Zion and Jerusalem favoured, he supposed, by Jewish interpreters.[54] On one occasion he stated strongly that

to think of the metropolis of the Jews in Palestine as the city of God is not only base, but even impious, the mark of exceedingly base and petty thinking'.[55]

In contrast to this Christians were to show their distinct identity by eschewing such material and 'earthly' concerns and focusing instead on the 'heavenly Jerusalem'.

This is one of the predominant themes in all his exegesis of the Psalms and of Isaiah, as he seeks to show how the physical entities referred to in these books have now been

---

[53]See *e.g. Comm. in Isa.* [66.20], 407-8.
[54]See *e.g. Comm. in Isa.* [49.14-16], 313-4; *Comm. in Psa.* [64.2-3], 624c; *DE.* 4:12.4, 4:17.15.
[55]*Comm. in Psa.* [86.3], 1044b-c.

outmoded and fulfilled in the Christian understanding of the heavenly Jerusalem and the spiritual Zion. This necessity of drawing a sharp distinction between Christianity and Judaism is seen even more clearly in his apologetical work, the *Proof of the Gospel*. In fact, the contrasting attitudes of Judaism and Christianity towards Jerusalem (combined with the whole more 'spiritual' approach to scripture and to physical reality in Christianity) is for Eusebius one of the the key distinctions between the two religions. As such, this apologetical need to define Christianity as a 'spiritual' religion is perhaps the strongest reason why Eusebius plays down the significance of the earthly Jerusalem. For the issue at stake was one of the essential nature of Christian identity: any interest in the physical Jerusalem was more 'Jewish' than Christian.

Cyril, of course, was no less concerned to distinguish Christianity from Judaism. Yet, if he was to introduce into the Christian Church this new notion of Jerusalem's significance, it was going to be harder to make that distinction; for on this point, his thinking clearly had certain affinities with Judaism: Christianity could now be seen as following Judaism in believing that the physical Jerusalem was of present spiritual significance. This would result, as already noted, in Cyril using certain Old Testament passages in a far more literal way than Eusebius.[56]

How then could Cyril preserve the distinction between Christianity and Judaism? First, he claimed that fourth-century Jerusalem was a Christian city which 'now worshipped Christ' in contrast to the first-century city which had 'crucified him';[57] thus all the scriptural texts relating to God's judgement upon the city were applied to the Jewish people of the first century, leaving Jerusalem as such free to be a continuing vehicle of God's blessing. Secondly, he enhanced the notion of Jerusalem's significance by employing the distinctively Christian category of the Incarnation; this was the distinctively Christian reason, unparalleled in Judaism, for perpetuating the notion of Jerusalem as a 'holy city'.[58] The fact that Christ Incarnate had been in Jerusalem (and that Jerusalem had been the scene for his Cross, Resurrection and Ascension) gave

---

[56]See above n. 26.
[57]*Catech*. 13.7.
[58]See above at nn. 27 and 49.

Jerusalem a unique specialness in God's sight and for the Christian Church.

In noting these two different ways in which Christians distinguished themselves from Judaism, it can be observed that Eusebius' approach was marked by straightforward contrast, Cyril's by a more flagrant appropriation; Eusebius left Jerusalem to be the concern of Judaism, Cyril brought it back to be the birthright of Christians—a more confident approach reflecting the greater confidence of the Church in the post-Constantinian period. Again we must ask ourselves in our own day: in what ways are the differences between Christianity and Judaism to manifest themselves? Is the issue of Jerusalem one of these? Do we mark our differences by contrast or by appropriation?

V. Their Methods

In noting some of the reasons for their different approaches to Jerusalem we have inevitably begun to touch on some of the methods which Eusebius and Cyril used to defend their respective positions: for example, the emphasis in Cyril on the Incarnation, the emphasis in Eusebius on God's judgement of the city in AD 70. It will be valuable finally to summarise these and other methods, and to ask of them questions relevant for our own enquiry into the continuing spiritual significance of Jerusalem. For these are some of the key questions which need to be asked in any age as Christians seek to formulate their understanding of the theological status of Jerusalem in the present.

a) The Incarnation

The Incarnation was central in Cyril's thinking. How relevant is this to the question of Jerusalem's significance? Can this truth be over-emphasized or used in ways which would be contrary to other (equally) scriptural truths? Is scripture a final truth or can other truths supplement it?

b) The events of AD 70

Eusebius had reflected quite deeply on the Fall of Jerusalem in AD 70, but how are Christians to interpret this? Through the destruction of the Temple, these calamitous events confirmed the more spiritual emphases of the New Covenant in Christ (as outlined, for example, in Hebrews), but Christians such as

Eusebius, influenced by the prophetic teaching of Jesus, have gone further and seen it also as an act of divine judgement. Is this legitimate, and if so, what was being judged?—the Jews of that day? Judaism as a religious system? or, Jerusalem as a religious symbol? Most importantly of all, if the Fall of Jerusalem is to be seen as a divine judgement, was it a final and definitive judgement (a complete 'rejection' marking the 'end of an era' in God's purposes) or was it but a temporary judgement, similar perhaps to that experienced in 587 BC after which God's people were encouraged to return?[59]

c) The Temple in Jerusalem

Eusebius began to suggest that perhaps the whole notion of Jerusalem's 'holiness' was a false inference made in Old Testament times because of the location of the Temple in its midst: this was indeed the place where 'God's name dwelt', this was truly 'holy', but was that really true of the city as well?[60] If this distinction between city and Temple needs to be borne in mind, how does it affect our interpretation of AD 70? Cyril believed that the Fall of Jerusalem was a judgement simply on the Jewish Temple, thus allowing the city as such to be deemed free of judgement. Was he correct? In the imagery of Ezekiel, when the *shekinah* glory departed from the Temple, did it not depart from the city as well?

d) The Cross in Jerusalem

What affect does the fact that Jesus was crucified just outside Jerusalem have on the theological status of the city? Cyril saw the Cross as being to the greater glory of Jerusalem, but others might with equal right see it more truly as the moment of Jerusalem's most profound judgement. In what ways can the city of the crucifixion ever be 'holy'?

e) The inter-relation of the Old and New Testaments

Eusebius allowed the negative thrust in the New Testament to be the definitive prism through which he assessed the whole of scripture. Cyril approached the biblical text more uniformly. What is the appropriate hermeneutic? How is the Old Testament to be read in the light of the New?

---

[59]On interpreting AD 70, see further above ch. 2, p. 74.
[60]See above n. 9.

VI. Some final questions

In addition to the questions already raised, through comparing both the reasons and methods of Eusebius and Cyril with our own, there are finally some more general questions to be asked.

In assessing the theological status of Jerusalem, Eusebius and Cyril manifest the two opposite extremes which are possible within Christianity. How do we cope with two such extremes within the one faith? Are they reconcilable? Which is more authentically Christian, more truly 'biblical'? In the light of such apparently irreconcilable views, can there ever be such a thing as a 'Christian' approach to Jerusalem?

If some are inclined to espouse Eusebius' more negative approach, are they really saying that Jerusalem can be given no positive function at all? Or might they be able to say with some legitimacy that some positive roles can be found for the city, but only when this negative foundation has been adequately laid?

If some are inclined to espouse Cyril's more positive approach (even if for very different reasons), are they committing the Church to a theology which may (as Cyril's did in due course in the Crusades) have unforeseen and undesirable consequences in the future? Can a positive Christian approach to Jerusalem ever be formulated in such a way that it serves to decrease, rather than to increase, the territorial tensions which already exist over the city because of the city's 'holiness' to both Jews and Muslims?

In other words, given that the situation of our own day is vastly more complicated than it was in the period of Eusebius and Cyril (partly as a result, in fact, of Cyril's theology), how are Christians to show their natural concern for the city in a way which is truly Christian?

CHAPTER 5

JERUSALEM IN JUDAISM AND FOR CHRISTIAN ZIONISTS

Margaret Brearley

I. Jerusalem's History from the 7th to the 18th Century

Jerusalem was under Christian Byzantine rule from the time of Constantine through to the time of the Persian invasion in 614. Palestine was recaptured, however, by the Emperor Heraclius in 627, and he re-entered Jerusalem with much pomp in 629. Under pressure from the Church, many of Jerusalem's Jewish inhabitants were forcibly converted or killed, and the rest expelled. Byzantine Jerusalem soon faced a new danger—that of conquest by Arab Muslims. Following Mohammed's death in 632, Arab armies invaded Palestine, and Jerusalem fell in 638. The majority population, however, remained predominantly Christian for hundreds of years and the Church had comparative freedom. Jews too were allowed once again to live in the city and experienced a far greater freedom than under the Byzantine rulers.[1]

Yet, for all concerned, Jerusalem gradually sank to become an economic and political backwater. Despite the importance of Jerusalem to Muslims, Jerusalem was never the capital for Arab rulers and never became an intellectual or spiritual centre of Muslim learning. Life under the Muslim Caliphs became increasingly unstable from the eighth century onwards, with sporadic warfare between different Muslim tribes and the threat of Bedouin marauders. Moreover, Jews and Christians were subject to punitive poll taxes (*jizya*) and under Caliph Omar II (717-720) a strict code was introduced,

---

[1] Readily available books on Arab history include: E. Atiyah, *The Arabs* (London, Penguin 1955); P. Mansfield, *The Arabs* (London, Penguin, 2nd. ed., 1985); A. Goldschmidt, *A concise history of the Middle East* (Boulder, Colorado, Westview Press, 4th. ed., 1991); S.N. Fisher, *The Middle East: A History* (London, Routledge & Kegan Paul, 2nd. ed., 1971). On the significance of Jerusalem in Islamic thought, see below ch. 6 (ii). For a history of Jerusalem under Jews, Christians and Muslims until the 12th. century see *e.g.* M. Join-Lambert, *Jerusalem* (Eng transl., London, Elek Books 1958).

regulating the behaviour of non-Muslims.[2] Violent persecution was relatively rare; in 1009, however, the Fatimid Caliph al-Hakim destroyed the Church of the Holy Sepulchre and other churches, and persecuted both Christians and Jews.

Despite these pressures and the poverty of many in Jerusalem, the city remained a centre of Jewish learning: the great Talmudic academy, for example, transferred from Tiberias to Jerusalem, probably in the ninth century. Yet the background was one of increasing violence, as in the eleventh century Fatimids warred against the Bedouin, the Turkish Seljuks (who captured Jerusalem in 1071) and, finally, the Christian Crusaders.

The First Crusade was proclaimed by Pope Urban II in 1095 to recover the Holy Land. The cavalry army successfully besieged Jerusalem and on entering attacked the Jewish quarter first, massacring virtually the entire population of 20-30,000; others were sold into slavery and few escaped. Their property was looted by Crusading soldiers and their homes taken over by Christian Arabs brought in from Transjordan. From then on, as under Christian Byzantium, Jews were officially forbidden to live in Jerusalem, being allowed to visit it only once a year, on the Fast of *Av* to mourn the destroyed Temple.[3]

The Crusaders established a Kingdom of Jerusalem and catered for the considerable influx of Christian pilgrims. Christian life in the city flourished and was multi-national, though predominantly European; many churches were built, monastic orders proliferated, and the Templars and Hospitallers created new traditions. Jerusalem remained in Christian hands until its recapture by Saladin in 1187. Despite continuing Crusader rule in the Holy land until the fall of Acre in 1291 (and two brief periods of occupation of Jerusalem in 1229-39 and 1243-4), and despite many subsequent abortive crusades, Jerusalem did not leave Islamic rule again until captured by British troops in 1917.

---

[2]*Cf.* Bat Ye'or, *The Dhimmi: Jews and Christians under Islam* (London and Toronto, Associated University Presses 1985).
[3]*Cf.* S. Runciman, *The First Crusade* (CUP, 1980) and *The History of the Crusades* (CUP, 1951); M. Gilbert, *Jerusalem: Illustrated History Atlas* (London, 1977); F. Gabrieli, ed., *Arab historians of the Crusades* (London, Routledge & Kegan Paul 1969).

Saladin invited Jews to return to Jerusalem, and in the 13th century a community developed, enlarged by Jews fleeing increasing persecution at the hands of Christians in Europe;[4] this community attracted great scholars, such as the Spanish Rabbi Nahmanides (1267).

Jerusalem continued to be the target of invasion and slaughter. In 1244 it was sacked by Turks and in 1260 attacked by the Mongols. Following their defeat by the Mamluks, who subsequently ruled until 1516, Jerusalem became a poverty-stricken, under-populated provincial town, in which Muslim theology and architecture flourished but poverty was endemic. Mamluk rulers championed both orthodox Islamic seminaries and communities of *Sufis*, and Jerusalem's religious role within Islam was greatly strengthened during their rule. Relatively few Christians and Jews lived there permanently, and both communities were subject to harassment, heavy taxation and occasional persecution.[5]

The entry of Suleiman the Magnificent into Jerusalem in 1517, following the Ottomans' defeat of the Mamluks, heralded a new period of relative prosperity: the city's population doubled within fifty years, and agriculture and industries prospered once again. In 1537, as Joseph ha-Kohen recorded, 'God aroused the spirit of Suleiman' to rebuild the ruined walls of Jerusalem, which remain to this day. Moreover, the Jewish community in Jerusalem experienced something of a revival from the sixteenth century onwards. For several reasons the spiritual centre of Safed in Galilee began to decline; in Jerusalem, however, new *yeshivot* (centres of advanced biblical and Talmudic studies) were created in the eighteenth century and the city became a focal point for many Jewish immigrants fleeing in the face of various persecutions.[6]

---

[4] The Fourth Lateran Council (1215), for example, decreed the establishment of ghettoes and the enactment of anti-Jewish laws, including hearing compulsory conversionist sermons and wearing a 'Jewish badge' or distinctive clothing, to separate Jews from Christians.
[5] Of Jewish immigrants from Spain or Portugal in the 1490's, for example, the majority settled in Safed or elsewhere. For the mediaeval and early modern history of Jerusalem see esp. *Encyclopaedia Judaica* (1971), 'Jerusalem', 'Israel'.
[6] For example, the massacres of the Jews in the Ukraine in the mid-seventeenth century. One result of this was the emergence of Hassidism, a movement of deep prayer and joyful spirituality which,

The scene was thus set for the dramatic events of the nineteenth century. From the time of Napoleon's invasion of Egypt (1798) Palestine became increasingly important to the European Great Powers, for both strategic and commercial reasons. Meanwhile, Jews and Gentiles flocked to Palestine in considerable numbers and with increasing religious or nationalistic fervour. In order to explain this unique phenomenon, we must first retrace our steps to note the religious significance of Jerusalem, both for Jews and also for many Christians.

II. Jerusalem and the Jewish people

The concept of holiness has always been inseparable from the concept of Jerusalem and Zion.[7] A people called to be 'a kingdom of priests and an holy nation' (Exod.19:6) was to dwell in a land where they could 'worship the Lord in the beauty of holiness' (1 Chron. 16:29). Jewish history has been inspired and hallmarked by a vision of holiness: from the past of Mount Sinai, when Aaron's mitre was engraved with the inscription 'holiness to the Lord' (Exod. 28:36) to the future of Mount Zion, the 'holy mountain' (Joel 3:17), when after the return of the exiles the very road to Zion would be called 'the way of holiness' (Isa. 35:8).

Zion was to be an utter contrast to the pagan world, with its divinisation of Nature and of man's basic instincts, and worship of the pagan gods and the cosmic forces of time. Within that pagan world, Zion—with its moral absolutes and ethical commands—was to be revolutionary. In their worship of the Creator, rather than Creation itself, the Jewish people were to be servants of the living God of holiness, whose people was to imitate him by reflecting his characteristics. The Talmud records: 'As the Holy One, is called righteous, be ye also

---

with its love for the land of Israel, inspired many Jews to emigrate to Jerusalem. See *e.g.* N. Efrati, *Homecoming; the Saga of Immigration to the Holy Land from biblical times to the present day* (Jerusalem, Kollek & Son Ltd. 1982).

[7]'Jerusalem' and 'Zion' are synonymous; 'they came to mean not only the city but the land and the Jewish people as a whole': R.J.Z. Werblowsky, *The Meaning of Jerusalem to Jews, Christians and Muslims* (Jerusalem, Israel Univ. Study Group for M. Eastern Affairs 1983) 11.

righteous; as He is called loving, be ye also loving'. Since the God of Israel was 'merciful and gracious, slow to anger, and abundant in goodness and truth' (Exod. 34:6), Jews were to imitate his love as a way of worshipping him: 'the beginning and end of the Torah is the performance of loving-kindness'.[8]

As Jews lived out the Torah in Canaan, they created a new society based on radical humaneness. Except when Israel itself lapsed into paganism, there were no human sacrifices, no immolation of widows and slaves. It was the first society where there was to be no temple prostitution and no inherent, permanent system of class or caste, and where bribery was forbidden. It was virtually the first civilisation which practised neither euthanasia, infanticide nor torture, and where capital punishment was rare. The Torah is unique in providing: the first code of responsibility for the welfare of the poor and the first organised system of charity; the first list of absolute moral commandment; and rules of extreme leniency towards slaves and servants. Neither were to work on the Sabbath and Jewish slaves were to enjoy the same food, wine and cushions as the master. By setting time limits, Judaic law ensured that, unless they chose, slaves could not be held in permanent bondage.[9]

Nor was it ever intended that Zion should be closed to Gentiles: it is clear from the Torah that strangers and aliens were to be an integral part of the state; it was, however, to be free of idols. Here the universality of Zion is clearly shown. For idols and pagan gods were almost always exclusive, being worshipped only by an initiated few. By contrast, worship of Almighty God in Zion was universal and available to all, as the dedication prayer of Solomon's Temple makes clear (2 Chron. 6:32-3). Zion was thus devoted not to the worship of man, but to his redemption; not to the worship of the land, but to its redemption through the Sabbath and Jubilee years. Zion was a vision of people worshipping the God of holiness in sanctified space, time and holiness.

That ideal of Zion remained partly unfulfilled, of course, because the temptation to worship the deities of nature

---

[8]*Cf.* A. Cohen, *Everyman's Talmud* (London, Dent 1968) 210-216.
[9]*Cf.* A.H. Silver, *Where Judaism differs. An inquiry into the distinctiveness of Judaism* (London, Macmillan, new ed., 1989); S. Belkin, *In His image: The Jewish Philosophy of Man as expressed in rabbinic tradition* (London, Abelard-Schuman 1961).

often proved too strong. Yet the creation of sanctified space and time, modelled on Zion, has been a hallmark of diaspora Jewry ever since. After the destruction of the second Temple in AD 70, the bulk of the Jewish people was cut off from the physical space of Zion. Yet as Jews celebrated their invisible God in those places far from Jerusalem, they effectively consecrated new spaces of holiness to him. The home became a reminder of the Temple sanctity, the sabbath a link with the hallowed time of Zion, the synagogue a sanctuary for the light of God's word embodied in the Torah. Moreover, with the loss of the system of animal sacrifices, the concept of worship deepened: every Jewish male had a priestly role, whether in Zion or in the diaspora, the space of every Jewish home was to be a dwelling place for God's presence, and every community was to be hallmarked by holy loving-kindness and love of the Torah. The spirit of Jerusalem was thus to influence every Jew exiled from her.

Furthermore, Jewish law (*halacha*) was designed to provide the framework within which the *mitzva*, the legal and religious deed of kindness should become the norm. Christianity has frequently misunderstood this role of Jewish law, seeing itself as a religion of love in contrast to Judaism, a religion of sterile rules. In fact, however, Judaism developed a society in which, in theory and often in practice, the permanent expression of practical love and the ideal of holiness were ensured.[10] This *halacha* enabled Jews to worship and imitate God outside the physical space of Zion.

Jewish communal patterns of holiness sought to reflect, however imperfectly, the holiness of Almighty God: 'You shall be holy, for I the Lord your God am holy' (Lev. 19:2). Yet they reflected his nature in another way: just as it was said of God that he had 'chosen Zion' (Ps. 132:13), 'loved the gates of Zion' (Ps. 87:2), would 'comfort' (Isa. 51:3) and 'build up' Zion (Ps. 102:16), so Jews sought to love and build up their own physical community in the diaspora. They were imitating God's own love for the physical land of Zion.

---

[10]*Cf.* I. Epstein, *Judaism* (London, Penguin 1959) ch. 3; P. Sigal, *Judaism: The evolution of a faith* (Grand Rapids, Eerdmans 1988) 236-8; S. Schechter, *Aspects of rabbinic theology: Major concepts of the Talmud* (New York, Schocken 1909, repr. 1961) ch. 13.

Yearning for Jerusalem, their lost 'Mother' was stamped on almost every aspect of Jewish communal life.[11] Daily reading of the Psalms, weekly readings of the Prophets reminded Jews of their God-given relationship to the Land. From Isaiah they learned to think of Zion as a widowed mother, bereaved of her children and yearning for them, anticipating their eventual return. They, in turn, prayed for that return in daily prayers in home and synagogue. One Sabbath benediction includes the lines: 'Have pity on Zion which is the home of our life...Blessed are you, O Lord, who makes Zion rejoice in her children'. In the *Mussaf*, an additional service appended to the Sabbath morning liturgy, Jews have pleaded over the centuries for God's eventual restoration of them to Zion and renewed worship there. Jewish festivals, such as *Shavuot* and *Succoth*, recalled the seasonal cycle not of the diaspora but of Zion.

Nothing, therefore, could be complete until Jerusalem was regained and redeemed. Thus an observant Jewish home has to this day not only an ornamental *misrach* (a picture or biblical verse recalling Jerusalem) on an east-facing wall, but often also an area of wall unpainted as a reminder of unredeemed Zion. No festive meal had its full number of courses. A shattered glass at weddings recalled the shattered Temple and the shattered dreams of Zion. Moreover, study of the Talmud and Midrash reminded Jews that 'the air of the Land of Israel makes one wise', that 'all who dwell in the Land of Israel are considered to be without sin', and that 'it is better to live in a hovel in the Land of Israel than in a palace in the diaspora'.[12]

Zion, however, was not only an ideal. It was a practical reality too, with a primacy over all other realities. For example, in demands on the communal purse, the poor of Jerusalem, took precedence over all other claims. Moreover, Jerusalem was the one object of Jewish pilgrimage, especially in the mediaeval period. For Jews, as for Christians, travelling to Jerusalem was always a hazardous enterprise. Yet often they went in large numbers; some would seek to stay at least

---

[11]*Cf.* Efrati, *Homecoming*, 19-32; A. Rubinstein, *The Return to Zion* (Jerusalem, Keter Books 1974); *Encyclopaedia Judaica*, 'Zionism'.
[12]*Baba Bathra* 158, *Ketubot* 111, *Bereshit Rabba* 39.

from Passover until after *Shavuot*, whilst others aimed to spend their remaining years in Jerusalem.[13]

Thus a modern writer could assert quite truthfully:

The restoration of Zion began on the day of its destruction. The Land was rebuilt in time long before it was restored in space. We have been building Zion daily for nearly 2000 years.[14]

David Ben Gurion echoed this, arguing that Israel had existed for thousands of years in the spirit, hearts and vision of the Jewish people. Jews have been rebuilding Zion in their hearts throughout time, by praying for it, by engraving it on their soul. Physical links with the land also remained unbroken. Throughout the past two millennia there have always been Jewish communities residing in Zion, whilst diaspora Jews have continually been rebuilding Zion through gifts, especially at times of special emergency and at the feast of Yom Kippur.

Jews have thus longed for and loved Jerusalem throughout their exile. Although, in the words of one rabbi, 'The Torah is the Jews' portable fatherland', hope of the promised Ingathering of the Exiles to Zion, their permanent motherland, has sustained them during their history of suffering in Gentile lands. This hope is clearly biblical. Over seven hundred verses in the Hebrew Scriptures relate to the time of the eventual Ingathering, when the wilderness will be

---

[13]See Efrati, *Homecoming,,* 39-46. Eye-witness accounts survive from the 9th to the 11th century, written by pilgrims from Italy, Persia and Babylonia, whilst six travel accounts were made by Italian Jews between 1434 and 1495. The most important scholarly study of the Land is *Kaftor Vaferah*, a geographical study by R. Ashtori Hafarhi (1313). It is also worth comparing the positive attitudes towards the Holy Land of Jewish pilgrims with the more negative ones voiced by Christians, who often saw its desolate nature as a sign of its being accursed by God. Conon de Bethune argued that if his body had to go on Crusade to Jerusalem, his heart would remain at home; whilst a 13th century French woman's song complains: 'Jerusalem, you do me a great wrong by taking from me that which I loved best. I shall never love you!'; see P. Dronke, *The Mediaeval Lyric* (London, Hutchinson 1968) 107, 127-8. By contrast, Judah Halevi wrote of Jerusalem in the 12th century while still in Spain: 'My heart is in the East and I am at the edge of the West. I am like a jackal when I weep for your affliction; but when I dream of your exiles' return, I am a lute for your songs': see *The Penguin book of Hebrew verse*, ed., T. Carmi (London, Penguin 1981) 347.

[14]One of the best books on Jewish religious Zionism is A.J. Heschel's *Israel: An Echo of Eternity* (New York, Farrar, Straus and Giroux 1969).

made a pool of water, the desert be filled with trees and the sons and daughters of the Jewish people will come from afar back to Zion (see esp. Isa. 41, 43).[15]

III. Jerusalem and Christians

Although in mediaeval maps (such as the Hereford *Mappa Mundi*) Jerusalem was shown at the centre of the world, although it was on a par with Rome and Compostella as a centre of Christian pilgrimage, nevertheless since Byzantine times Christians were far more preoccupied with Jerusalem as spiritual symbol rather than as physical reality. From hymns of the Church Fathers to negro spirituals, Jerusalem symbolised heaven, the soul's eternal home after its exile on earth, or the idealised perfection of the Church, the Bride of Christ, heralding the future kingdom of God on earth. Rome was the physical Eternal City, the sign of God's blessing the Church; the ruins of Jerusalem were the sign of God's cursing the Jews in perpetuity. Just as in Christian replacement theology the Church had replaced the Jews and become the New Israel, so too Rome had ousted Jerusalem.

Surprisingly, Christian poetry of the mediaeval period, during the two hundred years when the Holy land was under Christian rule, shows no traces of love for the Land. Its holy places, reminders of Jesus' life and, in the words of Conon de Bethune, 'God's holy inheritance', were valued, but as a land it was held in contempt. An anonymous 12th century poet expressed typical scorn: 'Sit, Zion, in the dust; sprinkle ashes on your head' (a mocking allusion to the Jews fasting in Jerusalem on *Tisha B'Av*). Christians went there to walk in Jesus' footsteps or, like Beckett's four murderers, to do penance. When Jerusalem fell again into Muslim hands in 1189, one impetus to build magnificent cathedrals in Europe sprang from the wish to recreate Jerusalem on Christian soil.

Following the Reformation, Christian attitudes to the Holy Land grew more nuanced. Gentiles for the first time had free access to the Bible, in Hebrew as well as in vernacular languages, and what has been called 'a new Hebrew spirit' began to influence European culture. Chairs of Hebrew were established at universities, scholarly Gentiles learnt Hebrew and the poet Milton even recommended that Hebrew should be

---

[15]*Cf.* L. Lambert, *The Uniqueness of Israel* (Eastbourne, Kingsway 1980).

taught in all English grammar schools. Increasingly, the Hebrew Scriptures were looked to as a source of ethics.[16] Moreover, as Protestants began to be persecuted and found themselves outsiders to the Church of Rome, there grew up a new understanding of and sympathy for the Jewish people as victims of persecution for their faith. Some gained a new respect for Jews and Judaism, and a sense of the unique Jewish mission among the Gentiles. Indeed, Amsterdam in the 16th and 17th centuries was a place so benevolent towards Jews that it was called by Jews the 'new Jerusalem'.

One of the responses to the regained Hebrew Scriptures was the movement which became known as Christian Restorationism—the belief, based on numerous biblical passages, that the Jews would ultimately return to Zion and establish a state there. This movement began with the writings of Frances Kett and Thomas Brightman in the late 16th century. It is still active today in many parts of the world, though less common in Britain, its original home. The long history of gentile belief in the Jewish return to Zion is little-known even among Christians, and only a brief outline can be given here of this international movement.[17]

R. Joseph ben Caspi had anticipated in the thirteenth century that the Return would be initiated, like the Return from the first exile in Babylon under Cyrus the Great, by a gentile ruler inspired by God. Many Christian Restorationists came to the same conclusion, and sought to encourage gentile rulers to assist practically in a future Jewish Return. Holger Paulli (1644-1714), a Danish pietist, wrote to the kings of France and

---

[16] The Levellers argued that the Torah should be made the sole basis for English law, whilst Oliver Cromwell wanted to reform Parliament with seventy members on the model of the great Sanhedrin.

[17] *Cf.* R. Sharif, *Non-Jewish Zionism: Its Roots in Western history* (London, Zed Press 1983); Y. Malachy, 'Christian Zionism' in *Zionism* (Jerusalem, Keter Books 1973) 231-6; M.J. Pragai, *Faith and Fulfilment: Christians and the Return to the Promised Land* (London, Vallentine, Mitchell 1985); N. Shepherd, *The Zealous Intruders. The Western Rediscovery of Palestine* (London, Collins 1987); B. Tuchman, *Bible and Sword* (New York, Funk & Wagnalls 1950); C. Duvernoy, *The Zionism of God* (Jerusalem, 1985); see also *With Eyes toward Zion*, ed., M. Davis (New York, Praeger 1986) vol. II, and most recently, K. Crombie *For the Love of Zion: Christian Witness and the Restoration of Israel* (London, Hodder and Stoughton 1991).

England, asking them to recapture Palestine in order to restore it to the Jews as the rightful heirs. In a detailed letter to William III of England, he addressed him as Cyrus the Great and the Almighty's instrument. A Swede, Anders Pedersen Kempe, wrote *Israel's Good News* in 1688, attacking Christians for their 'replacement theology':

You heathen Christians, you let yourselves be persuaded by false teachers. . .to believe that the Jews were forever disinherited and rejected by God, and that you were now the rightful Christian Israel to possess the land of Canaan forever.[18]

Occasionally Christian restorationists were persecuted (the British Francis Kett, for example was killed in the 16th century), but many were remarkably eminent men. Sir Henry Finch, was a legal authority in Britain and the King's Sergeant-at-Arms. imprisoned [19]

An essential part of many writings about the Jewish Restoration was a belief in the ultimate conversion of the Jewish people to Christianity. Nevertheless an English theologian, Thomas Brightman, while holding such a belief, also championed in the early seventeenth century the notion of Jewish Restoration

not for religion's sake,. . .but not to strive any longer as strangers and inmates with forraigne nations'.[20]

In other words, the Restoration should happen simply for the sake of the Jewish people and their safety. This humanitarian theme subsequently became a major strand of Restorationist thought. Meanwhile, almost all writers, both Catholic and Protestant, believed that the eventual Jewish state in Palestine would be in some measure utopian, with institutions distinct from and better than their Christian counterparts in Europe. Such a vision was created by Samuel Gott in *The Ideal City or Jerusalem Regained* (1648), in which the future Jewish Jerusalem is portrayed as an ideal and hospitable state. Moreover, from the seventeenth century onwards philo-semitism became more common: in his work *Samson Agonistes*

---

[18]Sharif, *op. cit.*, 28.
[19]He was imprisoned for his book *The World's Great Restoration or Calling of the Ieuues* (1621).
[20]Sharif, *op. cit.*, 18.

(1671) John Milton created a new phenomenon in Europe—the first subjective and sympathetic portrait of a Jew.

Distinguished scholars and thinkers who espoused the cause of Jewish Restoration included: John Locke, Isaac Newton, the philosophers Kant and Rousseau, and the scientist Joseph Priestley, who wrote in an open letter to the Jewish people:

> May the God of Abraham, Isaac and Jacob, whom we Christians as well as you Jews worship, be graciously pleased to put an end to your suffering, gather you from all nations, resettle you in your own country—the land of Canaan—and make you the most illustrious of all nations on the earth.[21]

Napoleon may have believed in an ultimate Jewish Restoration to Zion, though his motives were highly ambiguous. Describing the Jewish people as the heirs of Palestine, he was the first European statesman to propose a the creation of a Jewish state there. He called on the Jews of Africa and Asia to unite under his flag to re-establish the kingdom—and opened the ghettoes as his army marched through Europe.

In 1790 an Anglican priest, Richard Beere, wrote a letter to the English Prime Minister, William Pitt, urging him to assist in the 'final restoration of the Jews to the Holy Land', anticipating that Britain would be the first nation to convey Jews to their country. From then on, a succession of European thinkers, diplomats and statesmen could envisage the Jewish return eventually taking place. In 19th-century Britain there were many evangelical and other Christian Restorationists in the highest positions in the land.[22] One of the most important was the seventh Earl of Shaftesbury (the vigorous campaigner against slavery) who persuaded Lord Palmerston to appoint a fellow Restorationist William Young, as the first vice-consul in Jerusalem in 1838 with the specific brief of protecting the Jews in Jerusalem. Shaftesbury recorded in his diary:

> What a wonderful event it is! The ancient City of the people of God is about to resume a place among the nations; and England is the first of the Gentile kingdoms that ceases to 'tread her down'.

---

[21] *Ibid.*, 36f.
[22] They included the Duke of Kent, the Earl of Crawford, Earl Grey, Lord Grosvenor, Lord Bexley, Bishop Manning, and Gladstone.

Believing that the 'time for the turning of their captivity was at hand' and witnessing among Christians 'a new and tender interest in the Hebrew people',[23] he wrote:

Palmerston had already been chosen by God to be an instrument of good to His ancient people, and to recognise their rights without believing in their destiny'.[24]

Numerous theologians and preachers contended that God's covenant with Abraham and His promises relating to Jewish restoration to the Land were still valid,[25] and a number of pro-Restorationist religious groups were established, notably the Plymouth Brethren (1830), the Seventh Day Adventists (1830) and the Christadelphians (1844). Many Christians believed that the Return of Jews to their land was imminent and that they would be converted to Christianity there. As a result, the Church's Mission to the Jews established the first hospital in Jerusalem in the late 1830s, the first Anglican Bishop in Jerusalem was appointed in 1842 and some Christian agricultural settlements were established in the 1850s, although short-lived and ultimately unsuccessful. Christian travellers also came to Palestine in ever greater numbers including David Roberts and Mark Twain, and in 1865, the British Consul in Jerusalem, James Finn, a convinced Restorationist, established the Palestine Exploration Fund with the aim of mapping the country and pioneering the scientific exploration of the land.[26]

Mention should also be made of the following: George Eliot, whose last novel, *Daniel Deronda* (1874) was effectively the first Zionist novel;[27] Edward Cazalet, MP., who in 1887 suggested that there should be a Hebrew University in Jerusalem; Laurence Oliphant (1829-88), MP., who in *The Land of Gilead* (1880) detailed a settlement scheme for Jews in

---

[23]Pragai, *op. cit.*, 45-6.
[24]Sharif, *op. cit.*, 56.
[25]These included Bishop Hurd, Dr. Thomas Burnet, Joseph Eyre, Edward Whitaker, Charles Jerram, Pastor Crybbace, Edward Bickersteth and William Blackstone.
[26]Cf. *Britain and the Holy Land 1800-1914*, monographs printed by University College London Institute of Jewish Studies (1989).
[27]Other British literary figures whose writings reflect the Restorationist ideal include William Blake, Lord Byron, William Wordsworth, Walter Scott and Robert Browning.

Palestine, helped found a Christian organisation which supported the Jewish *Hibbat Zion* movement, and interpreted the arrival of the First Aliyah (1881) as a clear sign of the invisible working of God for the Jewish people; and the Revd. William Hechler, Anglican chaplain at the Embassy in Vienna, who predicted in *The Restoration of the Jews to Palestine* (1894) on biblical grounds that the restoration of Jews was imminent, and who became a valued friend of Theodor Herzl;[28] Claude Conder (1848-1910), an officer with the Royal Engineers, who surveyed the land and planned a network of roads which became the basis for its later infrastructure; Henri Dunant (1828-1910), the Swiss Christian philanthropist and founder of the Red Cross, who was the first gentile to be called a 'Christian Zionist' (by Theodor Herzl) and one of the few non-Jews invited to the First Zionist Congress; Lord Balfour, responsible for the Balfour Declaration, who was brought up by a Christian Zionist mother; and several of the Presidents of the USA (*e.g.* Wilson, Harding, Coolidge) who were inspired by the same ideals.[29] Unlike many of the earliest restorationists, almost all these Christians had close Jewish friends with whom they shared their Zionist ideal.

Christian Zionism, although not an organized movement, continues to this day through organisations such as the International Christian Embassy in Jerusalem and the Christian Friends of Israel, educating Christians about Israel, its role in biblical prophecy and God's love for His Jewish people. One contemporary example of this restorationist and humanitarian ideal is the practical and financial support given to Israel by Christian Zionists to enable Soviet Jews to settle in Israel.[30] Not surprisingly, in days when there is also a virulent

---

[28]*Cf.* C. Duvernoy, *The Prince and the Prophet* (Paradise, Calif., Land of Promise productions 1973). The views of these, sometimes eccentric individuals were nevertheless mirrored by a far larger Christian public: books such as J. Anderson's *Lays and Laments for Israel* (1845) and W.M. Thompson's *The Land and the Book* (1888) enjoyed wide popularity.
[29]Note too the military training offered by Major Orde Wingate to Jewish men in Palestine in the 1930s whose troops became the nucleus of the Hagganah: see L. Mosley, *Gideon goes to war: the story of Major-General Orde C. Wingate* (New York, Charles Scribner's Sons 1955).
[30]Two percent of the Jewish Agency budget for 'airlifting' Soviet immigrants has been contributed by Christian Zionists.

anti-Zionism, Christian Zionism too has been the target of some undeserved opprobrium.[31]

IV. The Rise of Jewish Zionism (to 1917)

Traditional Jewish thought held that Zion would be restored only when the Messiah would arrive. On the basis of such verses as Psalm 147:2 ('The Lord builds up Jerusalem; he gathers together the outcasts of Israel'), it was envisaged that the Ingathering of exiles to Zion (prophesied in Isaiah 43:6 and elsewhere) would occur only after the Advent of the Messiah.[32] However, Rabbi Joseph ben Caspi in the 13th century articulated the view that a gentile ruler might be moved by God to open the gates of Zion to Jews:

Perhaps a king will arise...proclaiming throughout his kingdom that the Jews shall return to their land. Even without all this, the Lord Himself may awaken the spirit of today's ruler, be it tomorrow or the next day, that he turn the land of Israel over to us wherein shall be gathered all Jews from all over his kingdom along with their colleagues from all four corners of the earth.[33]

Until the early nineteenth century, however, the view prevailed that the people of Israel should wait until the Advent of the Messiah before returning *en masse* to the Land of Israel; this advent itself would come about only with the spiritual return to God (*teshuva*—repentance) of the whole Jewish nation. Since then, there have always been groups of very orthodox Jews (*e.g.* some groups in Jerusalem's Mea Shearim today), who have been opposed to Zionism and the re-establishment of the Jewish state. Yet the fact that so many ardent rabbis and their followers settled in Palestine over the centuries demonstrates the power of the paradoxical belief that for a Jew the greatest *mitzva* was to settle in the Land.

---

[31] Since the Holocaust there has been much theological underpinning of Christian support for the Jewish attachment to Jerusalem and Israel. Leading writers include J. Parkes, *A History of the Jewish People* (Pelican, 1964); A. and R. Eckardt, *Encounter with Israel: A Challenge to Conscience* (New York, 1970); P. van Buren, *A Theology of the Jewish-Christian Reality* (New York, Harper & Row 1987).
[32] See A. Cohen, *Everyman's Talmud*, 352-5. Thus, whenever periods of Messianic fervour arose in some Jewish communities (as in the early sixteenth century), immigration to the Land always increased.
[33] In his work *Tam ha-Kesef*; see Efrati, *Homecoming*, 33.

Following Napoleon's opening of the ghettoes during his conquest of Europe, a German rabbinic scholar, Rabbi Zvi Hirsch Kalischer (1795-1874), interpreted these unprecedented (though short-lived) events in messianic terms as stages in the final Return, to be achieved through human agency:

The Redemption of Israel, for which we long, is not to be imagined as a sudden miracle. . .Everything will be fulfilled, but the Redemption will come by slow degrees. . .and will begin by awakening support among the philanthropists and by gaining the consent of the nations to the gathering of some of the scattered of Israel into the Holy Land.[34]

On the basis of Isaiah 11:11 and 27:6, 12-13, Kalischer believed that the Return would have two main phases: first, an initial pioneering stage (the blossom and buds) of preparing the land through agriculture, then secondly a mass return (the fruit). Kalischer himself appealed in 1836 to leading Jewish philanthropists, Meyer Anschel Rothschild and Sir Moses Montefiore, to buy either the whole land, or at least Jerusalem, from Muhammad Ali, the pasha of Egypt and in 1860 convened a conference to discuss financing the settlement of the Land.

Rabbi Judah Alkalai (1798-1878) was another forerunner of political Zionism.[35] In 1839 he put forward the revolutionary idea that the necessary precondition for redemption, *teshuvah*, should be interpreted literally as *physical* return to the Land. Further impetus was lent to his thought in 1840 by the infamous Damascus Affair[36] which Alkalai interpreted as further evidence that Jews should settle in the Land as a way of ending their plight in exile. Thereafter he published many pamphlets calling for agricultural

---

[34]From *Drishat Zion* (1862): cited in *The Zionist Movement*, ed., J. Kaplan, (Jerusalem, Heb. Univ. 1983) I, 6.
[35]For accounts of Jewish Zionism, see W. Laqueur, *A History of Zionism* (London, Weidenfeld & Nicolson 1972); S. Avineri, *The Making of Modern Zionism: the Intellectual Origins of the Jewish State* (London, Weidenfeld and Nicolson 1981). A selection of primary texts is in A. Hertzberg, ed., *The Zionist Idea: a historical analysis and reader* (New York, Atheneum 1982).
[36]The Capuchin Order falsely accused the Jewish community of murdering a friar and using his blood for baking Passover unleavened bread, resulting in Jews being tortured, imprisoned and many children kidnapped; surviving prisoners were eventually released in response to pressure from France, Britain and other European countries.

settlement, a Jewish army, resurrection of the Hebrew language, and for a Jewish state recognised by the nations. Like Kalischer, Alkalai's vision had little immediate success. Yet his writings and visits to Jewish communities in several European countries inspired other early Zionists and the creation in 1860 of the *Alliance Israelite Universelle*, the first supranational Jewish organisation, which in 1870 founded near Jaffa *Mikveh Israel*, the first agricultural school in the land.

In the meantime important political developments had occurred in Palestine. In 1832 Muhammad Ali's stepson, Ibrahim Pasha, had conquered Palestine for Egypt and amalgamated its various districts into one administrative unit: law and order were enforced more rigorously than before, rendering the land safer for travellers. Moreover, Christian missionaries were for the first time allowed to preach and establish schools ,and other institutions and European consulates were permitted in Jerusalem. From then on western powers began to be more heavily involved in the Middle East, France in support of the Ottoman Empire, Britain and Russia opposing it. The greater protection thus afforded to Jews by means of the consulates in Jerusalem encouraged an increase in Jewish immigration from the 1840s.[37]

Moreover Kalischer's call to Jewish philanthropists had borne fruit. Sir Moses Montefiore (1784-1885) was the leading British Jew of the 19th. century; a leading banker, philanthropist and Orthodox, he was highly regarded within Jewish circles, and admired by Queen Victoria. He used his considerable influence and wealth to assist his people in Britain and abroad, and in 1838 attempted to buy land in Palestine for Jewish agriculture. This failed because the Ottomans regained control from the Egyptians in 1840-1, but he continued to develop industry and was responsible for the first housing developments outside the walls of Jerusalem.

---

[37]For accounts of 19th-century Jerusalem, see Y. ben Arieh, *Jerusalem in the 19th century: the Old City* (New York, St. Martin's Press 1984). *Cf.* more general histories: S. Grayzel, *A History of the Jews* (New York, Signet 1968); B. Bamberger, *The Story of Judaism* (New York, Schocken Paperback 1964); P. Johnson, *A History of the Jews* (London, Weidenfeld & Nicolson 1987).

The majority of Jewish thinkers in the mid-19th. century continued to believe, like Montefiore himself, that the immediate Jewish future lay in Europe. Emancipation from the ghettoes had finally come in the 1840s and 1850s, and a period of increased security and prosperity seemed in sight. With the gradual lifting of discriminatory laws, Jews in Western Europe began to take a leading role in industry, commerce, politics and finance. Whilst there were still strong pockets of anti-Jewish feeling among some Catholics and Protestants, Marxists and right-wing Conservatives, the slowly lessening influence of traditional Christian anti-Judaism lulled many Jews into believing that Jews would be completely accepted in or assimilated into non-Jewish society.

However, the influential socialist, Moses Hess (1812-1875) was one Jewish intellectual who, having initially believed in such assimilation, came to disagree. He began to argue that anti-semitism was actually endemic in the gentile world.[38] As a result, the Jewish nation should be regenerated in Palestine, its spiritual centre, something which in fact would benefit the whole of humanity. The future Jewish state should be socialist and strongly ethical, with all working for the common good and the land communally held by the nation—ideas that would have considerable impact once the Zionist movement was established in the 1890s.

The Reform movement (founded in Germany in the early 19th. century) held that Judaism must follow the path of assimilation and be purged of particularist elements (including the Hebrew language and any references to Jerusalem and Zion in its liturgies and prayers). Others, however, such as Peretz Smolenskin (?1842-1885) were appalled at this process of disintegration of Jewish identity. Being more aware than some of his western counterparts of the power of antisemitism, Smolenskin became a passionate champion of the Hebrew language and literature: from 1868 onwards he published a Hebrew monthly, and, like Hess, asserted the necessity of a Jewish sovereign nation. After the terrible Czarist pogroms in 1880-1 a movement emerged under his influence called 'Lovers of Zion' (*Hibbat Zion*) which, dedicated to reclaiming the Land of Israel, encouraged fundraising for land-purchase in Palestine and taught the Jewish masses of the need for *aliyah*

---

[38]See Efrati, *Homecoming*, 90-2.

('going up' as immigrants to Israel). As a result, by the late 1890s about 4,500 Jews were settled in agricultural communities.[39]

In response to the 1881 pogroms and to the new racist antisemitism promoted by Richard Wagner and others, Leon Pinsker (1821-91) argued in *Autoemancipation* (1882) that antisemitism was endemic in gentile society:

For the living, the Jew is a dead man; for the natives an alien and a vagrant; for property holders a beggar; for the poor as exploiter and millionaire; for patriots a man without a country; for all classes, a hated rival.[40]

The only solution would be for Jews to have their own land—if not in Palestine, then in North America or elsewhere. Pinsker eventually became leader of *Hibbat Zion*; yet, as a philanthropic rather than political body, this group lacked the dynamic to create a united Jewish movement.

Only Theodor Herzl (1860-1904) could do that. His importance for Jewish Zionism is well-known. As a secular Jewish journalist, Herzl was shocked by the Dreyfus Affair (1894) and growing European antisemitism into a passionate commitment to what he was the first to call 'political Zionism'. In his book *Der Judenstaat* (1896) he stressed the unity of all Jews ('we are a people—one people')[41] and argued that only an independent Jewish state could bring Jewish persecution to an end.

At his first Zionist Congress (Basle, 1897) 197 delegates agreed on the necessity for large-scale *aliyah*, settlement of Palestine and international Jewish cooperation. Herzl argued convincingly that 'Zionism seeks to bestow upon a landless people both land and honour' and had good reason to claim in his diary: 'At Basle I founded the Jewish state'.[42] Subsequent Zionist Congresses endorsed his powerful impact on the movement. He inspired the creation of an international Zionist organisation and a Jewish bank, and had audiences with many European rulers (Kaiser Wilhelm II, the Pope, Joseph

---

[39]Cf. A. Yaari, *The Goodly Heritage: Memoirs describing the life of the Jewish community of Eretz Yisrael from the 17th to the 20th centuries*, abridged and translated by Israel Schen (Jerusalem, 1958).
[40]Cited in W. Laqueur, *op. cit.*, 72.
[41]T. Herzl, *The Jewish State* (Tel Aviv, M. Newman 1956) 38.
[42]W. Laqueur, *op. cit.*, 108.

Chamberlain among others). While Herzl had little impact on Jewish capitalists and assimilated leaders (particularly in Britain), the response among the Jewish masses was warm.

For Herzl the overriding need was simply for a Jewish state (in Argentina or Uganda if necessary). Congress delegates, however, were adamant: the Land of Israel was their only spiritual homeland. Following his own visit to Palestine in 1898, Herzl himself wrote a prophetic book *Altneuland*, envisaging the restored homeland as a Zionist utopia: Jerusalem would be rebuilt, the land rejuvenated through afforestation and draining of swamps, the people reunited under one flag.

By 1914 a second wave of immigration had occurred (the Second *Aliyah*); the Jewish inhabitants of Palestine now numbered 85,000, an eighth of the total population. Due to the ethnic policies of the Ottoman rulers, the population was very diverse and included Druzes, Circassians, Samaritans, Georgians, Armenians and other peoples in addition to the large Arab population. Jerusalem had long been a predominantly Jewish city; in 1889 there had been 25,000 Jews in the city, compared to 7,175 Christians and 7,000 Muslims.[43] Meanwhile the infrastructure of a future Jewish state was being laid, and biblical Hebrew revived by Eliezer ben Yehuda as a living language for daily use. Yet the Ottoman rulers normally placed heavy restrictions on Jewish immigration and building, and for many Jews, the idea of a free Jewish state seemed an impossible dream.

With the British conquest of Jerusalem in December 1917 and subsequent Mandate over Palestine in 1920, Zionist hopes were briefly renewed. Influenced by Lord Balfour and Lloyd George, (both convinced Restorationists and friends of the Zionist Chaim Weizman) the British government, seeing pragmatic advantages in the destruction of Ottoman rule, signed the Balfour Declaration in November 1917: this affirmed Palestine as 'a national home for the Jewish people'. Yet things were not so simple. As is well known, British policies proved equivocal. In 1915 the Sherif of Mecca had been promised that Britain would support the independence of the Arabs (though Jerusalem and southern Palestine were excluded). With an eye to future oil prospects and placating

---

[43]M. Gilbert, *Jerusalem*, 53.

incipient Arab nationalism, Churchill made Abdullah in 1921 Emir of eastern Palestine (Transjordan), where the concept of Jewish homeland was not to apply.[44]

Many of the troubles in the years after 1917 in Palestine would stem from this ambivalent approach of the British.[45] The long-awaited dream of Jewish Zionists throughout the previous century was now, through the Balfour Declaration, within the realm of political possibility. Yet the problems of how Jews and Arabs were to be reconciled began to loom large, and within years the awful spectre of the Nazi holocaust was on the horizon, with further painful consequences for this already difficult situation.[46]

Eventually the State of Israel came into being in 1948, and Jerusalem was reunited in 1967. In this way, at least in the eyes of many Jewish and Christian Zionists, the biblical prophecies were finally in the process of being fulfilled. The Ingathering of the Exiles had begun in earnest, the desert was beginning to flourish like a rose, and the beautifying of Jerusalem was under way. Powerless and at the mercy of Gentiles for so many centuries, Jews have again become farmers, soldiers and politicians in their own land.

---

[44]*Cf.* P. Mansfield, *op. cit.*, esp. chs. 7 and 10.
[45]British responsibility for many of the ensuing political problems in Israel/Palestine must be faced squarely. Britain's blockade, for example, on Jewish refugees seeking to enter Palestine—especially in the aftermath of the second World War—deservedly provoked a huge international outcry.
[46]See below ch. 6 (iv) and ch. 7 (v) for discussion of the period from 1917 to 1967 and the present day. In addition to the works cited there or above, see also: W. Laqueur and B. Rubin edd., *The Israel-Arab reader: a documentary history of the Middle East conflict* (Penguin Books, 4th revd. ed., 1984); T. Prittie, *Whose Jerusalem?* (London, F. Muller 1981); W. Frankel, *Israel Observed: an Anatomy of the State* (London, Thames and Hudson 1980); C. Cruise O'Brien, *The Siege: the story of Israel and Zionism* (London, Paladin 1988); M. Gilbert, *Exile and Return: the Emergence of Jewish Statehood* (London, Weidenfeld & Nicolson 1978). For a Marxist, pro-Arab view see M. Rodinson, *Israel and the Arabs* (Penguin, 1968). See also my pamphlet, *A Christian Response to Israel and the Palestinian Question* (London, Anglo-Israel Association 1989).

V. Three Points for Further Discussion

The above sections have been primarily historical, recounting the belief and practice of both Jews and Christians in relation to Jerusalem through the centuries. Some points of a more theological and contemporary nature are now in order.

1) The Theological Basis of Christian Zionism

A detailed exposition of the biblical and theological basis for Christian Zionism is clearly needed—especially in this volume where the contrary view appears to predominate.[47] Remaining space prevents the redressing of this imbalance and the reader is referred instead to the works of others.[48] Here it may simply be pointed out that those Evangelicals who today affirm the Jewish return to Israel do so on a theological and biblical basis which was accepted as thoroughly orthodox—even normative—by mainstream Evangelicalism in the nineteenth century. There has been a radical change within Evangelicalism on this issue which needs to be acknowledged. This should give grounds for caution amongst those who would now dub Christian Zionism as heretical. On the contrary, to claim that, because God's promises are fulfilled spiritually in Jesus, they therefore cannot later be fulfilled in literal way, is either to limit God's power or to imply that history ended with the Resurrection.

Many post-Holocaust theologians thus reject this 'replacement theology' which sees the New Testament as the total fulfilment of the Old and therefore superseding it.[49] Some see it as stemming from the triumphalist anti-Judaic tradition begun by the Church Fathers, contributing to the long history of what Littell terms the 'Christian crucifixion of the Jews', and even to the Holocaust itself.[50] Instead such theologians would wish to affirm God's continuing covenant with the Jews (based

---

[47]For these contrary views, see above, esp. chs. 1 and 3; for a further defence of Zionism, see below ch. 7.

[48]E.g. C. Duvernoy, *The Zionism of God* (Jerusalem, 1985); N.J. Dubois, *L'exil et la demur* (Jerusalem, 1984); see also the theological sections of the works cited in nn. 17, 31.

[49]They include, for example, J. Pawlikowski, P. van Buren, R. Eckhardt, M. Barth, M. Dubois, J. Parkes, F. Littell.

[50]Cf. J. Parkes, *The conflict of the Church and the Synagogue* (London, 1934); J. Gager, *The Origins of Anti-semitism: Attitudes towards Judaism in Pagan and Christian Antiquity* (Oxford/New York, 1985).

on such verses as Gen. 17:8; Isa. 54:10; Jer. 31:35-7) and the continuing validity of all the Hebrew Scriptures.[51] If this whole biblical perspective be accepted, the Jewish state today can then be seen as a partial fulfilment of God's explicit promises for the eventual restoration of Zion and a reuniting of Jews with their ancient land (Deut. 30:3; Isa. 14:1; Isa. 49, 51-6; Jer. 30-33 *etc.*).

The Christian Zionist position is that neither land nor Jerusalem is intrinsically holy; but that Jerusalem is the place where the Lord has 'chosen to place his name' (Deut. 14:23; 16:2,6,11; 26:2), and where he placed the Jews: 'and they shall put my name upon the children of Israel, and I will bless them' (Num. 6:27). As for the biblical curses regarding suffering and exile from Zion (Deut. 28; Jer. 19 *etc.*), these were *not* finished in 70 AD. Jews, the only people without a state for nearly 2000 years, endured exile and intense suffering until 1948 (in part because the Jewish people does in some mysterious way bear God's name and witness to His existence and ethical demand, thus arousing deep hostility). To believe that God's curses remain in operation but that his blessings cease would be to deny God's very essence, his mercy and everlasting love.

2) Christian Mission to Jews

Whilst, as noted above, there have been (and still are) some Christian Zionists who continue to be in favour of evangelism amongst Jewish people, there are many who oppose this; in taking this stance they are in agreement with most post-Holocaust theologians, such as those cited above. Three main reasons for this view should be noted.

First, *theological*: early Christianity was clearly not designed to replace Judaism; instead, as just noted, there is a continuing covenant with the Jewish people. Paul, Peter and other Jewish believers in Jesus remained orthodox Jews, worshipping in the Temple and observing the Law. Jesus affirmed the Law (Matt. 5:17-20; Luke 16:17), Paul affirmed observance of the Law for Jews, though not for Gentiles (Rom. 3:1-3; Acts 21: 20-6), and circumcised the Greek Timothy (Acts 16:3). Even after the Church became entirely gentile, some Christian Gentiles voluntarily continued Sabbath observance,

---

[51]It is hard to see how such verses as 'pray for the peace of Jerusalem; they shall prosper that love you' (Ps. 122:6) and 'do good to Zion, build the walls of Jerusalem' (Ps. 51:18) relate only to Jesus and not to today's Jews.

worshipping in synagogues and keeping biblical festivals at least until the seventh century, even though from 318 AD the Church tried to eradicate residual Christian links to Judaism by making such practices illegal, punishing Jewish proselytising with death, and preaching that Judaism was demonic.[52]

This distorted vision of Judaism has continued until today. If Christians knew Orthodox Judaism better, they would judge it more humbly. The Holy Spirit (*Ruah ha-kodesh*) has been widely taught and experienced in the Synagogue, and the Word of God loved, cherished and lived in countless Jewish homes since rabbinic times. The exiled Jewish people have been faithful to the Covenant, sensing God's forgiveness, love and blessing renewed each Shabbat and festival, sustaining them in their task of *tikkun olam*, mending the world. Yet they have understood themselves as suffering servants of God according to Isaiah 53, suffering not only for their own sins but as part of God's plan of redemption and to sanctify God's name in the world.

Secondly, *historical*: the Church has preached Jesus' love to Jews but practised hatred; it is time to change. Our record has been one of pride and often extreme cruelty. There have indeed been individual exceptions, but as a people, the record of history suggests that Christians have behaved not in a Christ-like but demonic way towards Christ's own people. Until the gentile Church, the Prodigal Son, repents of its past in humility and remorse, true brotherhood with our Jewish elder brother cannot be re-established.

Thirdly, *strategic*: the New Age movement today stands opposed to the Judeo-Christian tradition and seeks to destroy biblical monotheism and all orthodox worship of the God of Abraham, Isaac and Jacob; Christians and Jews therefore need to stand together against this common threat. From the perspective of the New Age, Orthodox Judaism (as well as Zionism and Israel) must disappear, and Bible-based Christianity subverted from within towards Goddess-worship, occult meditations, Creation-centred liturgies, and evident

---

[52]See e.g, E.H. Flannery, *The Anguish of the Jews* (New York, Paulist Press 1985); J. Gager, *op. cit.*; J. Trachtenberg, *The Devil and the Jew* (Philadelphia, Jewish Publication Soc of America 1983); L. Poliakov, *The History of Anti-Semitism* I (Eng. Trans. London, Routledge and Kegan Paul 1974).

paganism.[53] Christians therefore need urgently to recognise that observant Jews are their allies. If Christians seek to weaken Judaism or convert Jews from it, they will be aiding the New Age movement in its work. As fellow-worshippers of the one true God, Christians and Jews face a serious and imminent threat, and will find strength if we make common cause.

3) Acknowledging the Jewish mission to the world

Finally, Christians need to learn from observant Jews, for Judaism has much to teach the Church.[54] For Christian theology has tended to undervalue the Old Testament, and given insufficient emphasis to things such as biblical ethics, the laity, and the material world; by contrast, it has emphasised instead original sin, celibacy and Greek dualism. In comparison with Judaism, Christianity has often lost touch with true biblical traditions and standards, in valuing women, marriage and married sexuality, in education and democracy, in child-rearing and godly homes, in cherishing the poor and sanctifying the Sabbath. Observant Jews have retained this heritage intact, passing it on from generation to generation.

Orthodox Judaism, therefore, can be a helpful reminder of what should be (and often was) orthodox in Christianity. In synagogue services the Bible is central, read lovingly and at great length, and the liturgy, all biblically inspired, is focused on joyful praise and worship of Almighty God; every Sabbath morning service includes specific prayer for the Royal Family and for Britain. Yet many churches (even some evangelical ones) have lost that centrality of the Bible, that devotion to worship, and that fervency of prayer. The Church, God's gentile worshippers, vitally needs God's Jewish worshippers; for together we are the 'household of God' (Eph. 2:19). So too the Jewish people need Christians—not our missionising, but our prayer, our support, above all our self-sacrificial love.

---

[53]*Cf.* M. Brearley, 'Matthew Fox: Creation spirituality for the Aquarian Age' in *Christian/Jewish Relations* 22.2 (1989) 37-49; *idem*, 'Matthew Fox and the Cosmic Christ', *Anvil* 9.2 (1992) 39-54.

[54]The author has had the privilege (like that of early Christians but unusual today) of living within a Jewish community for many years, attending synagogue on festivals and Shabbat, fasting on Yom Kippur, working within an Orthodox synagogue, participating in Jewish family and community life.

In Judaism Zion represents the Sabbath, Jerusalem the major festivals—the heightened beauty of worship on Passover, Pentecost and Tabernacles. All Jewish art ultimately derives its inspiration from Psalm 118:28: 'You are my God, and I will adorn (exalt) you'. So Jerusalem today grows yearly more beautiful, as flowers, trees and fine buildings proliferate. Jews cherish and adorn Jerusalem, like a long-lost bride, in joy (Isa. 65:18; 66:10)—not from any sense of *apartheid* but knowing that it will again be, and indeed already is, a blessing to all Gentiles (Isa. 60:9-62:12)[55] and that, when God's messianic kingdom is finally established, again 'out of Zion shall go forth the law, and the word of the Lord from Jerusalem' (Isa. 2:3).

---

[55]Israel is, like all states, imperfect and deeply flawed, yet it is already a blessing to other nations: Carmel produce and irrigation technology are but the 'tip of an iceberg'. Less visible is the army of Israeli aid experts training in Africa and elsewhere in techniques of desert agriculture, its excellent record on the integration of immigrants, its educational and cultural achievements; its far-sighted treatment of women, children and the disabled. Israel values democracy and especially by Middle Eastern values is deeply humane.

CHAPTER 6

JERUSALEM IN ISLAM AND FOR PALESTINIAN CHRISTIANS

Naim Ateek

I. Introduction

The holiness of one place and its significance to the life and worship of a particular people is one of the oldest treasured beliefs of nations. Yet due to the passage of history certain places have become sacred to more than one group, resulting often in conflict and violence. Moreover, the way a people perceive that holiness becomes ingrained in their historical memory and religious consciousness. That holy space becomes uniquely theirs. It gives them identity and is hard to share; so it must be guarded and controlled.

Jerusalem is such a place. The surrounding land of Israel/Palestine is a beautiful country, but, because of its strategic location, it has been like a corridor—endlessly used by armies and people, open to constant attack, vulnerable to neighbouring powers. Its history reflects the constant movement of people. A great part of the pain and suffering in the Middle East today is caused by this long and changing history. For as a result, Jerusalem today is a unique place in the history of humankind, revered by millions. Yet this city has all the ingredients of driving people apart, because its sacredness to one group has somehow negated the others rather than included them.

The great challenge before us is whether humans can transcend exclusive historical claims and divisive religious understanding so that they can share sacred space. Or is it still impossible for sacred space to be shared in our modern world?

The following is a Palestinian Christian perspective on Jerusalem. Its purpose is both to explain a Palestinian approach to this subject and to show that Palestinians, though insisting on truth and justice, are working and hoping for a political solution that can be inclusive to all of Jerusalem's inhabitants rather than exclusive to one group.

Initially, some Western readers may find this approach to the land of Israel/Palestine somewhat strange. Yet there is a real sense in which, from a certain historical perspective, it can be claimed that Palestine has always been part of the land of the Arabs. Some scholars argue that the people of the Middle East originated in the Arabian peninsula:[1] the Canaanites, Babylonians, Assyrians, Phoenicians and Hebrews (Israelites) were people who populated the whole of the Middle East as a result of different waves of immigration arising from the Arabian peninsula. If so, this historical perspective emphasizes the common Arab roots of the people of the Middle East before they diverged into tribes and nations. It also encourages an awareness that in the land of Palestine there has been a constant influx of new ethnic groups, resulting in a population that throughout history has been both indigenous and foreign at the same time. Foreign elements have mixed with the indigenous population and have themselves in time become indigenous, whether Egyptian, Assyrian, Persian, Greek, Roman, Crusader, or whatever group came into Palestine.

The significance of Jerusalem for the ancient people of Israel and for Jewish people ever since has been covered elsewhere.[2] In the following we will examine: first, the role of Jerusalem within Islam; secondly, the significance of Palestinian Christians and the theological basis for their distinctive approach to Jerusalem; finally, the modern problem from a political perspective, with a concluding section outlining a vision for Jerusalem in the future.

---

[1] P.K. Hitti, *A History of the Arabs*, 10th ed., (New York, St. Martin's Press 1970) 3.
[2] See above chs. 2 and 5 (ii). To those accounts it is worth adding that Jerusalem evidently had a religious significance long before David's conquest; for it was the home of Melchizedek, who was subsequently described in the written tradition as 'King of Salem,...priest of God Most High' (Gen. 14:18). Moreover, Jerusalem's unique place within Israelite religion was augmented by its association with the 'Moriah' where Abraham was to have sacrificed Isaac (Gen. 22:2). On David's development of Jerusalem as a symbol of his rule and of Israelite sovereignty, power, and identity, see the excellent study by R.B. Coote and D.R. Ord, *The Bible's First History* (Philadelphia, Fortress 1989).

II. Jerusalem in Islam

There are at least three bases for the significance of Jerusalem to Muslims.[3] First there is the *theological* basis. Islam recognizes Adam, Noah, Abraham, Moses, Jonah, Jesus and others as 'prophets', and acknowledges that Moses was sent by God to the Jews with the Torah, and Jesus to Christians with the Gospel. Yet, according to Islam, both Jews and Christians corrupted their Scriptures. Islam therefore comes as the last and final religious revelation, fulfilling what came before it; Muhammad is the final prophet and apostle.

Moreover, Muslims believe that the Qur'an contains the exact words of God. As a result, where there are discrepancies in the way the Qur'an relates stories from the Old and New Testaments, compared with the biblical texts, Muslims assert categorically that these are due to the changes or corruptions which Jews and Christians have made in their Scriptures. The Quranic text alone is authentic. As a result Islam sees itself as the legitimate inheritor of both religions; indeed it points out their wrongs, since it is the final, correct and complete revelation of God. With this attitude, Muslims have never deemed it religiously wrong to build their religious shrines on places holy to Jews or Christians.

This affinity—especially between Muslims and Jews, and seen in their shared prophets—explains why it was natural for Muslims at the height of their power to build impressive religious shrines on sites that were equally holy to Jews, most notably the Dome of the Rock (on the site of Solomon's temple) and the Abrahamic Mosque in Hebron (over the tombs of the Patriarchs). Muslims did not consider themselves unlawfully impinging on the rights of the Jews; on the contrary, they saw themselves (and still do) as the valid and God-given inheritors of these sites from people who had corrupted their Scriptures and failed to keep God's law as originally given. In addition, since these same prophets are equally prophets of Islam, these holy sites are as much holy to Islam as they are to Jews. This same understanding then relates to the 'holy city' of Jerusalem.

---

[3] A full paper on this theme was given at the conference by Dr. Taysir Kamleh (available from the editor). See also O. Hasson, 'Jerusalem in Islamic Literature', in L.I. Levine, ed., *Jerusalem Cathedra* (Jerusalem, 1981).

Secondly, there is the *political* basis. A very interesting phenomenon developed in Islam almost from the very beginning: Muslims perceived an unbreakable and inseparable link between being an Arab and being a Muslim.[4] At the time of the advent of Islam, a number of Arab tribes had already been Christian and Christianity was flourishing in many places in the Arabian peninsula.[5] Yet Islam soon became indissolvably connected with Arabism. Muhammad was himself an Arab, and the Qur'an was for them God's own language, dictated from heaven in Arabic. This gave Islam its distinctive Arab rootage. Islam quickly coloured everything that was Arab, with the result that what was Arab but not Muslim was eventually marginalized and negated. Although Christianity among the Arabs in Arabia and the Middle East had preceded Islam by several centuries, it was soon disavowed as authentically Arab. Islam and Arabism were now intrinsically linked.

Furthermore, the Muslims were able within a relatively short period of time to conquer all the countries of the Middle East. Although in many places Christians remained numerically prominent well into the time of the Crusades, the Arab Muslim factor became predominant, with many Christians converting to Islam. The Arabic language and Islamic culture thus became imprinted in the lives of all the people of the Arab East. These countries became Arab Islamic countries, with Palestine being considered an integral part of them.

The 'Middle East' is therefore special in the eyes of its Muslim inhabitants. Whilst, it is true that Muslims see Islam as a world religion and many Muslims today are not Arab, the Middle East is for them essentially both Arab and Muslim. Jews and Christians can exist there as *Ahl-Al dhimmah*.[6] Any predominance or outwardly visible success of either Judaism or

---

[4] Kenneth Cragg, *The Arab Christian* (Westminster, John Knox Press 1991) 13-29.
[5] Christian monasteries and churches were familiar phenomena: for example, the large Church building in San'a, Yemen, was a very popular place of worship for Christian Arabs. See J.S. Trimingham, *Christianity among the Arabs in Pre-Islamic Times* (London, Longman 1979); I. Shaid, *Rome and the Arabs in the Third Century* (Dumbarton Oaks, Washington 1980), *Byzantium and the Arabs in the Fourth Century* (Dumbarton Oaks, Washington 1984), *Byzantium and the Arabs in the Fifth Century* (Dumbarton Oaks, Washington 1990).
[6] On this status of non-Muslims, see also ch.5. n. 2 and ch. 7 n. 20.

Christianity in the Arab world can be perceived psychologically by the Muslims as an infringement on the superiority of Islam. The point to emphasize here is that Palestine—and therefore Jerusalem—constitutes an integral part of the Arab world which is basically Muslim, and therefore, significantly theirs.

Thirdly, relating more specifically to Jerusalem, there is the *religious* basis. For Muslims believe that Muhammad miraculously left Mecca in a night journey to Jerusalem riding on a horse, and that from the large Rock of Abraham he went up on a visit to heaven.[7] On this rock, Caliph 'Abd al-Malik then erected in AD 691 the magnificent Dome of the Rock. Furthermore, at the beginning of Muhammad's mission, he asked his followers to face Jerusalem every time they prayed. In other words, he considered Jerusalem was already a 'holy city'. Later, according to *Surah* 2.142-150, Muhammad was divinely directed to change the direction of prayer (*Qiblah*) from Jerusalem to Mecca; having emigrated from Mecca it was necessary to keep the city of his birth and of Abraham's *Ka'bah* clearly in his sight. Yet Jerusalem was not forgotten, becoming the third holiest city of Islam after Mecca and Medina. The miraculous visit of Muhammad to Jerusalem and from Jerusalem to heaven, combined with the fact that Jerusalem was the first *Qiblah*, sealed the holiness of Jerusalem to Muslims and indelibly imprinted its link with Islam.

Though much more can be said, these three factors—the theological, the political and the religious—are the major reasons for the significant status which the land of Palestine and the city of Jerusalem have traditionally held for Muslims.

III. Jerusalem and Christian Palestinians

Palestinian Christians feel that many Western Christians are ignorant of the roots of their faith in the land of Palestine. Frequently it is assumed that Palestinian Christians must have been converted recently to Christianity from Islam. But where did the Church start?! Moreover, many Western Christians seem to have a subconscious feeling that Jews have a greater right to Israel/Palestine than Christians.

It must be emphasized therefore that Palestinian Christians do not consider themselves foreigners in Palestine.

---

[7] Qur'an, *Surah* 17.1.

They are not newcomers or converts from Islam. On the contrary, Palestinian Christians would wish to trace their ancestry to the original Christian community of Apostolic times that has lived in Palestine ever since.[8] The early Palestinian Christian community was not purely Jewish; it was composed of all those who accepted Jesus as Lord. This outreach of the Gospel beyond the Jewish people has been shown above to have been an integral part of Jesus' own mission.[9] Here it may be added simply that in his earthly ministry Jesus evidently related as well to Samaritans, Romans, Syrophoenicians, and others. Although there is no specific mention of Arabs, Jesus must have certainly been in touch with them:

Jesus withdrew his disciples to the sea, and a great multitude from Galilee followed; also from Judea and Jerusalem, and Idumea and from beyond the Jordan and from about Tyre and Sidon a great multitude. . .(Mark 3:7-8).

A great number of those who lived 'beyond the Jordan' were the Nabatean Arabs, and the Idumeans were Arabs who had adopted Judaism as a religion.[10]

Evidently, then, from the outset the early Christian community was composed of those who were ethnically diverse; they were Jews, Greeks, Romans, Samaritans, Arabs, and whoever else whose home was Palestine and its vicinity. This Christian community, speaking mainly Aramaic or Greek has never totally left Palestine; if some left, then other Christians moved in.[11] The importance of the Holy Land to Christians

---

[8]On this complex issue, see *e.g.* Trimingham, *op. cit.*, and Cragg, *op. cit.*, chs. 1 and 2. Part of the complexity, as there noted, rests on the issue of defining 'what is an Arab?'. Arabic was imposed as the principal language in Palestine only in the 690's, so that those speaking Greek or Aramaic previous to that time were of the same stock as those who spoke Arabic later; they can thus be termed 'Arabs', but only retrospectively. Moreover, the fact that many Christians in the early Christian centuries used Greek names does not necessarily mean that they were themselves Greeks; it is equally possible that they were indigenous 'Palestinians' (whether Jews or Arabs or others).
[9]See above ch. 1, p. 15.
[10]The Roman province of 'Arabia' was not far away but immediately adjacent to the south-east of 'Palestina', including the city of Petra and much of what is now in modern Jordan.
[11]Jewish Christians were indeed forced to leave Jerusalem under Hadrian's edict in AD 135, but the Gentile Church which continued in

in the fourth century, as seen in thinking of Bishop Cyril, has already been shown;[12] and by the the fifth and sixth centuries, Palestine could claim to be predominantly Christian, with hundreds of churches and monasteries built throughout the country. This was the situation when, in the seventh century the Muslim Arabs arrived, and the Christian community in Palestine became gradually Arabized in both language and culture. Yet it remained on its own soil, and though some Christians converted to Islam in order to avoid taxes and hardships, others remained loyal to their Christian faith.

These facts of history must be made clear to those who do not know them. Much of Western Christian support for Israel has been based on the assumption that Jews had a right to return to their country and that Palestinians were all Muslims and late-comers into Palestine—intruders on a Jewish territory. Many did not even realise that Palestinian Christians exist, that their Christianity goes back to apostolic times, that Palestine has always been their home, and that in the early years of Palestinian Christianity many of them suffered at the hands of non-believing Jews.

These important truths are easily missed by many Western Christians. From one perspective, it is possible to argue that Palestinian Christians are seemingly penalized by Western Christians because they have accepted the Messiahship of Jesus. If they had remained 'Jewish', they would be supported today by the West and would have a claim to Palestine. The fact that they have become believers in Christ and members of the Church, has almost seemed to forfeit them their right to their land. This seemingly ridiculous way of arguing only brings to light the comparative ignorance of many Western Christians when considering the Middle East—not least the so-called Christian Zionists. The Christian community of Palestine is not a foreign population that has been brought into the land to replace a Jewish one. With its multi-ethnic background it can legitimately claim to have always been in Palestine.

---

the city thereafter was conscious of a direct tradition going back into the first century: see *e.g.*, Eusebius, *EH.* 4.5, 5.12 and 7.19.
[12] See above ch. 4.

IV. Jerusalem and the Land: A Palestinian Christian Theology[13]

Anywhere else in the world a conflict like the present one in Israel/Palestine would have been considered a primarily political one. From a Palestinian perspective, the events leading up to 1967 are seen in the following terms: a people, living in their own country, were overrun by a group of people who came from outside; this was a violation of the political and human rights of the indigenous population. It had no special religious significance. As a result, arbitration should be based on international law.

Yet in this conflict, unlike any other, the Bible is brought into play. It is quoted in such a way as to give the primary claim over the land to Jews. For many religious Jews and for some Christians, the solution to the conflict lies in Palestinian recognition that God has given the Jews the land of Palestine 'forever'.[14] Palestinians are asked to accept this as a basic truth. Any settlement that is not based on such a foundation is seen by such people as contrary to the promises and covenant of God with the Jewish people.

Palestinian Christians are therefore forced to tackle the issue of land from a biblical perspective, not because they believe the religious argument over the land to be the very essence of the conflict, but because they are driven to it as a result of the religious-political abuse of biblical interpretation. This section offers some pointers towards a counter Palestinian approach to the theological issues of Jerusalem and the land.

In doing so, it will be immediately observed that there is a great difference between the outlooks of the Old and New Testaments on this issue. The issue of the land is very much

---

[13] Most of this section has been reproduced from N.S. Ateek, M.H. Ellis, and R.R. Ruether, edd., *Faith and the Intifada: Palestinian Christian Voices* (New York, Orbis 1992) 108-16.

[14] Much has been made of this word, 'forever'. As indicated above (ch. 1, p. 6) the Hebrew original does not necessarily carry a literal meaning that deals with an unending duration of time; sometimes it only applies to the length of a person's life (Deut. 15:17). The words reflect a Semitic Eastern expression—still used today in the Middle East—indicating a lengthy period of time but not an indefinite period. This is surely the meaning of the words in 1 Sam. 1:22. See D.M. Beegle, *Prophecy and Prediction* (Ann Arbor, Pryor Pettengill 1978) 183; see also W.W. Baker, *Theft of a Nation* (West Monrow, Jireh Publications 1982) 84-86.

bound up with the life of the people of the Old Testament; the same is not true for the New Testament. Given the general political abuse of the Old Testament material today, we would do well to emphasize the following points:

a) The Developing 'Universalism' of the Old Testament[15]

The Old Testament makes it very clear that the land belongs to God.[16] Many times in the Old Testament God is portrayed as the owner of the land. Indeed in one place the divine claim to the land is so emphasized that the Israelites are themselves regarded as strangers and foreigners:

Land will not be sold absolutely, for the land belongs to me, and you are only strangers and guests of mine (Lev. 25:23; *cf.* Jer 16:18).

Moreover, the Israelites were not supposed to defile the land. Yet in Jeremiah it is clear that this had already happened:

But when you entered you defiled my country and made my heritage loathsome (Jer. 2:7).

Those who live in the land must, therefore, obey the owner. Disobedience of God defiles the land. If the land is defiled, the inhabitants will be thrust out in consequence (see Lev. 20:22; Deut. 4:25-26; 28:63; Josh. 23:15-16).[17]

Furthermore, a reading of the Old Testament in its entirety reveals that the God who was initially thought to be one among many gods (Psa. 95:3) and then the greatest God above other gods, was eventually perceived as the one and only God who had created the world (Psa. 96:5; 97). There is a development in the Hebraic understanding of God and the extent of his sovereignty. In the light of this God is seen no more as the owner of the land of the people of Israel, but as the owner of the whole world. The whole world becomes sanctified because it is his:

To Yahweh belongs the earth and all it contains, the world and all who live there (Psa. 24:1).

In all this God can be seen as seeking to teach the ancient Hebrews the importance of understanding his promises correctly. Yet the Bible gives ample evidence of how they were

---

[15]*Cf.* above, ch. 1, pp. 1-3, 15.
[16]N.S. Ateek, *Justice and Only Justice: A Palestinian Theology of Liberation* (New York, Orbis 1989) 105-9.
[17]Discussed more fully below in ch. 7 (ii).

misunderstood. Chosenness, which was intended to be a responsibility for service, was interpreted instead as a privilege to hoard. From this point of view the first exile from the land can rightly be seen as God's way of shattering the people's narrow concept of himself and of the land. They had to learn that God existed without the land and outside of it. They needed to learn that God is concerned about other people besides themselves (a point eloquently expressed in the story of Jonah and God's concern for the people of Nineveh—that is, the Assyrians, who were one of the deadliest enemies of ancient Israel and Judah). The exile was meant to help them mature in their understanding of God. One observes that some post-exilic prophets now put the emphasis, not on the land itself, but on the people who are returning to it; the promises of God to the people after the exile are not about land and nationhood, but rather about the outpouring of God's Spirit on the people.

For I shall pour water on the thirsty soil and streams on the dry ground. I shall pour out my spirit on your descendents, my blessing on your offspring, and they will spring up among the grass, like willows on the banks of a stream (Isa. 44:3-4).

If the people are to be a 'light to the nations', then they have to be the carriers of that blessing, rather than hoarding it to themselves.

Unfortunately, however, the lesson of the exile was never fully learned: they lacked the realism that was needed to accept this important truth. Thus they continued in their attempt to restore the old dream, and to recreate their kingdom but to no avail. Politically the land was continuously vulnerable to outside powers, but this narrow theology of God and the land became fixed in the minds of many, leading eventually to the destruction of the nation in AD 70. Again, the people were given another chance to learn the lessons of history and the period extended to eighteen hundred years. Sadly, however, many Jews seem not to have been willing to learn that it is wrong to put one's heart on the land. To do so is to invite disaster and another exile.

In sum, within the pages of the Old Testament itself there is evidently a developing understanding of God and the land. There is a movement—albeit in a 'zigzag' way—from a narrow concept of God and the land to a broader, deeper, and more inclusive concept.

2. More than one Exodus

The famous exodus, when the children of Israel came out of Egypt, is not the only 'exodus' in the Old Testament. There was another when the exiles returned from Babylon in the sixth century BC. To many the first exodus is very familiar and its dramatic stories about the wonderful acts of God for his people cherished by many. The second exodus, however, is given little prominence—perhaps because it is quieter: it is significantly less dramatic than the first. Yet prophets like Jeremiah thought that it would be a greater exodus than the first:

> The days are coming when people will no longer say, 'As Yahweh lives who brought the Israelites out of Egypt,' but, 'As Yahweh lives who led back and brought home the offspring of the House of Israel from the land of the north and all the countries to which he had driven them, to live on their own soil' (Jer. 23:7-8).

One of the greatest points of contrast between the first and second exodus concerns their respective attitudes toward the indigenous peoples who were already living in the land. In the first exodus, these are entirely negative. Every time the indigenous people are mentioned, the language is very hostile: they are supposed to be displaced or destroyed, and there is no room for them in the land among the chosen people of God to whom the land was promised. The second is totally different. The returning exiles showed greater realism, being far more accepting of the people around them. In fact, one of the greatest biblical passages from after the exile is from the prophet Ezekiel, who spoke this word of the Lord to the people:

> You must distribute this country among yourselves, among the tribes of Israel. You must distribute it as a heritage for yourselves and the aliens settled among you who have fathered children among you, since you must treat them as citizens of Israel. You will give the alien his heritage in the tribe where he has settled (Ezek. 47:21-23).

What a remarkable contrast with the hostile language of Joshua! With the second exodus there is a new understanding of the people's relationship to the land. There is an acceptance of the changes of history. Certain demographic changes had taken place, and the prophet pronouncing the word of God exhorts the people to accept these changes and to share the land with those who are living on it.

Why then has the pragmatic nature of the second exodus not been emphasized? Why has so much emphasis been placed on the first war-like exodus, with its violent treatment of the indigenous people? In our own century many have tried to draw their inspiration from the first exodus—instead of living up to the ideal and realism of the second! This is, indeed, a tragedy. The 'third exodus' has glossed over the second, which expresses a greater understanding of the world. Instead it has clung to the first.

Part of the problem seems to relate to the central position of the Torah within Judaism. Although the Torah has in it a seed of a broader concept of God, much of it reflects a more exclusivist understanding of God. The book of Deuteronomy, for example, has made it impossible for a good Jew to live outside the land. Yet, we know that Jews had to live outside the land during the first and second exiles. In the nineteenth century some Jews in the Reform Movement were ready to break away from the land-bound faith and emphasize the prophetic and ethical demands of the Jewish faith; but they have been swamped by Zionism. The tragedy today is that there is very little use of the great prophetic material and its insistence on God's demand for justice; also that many Jews and (worse!) Christians have received their inspiration from the vocabulary of the first return to the land, rather than from the spirit of the second return. The first saw the indigenous inhabitants as those who had to be displaced. The second saw them realistically as those with whom they should be content to share the land; in fact, the returning exiles were happy to accept a very small territory between Bethel and Hebron.

3. The New Testament, Jerusalem and the Land

As a matter of plain observation, the New Testament is not preoccupied with the issue of the land as was the Old Testament. While scholars explain this in different ways (perhaps the evangelists 'depoliticized' their writings so as to decrease any tensions with the Roman authorities, or perhaps they intentionally 'de-Zionized' the tradition), this writer contends that the gospels reflect faithfully the message of Jesus and that the lack of interest in the land therefore stems from the very nature of the gospel and its basic difference with an Orthodox Jewish outlook.

Though some scholars have suggested that Jesus was a revolutionary or Zealot, others scholars have argued more convincingly that Jesus knew very well the position of the Zealots, but rejected it and consciously chose to go in another direction.[18] This throws new light on many biblical passages. For example, Jesus' third temptation (Matt. 4.8-10), which speaks about gaining authority over the kingdom of this world by following the strategy of the devil, can be interpreted as the attractive message of the Zealots that Jesus considered and was confronted with but, at the outset of his ministry, decisively rejected. Though this temptation resurfaced at other junctures, he was able to resist it. The gospel writers have surely remained faithful to the basic message of Jesus. The land was of very little significance to them.

Thus the New Testament in many places views the land, Jerusalem, and the Temple quite critically and negatively.[19] One way to illustrate this is by considering the four places in Jewish life that had an ascending order of significance: the land of Palestine, Jerusalem, the Temple, and the Holy of Holies. Working in reverse order, one notes first how at Jesus' death the veil in front of the Holy of Holies was rent from top to bottom (Mark 15:38): the way between God and humans has been opened in Jesus Christ, and so the Holy of Holies has lost its significance for the church.

Secondly, as predicted by Jesus, the Temple was destroyed in AD 70, being now redundant in the minds of Christians. Jesus had talked about his own body as a temple: 'destroy this temple and in three days I will it raise up' (John 2:19). So, for Christians, Christ takes the place of the Temple. Paul talks of Christians as constituting the temple of God when the Spirit of Christ dwells in them (1 Cor. 3:16). Again, he is calling attention to the significance of people who carry the witness of God by the Spirit in their life, rather than the witness of a geographical place. Thirdly, the city of Jerusalem was also destroyed by the Romans in 70 AD. Jesus himself predicted its destruction and wept over it because it did not

---

[18]See J. Yoder, *The Politics of Jesus* (Grand Rapids, Eerdmans 1972).
[19]I am heavily indebted to the excellent work of W.D. Davies, *The Gospel and the Land* (Berkeley, University of California 1974).

know 'the things that make for peace' (Luke 19:42). As a result, the whole land of Palestine is no longer of great significance, because no one area of the world is more holy than another; instead there is the holiness and presence of Christ. So the New Testament message transcends the land, Jerusalem, and the Temple. The significance and holiness of place has been replaced by that of a person, Jesus Christ.

Two further important points need to be emphasized. First, the ministry of Jesus was very much preoccupied with the concept of the 'kingdom of God'. Considered in our present context, this concept of God's kingdom implies Jesus' radical understanding of God's relationship with the world: it is the true corrective for any misunderstanding of God's concern for one land. For the kingdom of God stresses the reign of God in the hearts and minds of people, whoever or wherever they are. This is not dependent on one place or one region, but is dependent on faith: where Christ is acknowledged as Lord, there God reigns. The concept of the Kingdom of God, therefore, shatters any narrow concept of the land. Jesus' frequent use of this concept was intended to lift people's ideas and thoughts from a concentration on the land to the universality of God and his reign. This becomes an inclusive concept, fitting the whole spirit and ethos of the New Testament.[20]

Secondly, the New Testament is concerned with the spreading of the gospel into the whole world. The narrow concept of the land is replaced by a worldwide vision of God's concern for people in every country of the world. What started in the land in the ministry, death, and resurrection of Christ had now to be transported to every other place under the sun; the gospel must move from the vicinity of Jerusalem and reach the capital of the Roman Empire. In other words, the dimensions of the gospel have shattered the geographical focus on the land of Palestine. God's love for the world in Christ now encompasses all people (see *e.g.* John 3:16; Gal. 3:26-29; Eph. 3).

With the coming of Christ, therefore, Palestine is revealed as having been paradigmatic for the world. It is a microscopic replica of the way God is relating to the whole

---

[20]The words of Jesus, 'The Kingdom of God is within you' (Luke 17:21), reflect this same view. People carry within them the seed of the kingdom in their faithfulness and obedience to God. The land is no longer the focus, but people.

world. Yet the replica has no privilege over what it represents. 'God so loved the world'; not 'God so loved 'the Land of Israel' or 'Palestine'. Admittedly, one can only discover this truth when looking back from the vantage point of fulfillment. Yet it needs to be made clear and continuously emphasized.[21]

Thus God's concern is no longer for one land and one people, but rather for all lands and all peoples. The focus on one place may have been a necessary stage within God's economy (or due to the 'hardness of the human heart'?), but it was one that then needed to be transcended as human understanding of God's purposes matured. No longer is it a matter of the sacredness of the city of Jerusalem; it is the sacredness of the people of God wherever they are. No longer is it a matter of the physical presence of an impressive Temple, but the presence of 'living temples' of God in whom God's spirit dwells. It is not the holiness of one space but the whole world which has become sacramental. It is no more the Jewish people who are the focus of God's activity in the world but what God has done in Christ for the whole world.

Later in the life of the church the land of Palestine did indeed resume a greater significance. The church, after all, lives in the world, and geography is significant because of the incarnation. Bethlehem, Nazareth, the Sea of Galilee, all have unique associations for followers of Christ, and Jerusalem, above all, as the place of Christ's death and resurrection and the church's 'birth' at Pentecost. So the land gradually became important once again, because the church lives in history and because God in Christ had taken history very seriously. Though recent studies have shown that this shift in Christian attitudes to the land did not begin really to take hold until after Constantine,[22] Christians from early centuries have made pilgrimage to the land, because this land alone hosted the Holy One.

Despite this, the theological foundation of the Christian faith, as revealed in the New Testament, still resists being contained and tied down to certain 'holy places' or to Jerusalem. These have a limited benefit, reminding the believer of

---

[21]See more fully above in ch. 1.
[22]See P.W.L. Walker, *Holy City? Holy Places? Christian Attitudes to Jerusalem and the Holy Land in the Fourth Century* (Oxford, OUP 1990).

the historicity of the faith and the incarnation of the Holy One, but they are not places to which Christians should cling.

What does all this have to do with the whole issue of the land today in the Israel/Palestine conflict?

a) Many Jews have come to understand their identity as being very much bound up with the land and Jerusalem, emphasizing this link from a religious understanding; some would go further, concluding that there is no room for the Palestinians in the land. Such groups therefore need to be confronted with the challenge of a deeper investigation and study of their own Bible, so that they can discover that their *own* tradition has provided answers to this present dilemma: the land *can* be shared, one *can* live away from the land and still maintain faithfulness to God. The more open understanding of God and the land as it is found in the Bible must be encouraged, not the more narrow and limited view.

Sometimes the State of Israel gives the impression of selectively denying history—pretending that there was no history in Palestine between 135 AD and 1948.[23] However, the message of Ezekiel 47 (quoted above), as God speaks through the prophet, is effectively: 'do not deny history; there are now other people living on the land, and they also have a right to it'.

b) For Palestinian Christians the conflict over the land of Palestine is not on their side a religiously motivated conflict. Yes, Palestinian Christians cherish and pride themselves in the fact that they live in the land where Jesus was born, died, and raised to new life: such a historical fact has great significance for many of them. At the same time, this is not the reason which is paramount when they defend their right to the land. For most of these Christian Arabs the land is simply their *watan*, their homeland. This is the land of their birth. It is the land which God in his wisdom has chosen to give them as *watan*; just as God has chosen to give other peoples their own *watan*. Palestinian Christians are fighting to maintain the God-given right to their own land. Any *watan* is obviously a responsibility given by God to all the people of any country; it is not that they own their country, for in the final analysis God is really its owner, as God is the owner of the whole world. Yet because

---

[23]This is very clear when you visit the Israeli museum, for example: every period of Israelite history is well covered except the period between 135 and 1948—almost as if nothing had happened inbetween.

they have been given the land, they have a responsibility for it before God. So they would like to live on their land not only in dignity as human beings, but also as good stewards.

c) Many Israeli Jews must come to accept the fact that, in order to live their religious faith, they do not have to have exclusive political control over the whole of Israel/Palestine or indeed of Jerusalem. For even at the height of Solomon's reign there were certain parts of the land still not under Israelite control.[24] Palestinians would like to assure Israelis that, just as it is important to have a continued physical presence of Christian and Muslim communities in this land, they acknowledge it to be equally important to have a continued presence of a Jewish community. Yet, in the same breath, they must emphasize that, in order to live in the land and to fulfil one's religious duties here, no one party need have an exclusive political control over it all. The challenge before us is a challenge to hammer out a new understanding of our relationship to the land. We *can* achieve a full expression of our religious life by sharing the land. Once this principle is affirmed, then justice is not far off, and peace and reconciliation will become a welcome reality.

V. The Modern Political Problem: Two Conflicting Stories

The issue of Jerusalem and the land, however, is not simply a religious or theological one. A broader perspective of the general political context will now be given, emphasizing the crux of the conflict as perceived by Palestinians.

The Israel/Palestine conflict has brought together the stories of two nations that otherwise might have remained quite separate. Each story has carried the passion and legitimacy for its own group. Each has needed a solution to its problems and a fulfilment for its aspirations. Unfortunately, the two stories have become interlocked in our modern history, resulting in grief to countless thousands. These are the stories of the Jews and the Palestinians. If we exercise honesty and integrity, the legitimacy of each of these stories cannot be denied. Unless we are prejudiced and blind, we should be

---

[24] Parts of the western coastal area were not part of the Israelite kingdom during Solomon's reign.

driven to empathy for both, and strive as best as we can to point to a solution that can restore justice and dignity to both groups who have suffered in the process. At the same time honesty compels us to make certain judgements. We should name the wrong and call it as such. Yet that should not prevent us from looking at the situation pragmatically today and suggesting possible compromises and solutions. Let me briefly reflect candidly on these two stories.[25]

a) The Jewish Story
At the time of Jesus a sizable number of Jews were living in Palestine. Yet Jewish life was not only confined to Palestine. Already, substantial Jewish communities had for centuries been living in the *diaspora*, in Egypt, Iraq and Syria as well as other countries of the Middle East; many were also scattered throughout Asia Minor and other parts of the Roman Empire.

With the failure of the two Jewish revolts against Rome in AD 70 and 135, many Jews left Palestine and settled in other parts of the Middle East as well as Europe—though some settled in other parts of Palestine, away from Jerusalem. After the rise of Islam, Jews and Christians living in the East were both dependent on the whim of Muslim rulers. The life of minorities in those days, and even today, has never been easy. They survived by living cautiously, wisely, and shrewdly.

In the West, and as Christianity grew into Christendom, religious prejudice against Jews became evident. They were blamed for the death of Christ and their suffering and marginalization was attributed to God's judgement on them. This prejudice produced what eventually became known as anti-semitism—a venomous attitude of hate and prejudice directed against Jews for being Jews. By the nineteenth century, Jewish leaders had become concerned about this phenomenon—especially when the ghetto walls were breaking down and Jews were free to move into European society. Some of their leaders concluded that the movement in the European countries of 'liberty, equality, and fraternity', as declared by the French Revolution, was not a guarantee that Jews would be treated as equals. Some Jews felt that the only way open to

---

[25]For a contrary perspective on Zionism and Palestinian nationalism, see above ch. 5 (iv) and below ch. 7 (ii and iv).

them was conversion to Christianity; others would have opted for a return to ghetto life.

Others, however, such as Theodore Herzl, felt that Jews must have a place where they could have their own State, and run their own affairs away from the prejudice and bullying of Christians. Herzl assumed that Jews constituted a 'nation' in the European sense of the word; so they needed a country to go to, and the sponsorship of a European power. He was thinking in the context of colonialism and was sure that a place on earth could be found to accommodate Jews. He felt that Jews would be pleased to go to such a place and that their host countries would be glad to see them go. He saw the problem as real and acute, requiring urgent answers. Not being able to foresee the development of constitutional democracies in Europe as an answer, he wished to seize the moment. So he started his 'shuttle diplomacy' seeking the support of a government that would help him bring his Zionist dream into fruition.

It gradually became clear to Herzl that if his dream was ever to see the light of day, it would stand the greatest chance if it was linked with Palestine. This was a spark of genius. Some of his Christian friends were already encouraging him along these lines: Palestine was, after all, the original home of Jews; it would, therefore, make sense to the Western Christian leaders, and would be supported by many Christians, especially among those Protestants who had already concluded from their study of the Bible that the Jews must return to their ancient homeland. It was a perfect idea which Herzl set out to implement. After several unsuccessful discussions with other countries, Britain eventually offered the promise for sponsorship. Recent studies have shown that some of the British leadership who were responsible for the Balfour Declaration were already influenced by a Christian form of Zionism.[26]

It is really at this point that the Jewish story became intrinsically connected with the Palestinian story, and the clash between Jews and Palestinians became inevitable. Jews were coming from Europe to impose their dream on a Palestinian

---

[26]H. Haddad and D. Wagner, edd., *All in the Name of the Bible* (Chicago, The Palestine Human Rights Campaign, 1 Quincy Court, 220 South State St, Suite 138, Chicago, Ill 60604, Report No. 5, April 1985) 16-17. See also above ch. 5, iv.

population that was itself looking for independence and freedom. Undoubtedly, what eventually hastened the fulfillment of the dream was the tragic events of the holocaust when between four and six million Jews were killed by the Nazis. Though many European and North American countries did not wish to absorb the Jewish refugees, in a sense this suited the purposes of the Zionist leadership which wanted the refugees to come to Palestine; and come they did. The fate of the two groups—Jews and Palestinians—was tragically sealed for many years with strife and blood.

b) The Palestinian Story

The Palestinians were, as the rest of the Middle East, a part of the Ottoman Empire for four hundred years, a period considered by Arab historians as by and large an age of decadence and frequent Ottoman brutality. By the mid-nineteenth century, European powers were gaining influence in the Middle East, and the flow of ideas between East and West was increasing. There was already agitation among many Arabs for greater political freedom and by the beginning of the twentieth century Arab nationalism was very much on the rise.

The Arabs were willing to support the Allies during the first World War against Turkey in exchange for their freedom and independence. They made a significant contribution only to find themselves, after the war, simply experiencing colonial rule in place of the Ottomans. Meanwhile, Palestinian nationalism, though a part of the general trend of Arab nationalism, developed unique features which gained momentum as Zionist aspirations became clearer. Palestinians were aiming for independence from the British Mandate as well as from the greater creeping menace of Zionist presence in Palestine. Thus the two nationalisms—Zionism and Palestinianism—had to clash.

The Palestinians saw themselves as having no part in the development of anti-semitism in Europe. They had had nothing to do with what was going on in Christian Europe in previous centuries and, later, they had nothing to do with the massacre of millions of Jews in Europe. Yet they felt that the world wanted them to pay the price for European atrocities. The lot had been cast. It was Palestine and Palestinians who were expected to bear the brunt. Soon Palestinians were being blamed for even resisting the onslaught of the Zionists.

The Zionists proved to be better equipped than the Palestinians. They were able to occupy approximately 77% of the area of mandated Palestine. Hundreds of thousands of Palestinians fled in terror as the Zionists moved in, while hundreds of thousands were forced out of their homes by the Zionists. A total of 750,000 Palestinians, both Christian and Muslims, were displaced to make room for the many Jews who were coming into the country. Hundreds of Palestinian villages and towns were razed to the ground by the Zionists—a deliberate policy of the Zionists, preventing the Palestinian Christians and Muslims from returning to their homes.

Many people throughout the world were not aware of the tragedy of the Palestinians at the time; they were pleased that the Jews had finally been able to return to their 'rightful home'. Many were delighted that the world had found a solution to the Jewish refugee problem after the second World War; it appeared that the evils of anti-semitism were at long last being addressed effectively.

Many people today still blame the Palestinians for refusing the 1947 United Nations Partition Plan of Palestine. They ask the Palestinians: 'Why did you reject the division of Palestine into two states—a Jewish and a Palestinian? Are you not today asking for much less than what you would have received then? Would you not have saved yourselves and others all the bloodshed and violence of the last 50 years?'

Such people would make poor Solomons. The wise King realised that the mother who was willing to see the baby divided into half was the false mother (1 Kgs. 3:16-28). The true mother resisted the partitioning of her child. Similarly, in 1947, the Palestinians refused the partitioning of their country and called for the establishment of a single State of Palestine where Muslims, Jews, and Christians could live together. But the world, through the United Nations, reversed the wisdom of Solomon and declared the true mother to be the Zionists who wanted the partitioning of Palestine. Many Zionists were interested in getting a legal foothold that would allow them to usurp the whole of Palestine and the surrounding area in accordance with their original Zionist scheme of 1919.[27] There then followed the tragic events of 1948 and after.

---

[27]In 1919 the World Zionist Organisation submitted to the Versailles Peace Conference an official plan which specified the minimal territory

Palestinians therefore claim that the State of Israel has clearly been founded on injustice, an injustice which first and foremost is political, not religious. They believe their country of Palestine was overrun by outsiders who were determined to transform it into a Jewish state against the will of the majority of its Palestinian population.

No one should deny the evil of anti-semitism and the grave injustices done to Jews in Europe. But the solution should have been resolved in the development of political democracies in Europe, in which Jews would have been considered as human beings entitled to full human rights and democratic freedoms. No doubt Palestine could have absorbed some Jewish refugees to live as Palestinian Jews in a country sacred to the three monotheistic religions. That, however, is totally different from carving a Jewish state out of Palestine, negating Palestinian identity and existence, and denying Palestinians the right and international legitimacy to independence and freedom.

The stage was Europe, the problem a European one. The victims were the Jews, but the victims were transferred to the unrelated stage of Palestine. On this stage a new tragedy was enacted and the Palestinians became the new victims. In essence, Palestinians see themselves as the scape-goats of a guilty Europe; they have been asked to pay for the Jewish problem. One injustice had been solved, but another created.

Since 1967, when Israel occupied the rest of British-mandated Palestine, there has been a strengthening of Palestinian identity, as the population of the West Bank and Gaza has naturally reacted to being under Israeli occupation; this has spilled over to the Arabs living in Israel. The continuing existence of Palestinians was seen by many as an obstacle to the fulfilment of the Zionist dream; they therefore needed to be controlled—by the confiscation of Palestinian land, the building of illegal settlements, and many other things which denied

---

which was required for a Jewish homeland in Palestine. This included 'the headwaters of the Jordan river in Syria and Lebanon, the south of Lebanon up to the town of Sidon, the southern Bekaa Valley in Lebanon, the Hauran Plain in Syria, and the control of the Hijaz Railway running north-south considerably east of the Jordan from Derra in Syria to Amman and Aqaba in Jordan'; cited in Frank Epp, *Whose Land is Palestine?* (Grand Rapids, Eerdmans 1970) 15.

them their humanity and dignity. Not surprisingly, the West Bank and the Gaza Strip, like a pressurized powder-keg, exploded in the events of the *Intifada*, when the Palestinians tried to 'shake off' the yoke of Israeli oppression and to send a clear message to the Israeli government and the international community.

Since the end of October 1991, the Palestinians, and some Arab States, have entered into peace negotiations with Israel. The Palestinians are asking for the implementation of the United Nations resolutions regarding Palestine, insisting that Israeli forces should withdraw from the area of the West Bank and Gaza, and after a transitional period of a few years, that a Palestinian State be established on the remaining 23% of the area of Palestine. They know full well that the only possible peaceful solution is to share their country with Israeli Jews. They are struggling to achieve that peacefully and are ready to normalize relations with Israel. For the sake of peace and the future of their children, the Palestinians are willing to carry the scars of a painful and unjust past, accept a small state on one fourth of the area of Palestine, and live in peace with Israel.

VI. Jerusalem: Hope for the Future

Jerusalem lies at the heart of the conflict and probably its solution is a key to the solution of the whole. Whatever one's personal conviction as to religious truth, the present situation in regard to Jerusalem and the land of Israel/Palestine is now such that there can be no prospect of peace if in the realm of politics any one religious viewpoint or any one nation predominates to the exclusion of others. The city of Jerusalem itself, in light of its long multinational, cultural, religious and historical background defies any one group which dares to view it exclusively. In other words, its innate inclusivity will defy, frustrate and exasperate all attempts to impose the dominance of one group. Such an action would only defer the problem, project it into the future and prolong the conflict.

This is precisely what Israel has been doing since 1967. Palestinian land has been confiscated in and around East Jerusalem and throughout the Occupied Territories. A ring of illegal Jewish settlements (according to international law), has been built around Jerusalem, and every possible attempt made to create new facts on the ground, 'judaizing' the city. Jewish extreme religious groups have been using all sorts of immoral means to purchase Palestinian homes in Jerusalem, especially inside the Old City.[28] Yet the very nature of Jerusalem will surely resist such attempts in the end.

The way forward for Jerusalem is the way of sharing. There is no future that can last for long if it is imposed by force—in Jerusalem or anywhere else. There has to be a change of attitude *vis-a-vis* Jerusalem. There has to be a recognition of the past, rich, and yet painful mosaic of the city. There has to be an acceptance of the equal rights of others. There has to be an abdication of the use of force as a means of imposing sovereignty. There has to be an understanding of the equal significance of the city to Judaism, Islam, and Christianity, both for those who live in the Middle East and for the millions who live in the rest of the world.

It is this new mental framework and attitude, more than anything else and before everything else, that holds the key to the future of Jerusalem today. It is, however, an attitude that does not lend itself easily to many people. Therefore, it has to be taught, preached, explained, and emphasized to all, in mosques, synagogues, churches, schools—and opportunities such as this. It is an educational process that must start now.

The burden today lies primarily on the shoulders of Israel. How can Israel, which has conquered Jerusalem by force, annexed it, and considers it to be the eternal capital of Israel, share its sovereignty over Jerusalem with others?

Some might even ask, 'had Jerusalem been in the hands of Arab rule, would they have been willing to share sovereignty with others'? This is a good question and the answer is probably 'no'. Yet the fact has to be emphasized that Israel's control of Jerusalem has never been accepted by the international community. In fact, Jerusalem, including the Old City, is as much a part of the Occupied Territories, just as the rest of the West Bank and Gaza are. Moreover, in the interest of peace, one needs to be innovative, forthcoming, and willing to take risks. Today, there is a climate for peace and we must seize the moment. The following are some suggestions:

---

[28]One of my parishioners and his family have been the victims of such harassment, as Jewish settlers, eager to gain more footage within the city, have been trying to force him out of his house.

1) As indicated just now, Israel has been constantly 'Judaizing' the Old City, thereby creating more tension and deepening the injustice. This should now stop. Israel should recognize that in order to exist in the Middle East, it cannot persist in this kind of action. Her continued existence can better be guaranteed by acting according to what is right, than by might. Jerusalem cannot be totally Jewish, with all others marginalized. Israel now has the opportunity to take the initiative, along with the world community, and to legalize the status of the city for the three religions that will never leave it.

2) The significance of re-building the temple in Jerusalem must be recognised. For many Jews this is an urgent necessity, but its ancient site is now covered by the Muslim Dome of the Rock. If Jews wish to build their temple they should make it as magnificent as they desire, but they must accept the changing facts of history. The Dome of the Rock has stood on that site for the last 1300 years—a period longer than the duration of the Jewish temple. This fact cannot be reversed. Is it quite inconceivable that a Jewish temple could be built next to the Western Wall, within the Jewish Quarter, and as close as possible to the original place? Is such a possibility categorically rejected by Jewish theology and the Jewish scriptures (our Old Testament)?[29] Is it beyond the realms of theological possibility for Jewish rabbis and scholars to argue for the building of the temple *close* to where it once stood? Such a religious site could gradually become an important focus for Jewish faith. It would also put the Muslims' mind at ease that the Dome of the Rock and the Al-Aqsa Mosque were not under threat, and set an important new trend in religious relations.

3) The unique character of Jerusalem's Old City should be established and preserved, making it a model for religious tolerance. The following suggestions should be considered:

a) The boundaries of the four quarters (Muslim, Jewish, Christian and Armenian) should be clearly defined and respected. Any attempt to change them should be resisted and reversed.

b) Needed renovation work, similar in part to what was done within the Jewish Quarter, must be carried out in all parts of

---

[29]Isaiah (1:10-17) expressed God's displeasure with people's sacrifices because of their injustice; evidently God was less concerned with where the temple stood, more with justice and morality.

the Old City so that the city's unique character and special status can be preserved.

c) A special formula must be found for Jerusalem's jurisdiction and governance. This should be shared by the three religious communities, Israel, the Palestinians, and the United Nations.

4) The city of Jerusalem must remain open and united. However, its unity has very little to do with the issue of sovereignty. Excluding for now the Old City and the special constitution that should govern it (above 3 c), we need to look at different stages of development for the wider city. As a first stage, the West and East parts of the city might be administered under two municipal areas of control—the former Israeli, the latter Palestinian. Both would have to work together, co-ordinating many practical issues. It would be one City with two municipalities and two flags. Such a scheme should be a part of a second and broader vision that looks down the future to a period when Jerusalem will be governed by one municipality, equally representative of its inhabitants and with no discrimination, a municipal council which is elected democratically, and where the dynamic of its rule is not that of an occupier and occupied, but fellow citizens with equal rights.

A further vision down the road of history could be that of making Jerusalem the federal capital of a federation of states of the Middle East that would bring together Lebanon, Israel, Palestine, and Jordan, thus raising the city's political status to a new height.[30]

Whatever the precise details, any alternative that would give one group dominance over others will never bring peace to our area. The present period has been a long and devastating nightmare. It must be replaced by a period when old and young are dreaming dreams and seeing visions of a better future, when people 'beat their swords into ploughshares, and their spears into pruning hooks' (Isa. 2:4). This land requires dreams and visions that can be translated into real strategies of justice and peace that would restore to the peoples of Jerusalem and the land of Israel/Palestine the dignity and humanity that God has given them. It is only then that people will experience peace, stability and reconciliation.

---

[30]This point is elaborated more fully in my *Justice and Only Justice*, 170-175.

POSTSCRIPT
(June 1994)

Events in the Middle East occur at such a fast speed that render any writing about it partially obsolete before it is even in print. Since the writing of this chapter, a number of changes have happened that have altered many things.

The Gulf War led to the convening of the Madrid Conference in October 1991 which was perceived by many as a sign of hope for the people of Israel/Palestine and a real opening for a negotiated solution to the Arab-Israeli conflict. After eleven rounds of negotiations between the parties, however, it was clear that the negotiations were stalling and no real breakthrough was in sight. Then suddenly, one morning at the end of August 1993, the world woke up to the news that Israel and the PLO were secretly conducting direct negotiations in Oslo, Norway. These negotiations led to the mutual recognition between Israel and the PLO; and culminated in the historic handshake between Rabin and Arafat on September 13th 1993 on the lawn of the White House in Washington.

That handshake marked another turning point in the history of the Middle East. Israel and the PLO signed a Declaration of Principles that started them on a perilous road of strenuous and tedious negotiations which lasted for eight months. On May 4th, 1994, the two sides signed the Autonomy Agreement in Cairo in the presence of many invited dignitaries, both local and international, including the foreign ministers of the United States and Russia. The agreement was conceived as a first step in giving Palestinians autonomy in the Gaza Strip and Jericho. Furthermore, the two sides agreed to postpone some of the more thorny issues to a later stage. The two most important of these concern the Jewish settlements on the West Bank and Gaza and the status of Jerusalem.

These two issues have often cast a shadow on the negotiations and exacerbated them. The massacre of over forty Palestinians in the Abrahamic Mosque of Hebron by a fanatic Jewish settler on February 25th, 1994, raised the whole issue of the settlements and revealed the real threat which they pose to lasting peace. Meanwhile Israel's policy since March 1993 of closing off Jerusalem from the rest of the West Bank (preventing Palestinians in the West Bank from entering the city) has called seriously into question Israel's intention for peace and has naturally deepened resentment amongst local people.

Palestinian East Jerusalem is the life-line of the West Bank; it is the natural link between the north and south of the occupied territories of the West Bank. To close it off and forbid Palestinians a free access to their city is cruelly to sever the Palestinian community in half and to subject it to harsh and inhuman sufferings. Furthermore, the Palestinians of the West Bank are integrally and inextricably dependent on Palestinian institutions in East Jerusalem—whether medical, economic, education, or religious. People have been refused permits to enter Jerusalem to worship in their churches. Any tourist from all over the world can visit Jerusalem, not so the Christians who live just six miles away in Bethlehem!

So the closure has hit the Palestinian community very hard and paralysed much of its life. Yet this closure has supposedly been imposed in the name of 'security'. Many people, however, are convinced that its true motivations go deeper to include both political and psychological considerations, weakening Palestinians' morale and also their claim on Jerusalem.

Moreover, Israel has continued unabated in its policies to judaize Palestinian East Jerusalem and to 'create new facts on the ground' (above, p. 147). Palestinian lands are confiscated as a matter of fact; hardly any building permits are issued to Palestinians. As to the Old City of Jerusalem, attempts are constantly being made to squeeze out its Palestinian inhabitants. According to one study, there are no less than five different Jewish settler groups operating within the Old City.[1] The two most prominent groups among them are *Ateret Cohanim* and the 'Temple Mount Faithful', who have been working tirelessly to increase the number of Jews living within the Old City. They are also planning to replace the Dome of the Rock by rebuilding the Jewish temple in its place; by doing so they believe that they are paving the way for the coming of the Jewish Messiah.[2] By 1987 *Ateret Cohanim* claimed to own 70% of the Muslim

---

[1] Ulf Carmesund, *Two Faces of the Expanding Jewish State* (Sweden, Uppsala Univ., 1992) 35.
[2] *Ibid.*, 13.

Quarter of the Old City.³ Apparently these Jewish religious groups have huge amounts of money at their disposal—including funds that they receive from the Ministries of Housing and Religion.⁴

This is a very revealing study that reflects the commitment and determination of these groups to do all that they can to change the demography of the Old City in the name of their religion. Whether it is religious militants or municipal and government officials, it is clear that there is a meticulous and calculated plan to judaize the city of Jerusalem and make it irreversibly Jewish in character and sovereignty.

Nor can one forget the zeal of Christian Zionists in general and more specifically Christian dispensationalists who have been supportive of the state of Israel because it fits in with their biblical interpretation of God's plan for history. Interpreting some passages according to a certain biblical scheme and linking verses and passages together like a jig-saw puzzle, these groups insist on the inevitability of the rebuilding of the Jewish temple in place of the Dome of the Rock and the Al-Aqsa Mosque.⁵ Sitting in their comfortable homes and churches in the West they concoct biblical schemes and draw up future plans when these are matters of life and death for people in Israel/Palestine. Clinging to a literal interpretation of the Bible they expect a violent end to history without paying sufficient attention to God's mercy and concern for all people in Christ, and without responding to God's call to be agents of justice, peace, and reconciliation.⁶

When one reflects on the policies of the state of Israel in East Jerusalem including the Old City, one is reminded of the words of Micah 2:1-2:

Alas for those who devise wickedness and evil deeds on their beds! When the morning dawns, they perform it, because it is in their power. They covet fields, and seize them, and houses, and take them away; they defraud a man of his home, a fellow-man of his inheritance.

---

³*Ibid.*, 33.
⁴*Ibid.*, 94-95.
⁵A number of books have been written on this topic; see *e.g.* Thomas Ice & Randall Price, *Ready to Rebuild: the imminent plan to rebuild the Last Days Temple* (Oregon, Harvest House, 1992).
⁶See, for example, the writings of Hal Lindsay, including *The 1980's Countdown to Armageddon* (Bantam Books, 1981).

These words describe in a remarkable way precisely what is happening to many people within Jerusalem as well as the rest of the occupied territories. It is important, therefore, to stress the need for the international community—indeed, for all people who are concerned about a just peace—to do everything they can to stop Israel from its expansion in Jerusalem. A clear message must be communicated to the Israeli government that such practices will have to be reversed. Injustice cannot be legitimised; it is evil and ultimately self-destructive. East Jerusalem is an occupied territory and belongs to the Palestinians. The sooner Israel acknowledges this fact and agrees to share its sovereignty over Jerusalem with the Palestinians the nearer we will be to justice, peace, and security.

For in the final analysis, even the 'holiness' of the city of Jerusalem will not save it nor guarantee its survival. Many in the days of Jeremiah thought that Jerusalem was invincible and inviolable (Jer. 7). Injustice, however, led to its destruction; for ultimately, God's eye is on justice, and what is unjust can never last. Thus neither the holiness of Jerusalem today nor its beauty and charm (in spite of the billions of dollars spent) will be enough to guarantee its safety and survival. For, according to Isaiah, the very nature of God is expressed supremely in justice and righteousness:

The Lord Almighty will be exalted by justice, and the holy God will show himself holy by his righteousness (Isa. 5:16).

CHAPTER 7

JERUSALEM AND JUSTICE: A MESSIANIC JEWISH PERSPECTIVE

Baruch Maoz

I. Introduction

The Christian faith requires us to be utterly worldly in the best sense of the term: we look forward to the day when the 'kingdom of this world becomes the kingdom of our Lord' (Rev. 11:15). So Christians must be opposed to the appearance of evil in the world. They have a prophetic calling to address all mankind with the Gospel and to call both Jew and Gentile to repent, believe the Gospel, and live in this world in obedience to God's perfect will. Christians must inevitably be concerned with the Arab-Israeli conflict and be aiming at some solution of the problems, whilst acknowledging that in this sin-damaged world no perfect solution will ever truly be found.

As Christians our method of finding solutions will inevitably stem from a prior examination of the scriptural teaching and an awareness of both the recent history and the inevitable political implications of our theology. Our ultimate authority is unashamedly the Bible; yet we must deny any temptation to proof-texting and interpret the ancient texts carefully in the light of their historical contexts.

Many Christian contributions to this subject have been made from one of two prevalent positions: first, those who believe that eschatology (particularly pre-millenial eschatology) must be the primary consideration in any discussion of the Middle East conflict; alternatively, those whose evangelical commitment is less than firm and whose *a priori* assumptions cause them to be highly selective when dealing with the various biblical data.

Both positions ought to be avoided. Eschatology must indeed be one of our considerations, but why should it be the primary one? There is much less prediction in the biblical text than is commonly assumed; if the texts are read in relation to their respective historical contexts, it emerges that our task has more to do with religious (that is to say, spiritual and moral) obligation than with fortune-telling. The primary issue turns out to be one of justice.

From the outset I acknowledge my lack of objectivity. I am a Zionist who believes the best interests of my people are served by the existence of a Jewish state, that such a state should continue to be in the land of Israel, and that there are moral grounds upon which such a Jewish state can be defended, according to which it may and must conduct itself. However, I am not a Zionist because I am a Christian. My Zionist convictions issue out of the fact that I am a Jew and am convinced that Zionism offers the most correct solution to my people's predicament in this imperfect world.

One does not have to agree with all that assumes the name of Zionism or with all that has been done in its name—any more than one has to agree with all that has been done throughout history in the name of Jesus. Above and beyond one's loving obligation to one's people there exists a greater obligation to God. For that reason, many Jewish-Christians should be critical of much that has been done in the name of Zionism: Israel as a nation will yet have to answer to God for its behaviour.

II. The Bible and the Land

Those who wrestle with the issue of justice and the land cannot afford the luxury of merely theoretical meditation. Reality impinges upon our thoughts, demands our immediate decision and threatens to expose our prejudices. Each side in the current dispute insists upon divine justification for its position and seeks to enlist God's support for its cause. What follows is an attempt at political theology, tentative in its results.

In turning to the Bible one notices immediately God's very 'earthy' concerns for human faithfulness in his created world. This is especially true of the Old Testament. For that reason we focus in this section upon the Old Testament, though we do so because of our firm belief that the Old Testament serves as the raw material out of which the final form of truth is established in the New.

Land is not incidental to biblical revelation. It occupies a large part of God's message to mankind. Man himself came from the earth (Gen. 2:7) and therefore has an inseparable bond with it. Man was called, within the limits of his capacity, to be like God in relation to the earth (Gen. 1:26, 27). The earth was to be replenished and cared for by man (Gen 1:26).

When man sinned, the earth itself was affected both directly, with a curse (Gen. 3:17-18), and indirectly, by the loss of its caretaker (Gen. 3:23-24, *c.f.* 4:11). In spite of man's sin, the call to fill, subdue and replenish the earth was not withdrawn, though its final accomplishment was postponed (Rom. 8:19-21). The earth is involved in man's blessing and in his curse: in the Noah saga God warns, 'I am surely going to destroy both them and the earth' (Gen. 6:13, *c.f.* Lev. 19:22), whilst man loses the privileges associated with the earth when he sins (Gen. 4:11-12; Num. 20:12, 24: Lev. 26 *et al.*). Man and the earth are evidently so closely related that the latter partakes of the moral consequences of the former. When man sins, the earth becomes 'corrupt' (Gen. 6:11-12; Lev. 18:19, 24-25; 19:29). When he follows God's commandments, the earth is blessed (Lev. 26:3-10).

All of these principles find their later outworking in the history of the nation of Israel in relation to the land (as seen especially in Leviticus, Deuteronomy and Jeremiah). In this regard, as in all others, Israel is no exception; rather, it is the example from which all other nations are to learn. Israel was given a land, a specific place on earth, in which to serve God. Israel's enjoyment of the land was not so to absorb the people's attention that God's will and honour would be forgotten (Deut. 6:10-13). They were brought to the land in order to serve him, and if they forgot this central purpose they would be guilty of a sin which would not go unpunished.

Yet the land is also a gift of God's grace (Deut. 9:4-6). God began the process, through which he gave them the land even, when his people were in Egypt and neglecting to serve him. He assures them of his faithfulness to that covenant promise for as long as the sun and the moon abide in their courses (Jer. 32: 42-44; 33:23-26). Grace is fundamental to the Biblical message.

The land is also a sovereign gift: God is under obligation to no one. He can make of the same lump of clay some to honour and some to dishonour, and who dares challenge him? He chooses Israel by the free action of his own will. Israel is not chosen due to any attribute or accomplishment—past, present or future; rather, Israel is the 'very least of all the nations' (Deut. 7:7). God chooses Israel for reasons which lie wholly in himself. Nor is Israel chosen for its own sake. The nation is set apart for a demonstration of God's grace, as it becomes a 'light to the nations' (Isa. 42:6) and a blessing to the world (Gen. 22:18). And, in order to fulfill that task, it is apportioned a land.

'The earth is the Lord's' (Psa. 24:1); so he disposes of it in part or as a whole in the free exercise of his sovereign will, unfettered by human expectations or accomplishments. One expression of this, carved into Israel's annual calendar by divine decree, are the rules of the Year of Jubilee, when all debts were annulled because God reigned supreme in Israel's (earth-based) economy. For the land is the Lord's (Lev. 25:23).

Since the land is not only a gift of grace but also one exercised under the sovereignty of God (Ezek. 36), living in the land necessarily implies obedience.

Judaism's insistence that the occupancy of the land is not absolute but conditioned. .. points to the truth that ecology is indissoluble from morality, land and law being mutually dependent, and that a people is ultimately responsible for the maintenance of its 'place'.[1]

If Israel sins, they will be sent out of the land and forego the privileges attached to it; if faithful, they will enjoy its blessings. Living in the land implies real duties (Lev. 2:24-25; 23:22).[2]

Israel was not at liberty to choose whatever part of the earth it fancied. The history of Israel as a nation begins with a journey to a specific earthly real estate;[3] from then on, Israel's history and fortune are inextricably bound up with the land—so much so that land and people are often indistinguishable in biblical parlance.

---

[1] W.D. Davies, *The Territorial Dimension of Judaism* (Berkeley, California University 1982).
[2] This is not to say that people earn a right to dwell in the land by virtue of their goodness. No man or nation has 'rights' before God; the modern pre-occupation with 'human rights' is unbiblical in that the Bible never speaks of 'rights' but of duties both in relation to God and to our fellows.
[3] It is important to note that the actual borders of the land apportioned to Israel were more fluid than is often acknowledged. The people generally lived to the west of the Jordan, although the promises (in Gen. 15:18 and elsewhere) had indicated borders stretching as far as the Euphrates. In *e.g.* Num. 32-34 it is clear that the east bank of the Jordan did not even figure in Moses' considerations until the two tribes of Reuben and Gad with the half of Manasseh requested permission to settle there.

The quintessence of Israel's national territorial hopes came to be focused on one place: the city of Jerusalem. Time and again Jews repeated the Psalmist's vow:

if I forget you, O Jerusalem, may my right hand forget its skill; may my tongue cling to the roof of my mouth, if I do not remember you, if I do not consider Jerusalem my highest joy (Psa. 137:5-6).

Jerusalem was not only Israel's capital and the site of God's Temple; it also embodied everything that the people hoped for. In this Israel followed the example of the prophets, who spoke of Zion and of Jerusalem as representative of both the land and the people as a whole (Isa. 10:24; 46:13 *etc.*).

The New Testament builds upon these foundations. The New Testament never describes itself as superseding Old Testament religion, nor Jesus as coming to annul the Old Testament, but rather to fulfill it (Matt. 5:17). It is therefore legitimate to think of Israel remaining as a distinct nation in the purposes of God and still to be a blessing to the world. It is of national Israel that we read that, 'if their rejection is the reconciliation of the world, what will their acceptance be but life from the dead?' (Rom. 11:15). In this important chapter Paul still describes the people of national Israel, in spite of their sins, as 'beloved' (v. 28): 'for the gifts and the call of God are irrevocable' (v. 29).[4] Moreover, the continuity of God's purposes towards the Jewish nation are surely seen in the mere fact that, when the time came for the revelation of his Son, Jesus was born to a Jewish family in the land of Israel, died in Jerusalem on the eve of Passover and appeared after he rose to his Jewish disciples in Jerusalem.

The land therefore in no sense loses its importance. Where is the drama of the New Testament revelation of God's love played out but in the area of Jerusalem, Galilee, Judea and Samaria? So long as the people of Israel, even in their rejection, are deemed 'beloved' by God's grace, so long will the land of Israel continue to figure in the purposes of God for the world. Palestinian Christian discussions of the land are weak here, because they either dismiss the emphasis on a particular land as belonging to a 'primitive layer' of revelation within the Old Testament, or (more commonly) they accord authority in this realm to the New Testament alone. This leads to a kind of

---

[4]For a contrary approach, see above pp.17f. and 62-4.

doceticism in which the tangible world is in danger of losing any real meaning—at least so far as the worldly aspirations of the other person are concerned. The church rightly rejected doceticism as heresy, and so should we.

III. The Bible and Justice

Our conclusions concerning the Middle East conflict will inevitably be 'critically affected by what justice is.'[5] The Bible nowhere gives us reason to think of justice in abstract or objective terms. Righteousness is existential, in that it is a working out of unchanging principles within the context of variable human situations. 'Justice' is not a mere juridic term, it has to do with given circumstances: thus God's law to Israel was case-law rather than juridic abstraction. This is an aspect of the beauty of divine self-revelation. God did not disclose himself to mankind in a set of systematic assertions; he came to man within the ongoing circumstances of life and declared his unchanging lordship among the vicissitudes of human experience.[6] The word came from without, apart from time, and is therefore timeless; yet it was given within the context of time, and is therefore relevant.

God's justice is no abstraction; it seeks to express his mercy concretely and to accomplish his salvation. The kind of justice that accords with God's character is dynamic rather than static, creative rather than codified, realistic rather than idealistic.[7]

God requires mercy, not sacrifice. Nor is this a lower standard. On the contrary, God requires more than rigorous pedantry, not less. The Scriptures repeatedly state that God required justice in the land, and that the justice required was not mere

---

[5] From the introduction to J. Peters, *From Time Immemorial: the Origins of the Arab-Jewish Conflict over Palestine* (London, Michael Joseph 1984).
[6] This does not deny the value of systematic theology or of distilling God's truth into propositional form. Yet God has clearly chosen to reveal himself to mankind in terms which are more often situational than otherwise.
[7] G.W. Bromiley, 'Justice', *International Standard Bible Encyclopedia*, II (Grand Rapids, Eerdmans 1982); *c.f.* such texts as Isa. 46:13; 51:5 *etc*. The 'unjust' judge in Jesus' parable is described as such although he ultimately decreed what was legally right, because he did so with neither concern for man nor fear of God.

juridic rectitude but a vibrant concern for the needy, the widow, the stranger and the orphan. Israel was warned that, if she fell short of God's requirements in this area, she would be liable to exile. No amount of military prowess would protect the nation from God's righteous wrath: the Lord had declared their destruction, and it would surely come.

Israel's history is an outworking of the principles outlined above concerning the land. Jeremiah in his day countered those who, inspired by an abstraction of the divine covenants without regard to duties enjoined, assured the people:

You will not see the sword or suffer famine. Indeed, I will give you lasting peace in this place (Jer. 14:13).

There is no 'peace to the wicked', be they Jews or Gentiles, and no divine covenant has ever promised otherwise. Whoever has truly 'stood in the council of the Lord' will seek to turn sinful people 'from their evil ways' (Jer. 23:22).

This obligation is not true only of Israel. God, who apportioned to the nations their inheritance, calls them also to account for the manner of life they lead in their respective lands. The fullness of the Amorites' sin brought about their exclusion from the land; Sodom and Gommorah, Assyria, Babylonia, Moab, and Egypt are all called into account by the righteous God and punished according to their deeds.

On the other hand, let none make light of the goodness of God, who is both a just God and a Saviour. He is as merciful as the justice he requires. Nowhere is it intimated that God's punishment to Israel implies the people's final rejection. God has not rejected the people whom he foreknew, nor can he, for he cannot deny himself (Lev. 26:44-45). Nothing can separate his chosen ones—whoever they may be—from his love.

As the terebinth and oak leave stumps when they are cut down, so the holy seed will be in the stump in the land (Isa. 7:11-13).

God promised to restore the people both to the land and to his good favour. He will transform them into his image, for the glory of his grace.

The book of Jeremiah, so remarkable for its repeated statements of divine rejection, is all the more remarkable for its repeated assurances of God's unilateral mercy.

After I uproot them, I will again have compassion and will bring each of them back to his own inheritance (Jer. 12:15).[8]

This then is the background to Paul's jubilant assertion that God is both just and the 'justifier of the ungodly' (Rom. 3:26; 4:5). God's dealings with Israel is the divine demonstration *par excellence* as to the nature of true righteousness.

Here, too, Israel is but a reflection of God's grace toward the nations, for the prophets often speak of the day when nations will walk in the light of God's goodness, serving him with hearts made new by his sovereign mercies. Thus

the terms of Old and New Covenants refer to two forms of the one eternal covenant of grace. The external details may change, but there is an underlying consistency and coherence to the Word and Acts of God.[9]

According to the Bible, therefore, Israel's calling and identity are inextricably linked to land. Hence we are not free to expect Israel to be indifferent to that land to which God led their fathers, and to which he attached so many of his promised blessings. On the other hand, land also implies responsibility. Israel's claim to the land—in whole or in part—must be supported by godly living, the lack of which renders the nation unworthy of the land and liable to be cast out. Godly living implies a just society, and justice is not mere legal rectitude; it involves mercy and kindness. Sinning in order to obtain land or while retaining it are sins to which God often responds by causing the land to disgorge its inhabitants. This is as true of the Jews as it is of any other nation on earth. God holds the nations accountable.

Nevertheless, while sin is real, grace often abounds. Grace is of the essence of God's relations with man, a truth exemplified for mankind in God's dealings with Israel: while Israel can forfeit the right to God's blessing, it can never sin so as to put itself beyond the reach of God's mercies.

If we are faithless, he remains faithful—for he cannot deny himself (2 Tim. 2:13).

---

[8] *C.f.* Jer. 17:9-15 *etc.* and Deut. 32:43: 'Rejoice, O nations with his people, for he will make atonement for his land and people'.
[9] J.B. Walker, *Israel: Covenant and Land* (Edinburgh, Handsel 1986), 1. For an alternative approach to Israel and the Gentiles, see above pp. 2, 15f.

Many would wish to see the establishment of the state of Israel as an obvious fulfillment of the prophetic promises. Surely we must remain agnostic on this issue. Even if, as I believe, God's promises to the people of Israel indeed include political independence in the land of their forefathers, it is 'not for us to know times or seasons' (Acts 1: 7), and any theory of eschatology that weakens Israel's sense of moral responsibility towards others is faulty. Nor can it serve Israel's true interests: the Jewish people have twice been sent out of the land because their society had become cruel, unjust and ungodly. Any view of the present or future that assures Israel of possession of the land in spite of its sin misses the true burden of biblical prophecy. The prophets were concerned, as we should be, that the land should be filled with justice.

IV. The Modern Political Problem: Eight Important Points

1) Jewish Suffering and the Rise of Zionism

The history of the Jewish people and their two millenia of suffering is well known (and has been touched upon in chapter 5). Jews were frequently treated as second-rate citizens, liable to being treated as scapegoats, used but seldom respected; their Scriptures burnt and their persons subjected to repeated indignities. Such experiences, undergone for so long, cannot but enscribe themselves upon the national soul of a people. They explain the Jews' attitudes towards other people, and they explain the appeal of Zionism.

This experience of suffering has naturally led to a certain distortion in the way the Jews view themselves and the world around them: all the more so when these experiences have been hardened in the recent crucible of Auschwitz and Treblinka. The attitude of the Jewish people toward its fellow nations is sometimes deemed slightly perverted, not without cause. Yet is it ill-founded? Has it no logic? For the suspicion with which modern Israel regards the nations at large is the result of much pain and will need much healing. Inevitably, before it can relax its defensive stance, Israel must first be allowed to undergo the unfamiliar experience of being accepted as one of many among the nations. The State of Israel is indeed driven by a sense of threat, but that is not the product of an illusion. Its citizens are convinced that their state's security lies in its ability to maintain a viable independence within which Jews will be assured of their corporate and individual welfare.

This desire for freedom and independence lies at the very core of Zionism—the desire of the Jewish people to be one among the family of nations, living in their own land, administering their own government and conducting their life freely according to their own customs. Again, the rise of Jewish Zionism and its causes (both political and religious) have been outlined above.[10] Here some points will briefly be underlined and others added.

In addition to its being the result of the experience of persecution in other lands, Zionism has also been fuelled theologically by the continued significance of the land of Israel and of Jerusalem in Jewish thinking throughout the last two thousand years.[11] No other people have been removed from their land for so long and yet continued to exist. No other people has so consistently maintained its link to a land.

Whatever one may think of a spiritual calling subject to geography, we must take this tradition for what it is: not only a protest against a disincarnate spirituality but, more specifically, an unconscious testimony to the inability to affirm any sort of Jewish spirituality other than that of a people—it being understood that this people fully realised its existence only in hypostatic union with the land. [Moreover the land is not] an end in itself, but a means whereby the people of Israel are the better to fulfill their destiny.

This then is the added complication to the 'Jewish Problem': not only is a state needed, but a Jewish state, and such a state can only be truly Jewish in the land of Israel

Moreover Zionists would wish to point out that (with the exception of the Philistines and the Crusaders) no nation apart from the Jews has maintained political independence in the land since the days of Saul—some 3000 years; nor has any other nation treated the land as home. Stronger nations have administered it from afar, but no people other than Israel have

---

[10]Much of the historical data concerning Zionism is outlined in ch. 5 above, though it should be observed that our perspectives differ in many points, not least in the conclusion that the Gospel of Christ need not be presented to the Jewish people.
[11]See more fully above ch. 5 (iv).

looked upon the land as 'motherland'. This is all the more remarkable in light of the land's geopolitical importance.

2) Issues of Demography

Against the charge that the Jewish population has only ever been a minority, it needs to be made clear that the small number of Jews relative to that of other residents was the product of forced exiles and insufferable circumstances under which the Jews were forced to live by Muslim and Christian invaders.[12]

After the First World War, due to Jewish development of the land and extensive military works, some 60,000-100,000 Arabs immigrated to Palestine in order to take advantage of the employment opportunities offered by the Jewish settlers, many of whom 'entered Palestine without their presence being officially recorded'.[13] In consequence, the non-Jewish population of Palestine expanded by more than 75% between the years 1922 and 1929.[14] The Palestine Royal Commission Report (1939) stated that:

> the shortage of land is due less to the amount of land required by Jews than to the increase in the Arab population...The Arab charge that the Jews have obtained too large a proportion of good land cannot be maintained. Much of the land now carrying orange groves was sand dunes or swamp and uncultivated when it was purchased.

3) The Rise of Palestinian Nationalism

Many Zionists would wish to assert that Palestinian Nationalism and the Palestinian desire for self-determination is a comparatively new phenomenon, which must therefore be seen in a different light from the age-long hope of the Jewish people for a return to their land. Any Arab nationalism was not at first a distinctly Palestinian nationalism, and an Arab Palestinian theology of the land has appeared only recently.

This perspective is confirmed by anti-Zionist writers such as Herman and Rosemary Ruether, in their book *The Wrath of Jonah*. Palestinian nationalism, they argue, only em-

---

[12]M. Comay, *Zionism and Israel: Questions and Answers* (Jerusalem, Ketter 1976), 24-25.
[13]UNWRA, 1962.
[14]Na'im Ateek records a growth in the Jewish population from 56,000 in 1918 to 553,600 in 1944: see *Justice and Only Justice* (New York, Orbis 1989), 53.

erged alongside the expansion of Jewish settlement in Palestine. Before that time there was no indication of a national Arab Palestinian consciousness; the Arab nationalist movement spoke in terms of a pan-Arab state stretching over the whole of the Middle East and beyond. 'Particular Arab nationalisms emerged out of the colonial fragmentation of the region'.[15]

There was no distinctly Palestinian culture, language, literature or history; Arab Palestinians had neither national institutions of any kind, nor a corporate sense of belonging. It was Jewish immigration and the improvement of job opportunities which together served to lay the grounds for what was to become after 1948 a growing national Arab-Palestinian consciousness. In 1948, however, no such consciousness was in evidence. Arab nationalism in Palestine was part and parcel of the Arab hope for a greater Arabia. It was only after that date, in the denigrating conditions of the refugee camps, that Palestinian nationalism was finally born.

Yet this Palestinian desire for self-determination, albeit modern, is a factor which must now be taken into account. Yet there remains a marked difference between Israeli and Palestinians in their desire for such self-determination. For the Jewish people, after two millenia during which their physical survival has often been in jeopardy, the issue is one of survival: only a Jewish state in Jewish hands can ensure that. By contrast, Arab Palestinian existence, culturally and physically, is not threatened by the lack of an Arab Palestinian state; indeed there is a real danger that such a state, if it came into being, would be soon swallowed up by pan-Arab nationalism. In the struggle between Arab pride and dignity and Jewish survival, survival must take precedence.

4) The Events of 1948 and After

Nazi atrocities were a final impetus towards the establishment of an independent state. Already, however, the Peel Commission had published its report in 1939, recommending a partition of the land between Jewish and Arab settlers. The Arab nations, acting on behalf of the Arab population in Palestine, unanimously rejected the proposal; the Jewish settlers expressed their willingness to negotiate. Eight years

---

[15]R.R. and H.J. Ruether, *The Wrath of Jonah: the Crises of Religious Nationalism in the Israeli-Palestinian Conflict* (New York, Harper and Row 1989), 103.

later the United Nations decided to partition Palestine. Once again, despite the economically and militarily untenable positions the partition plan imposed upon the Jewish settlers, they accepted the plan. The Arab nations declared their rejection and threatened to invade as soon as the plan was realised.

The borders which pertained until 1967 were the result of the ensuing conflict. Much of what would have belonged to an Arab Palestinian state, had the United Nation's proposal been implemented, was now under the control of Egypt and Jordan. Neither country took steps to establish a Palestinian state: Jordan annexed the West Bank and held its inhabitants under firm repressive control (denying them even the right to vote) and Egypt kept the Gaza Strip under military command. Squalid refugee camps were built and their inhabitants were forbidden to own land, settle outside the camps or develop their own institutions and industries. Their plight was cynically used by the Arab host nations as a means for constant pressure on the more squeamish Western world.

5) Israel and the Israeli Arab Population

Early in its history the Zionist movement had found itself torn between hopes for a truly Jewish state and a human concern for the growing Arab population in the land. Some called for their deportation, others for granting them a secondary status in the land. A majority insisted that equal civil rights be granted to all and any residents of the Jewish state-to-be. In theory, the majority carried the day, although Israel's record of achievements in this area falls far short of the ideals which motivated their decision.

The invasion of Israel on the part of the surrounding Arab nations in 1948, and the consequent struggle between the two peoples resident in the land, contributed little to Israel's goodwill toward its Arab citizens; the national selfishness of which all mankind partakes also had a part to play. As a result, Arab villages within Israel, while enjoying higher standards of life than in any other country in the Middle East, are still markedly poorer than the neighbouring Jewish settlements.[16] Israel has much yet to improve in this respect. Yet Israeli Arabs

---

[16] Arab schooling is on a much lower level. Electricity, running water and sewage are lacking in many Arab villages. Their roads are unpaved and their industry is on the whole poorly supported in comparison to Jewish industries.

have equal right to vote and their own representatives in the House of Legislature. Their religious institutions receive government support and their holy places are protected with equal devotion—something more than can be said in most Arab states today.

6) Israel and the 'West Bank'

Since 1967, as a result of defeating the Arab invasion of its land, Israel has found itself in possession of the Golan Heights, the West Bank and Gaza, which have been administered by Israel ever since. Jewish national aspirations, dormant in the light of historical reality, now burst into flame: Hebron! Bethlehem! Judea and Samaria!—all replete with Jewish historical memories—and, above all else, Jerusalem!

Yet these areas were not uninhabited. Some one million Arabs live in the land. What is to be done with these two realities—a land much desired and now in one's possession, and the presence of a people with human right, longings and needs themselves? As the years have gone by, Arab intransigence and Jewish fears have coupled to make a resolution impossible. A nationalist Israeli government, as well as the undemocratic regimes among the Arabs, added to the difficulty.

Meanwhile, Jewish settlers embraced the land, at times at the expense of Arab welfare. The close proximity of the two peoples and the Israelis' determination to take advantage of Arab and Palestinian hesitation, promoting their own interests with little regard for those of the Arab Palestinian population, have exacerbated tensions. The Arab Palestinians responded with the *Intifada*. A growing number of Israelis have responded with equal anger, toying with ideas such as mass deportation or continued military control.

These developments have not been met without remorse or internal conflict. Israeli society today is torn in a struggle between those who are willing to compromise so as to secure the democratic nature of the State of Israel, and those who wish to secure 'Jewish interests' with less regard for those of others. Every act of terrorism, every stone thrown in the *Intifada*, every young Israeli soldier who is forced to deal with the violent hatred now so evident among the Arab Palestinian populace, threatens to increase the number of the latter group. Every act of suppression, every new settlement and every indication of Israeli intransigence enlarges the gap between the two peoples and adds strength to the hatred felt by both sides toward each other. The Middle East is caught up in a whirlpool of human stupidity which threatens to engulf both Jew and Arab in a storm of self-destruction.

Israel had administered the West Bank and Gaza Strip for twenty years before the outbreak of the *Intifada* in December 1987. These areas were administered under a firm, military hand, yet this Israeli military administration was the most enlightened, the most generous of any military occupations that the world has ever seen. In twenty years the standard of living in the West Bank and Gaza attained the highest average in the Middle East, with the exception of Israel. New industries were established, agriculture advanced and agricultural produce grew by leaps and bounds. Tens of thousands of Arab Palestinians were employed in Israel and the Government expended constant efforts in trying to bring an end to illegal employment, which paid shameful salaries and accorded no social security.[17]

Yet the emerging Palestinian national consciousness had no outlet. Moreover, extensive contact with Israeli Jews exposed many Palestinians to a kind of arrogance that one would have thought Jews could never display toward another people. The added restrictions of an uncompromising military government and the threat of Jewish expansion into the West Bank and Gaza created the fear that Israel was determined to displace Arab Palestinians or to transform them into a permanently subject people. Unfair employment practices, repeated indignities from Israeli Jews and the cynical use by Arab states of the Arab Palestinians plight were increasingly painful.

Israel's policy of settlement in the West Bank and Gaza has been a focal point of controversy both in Israel and abroad. Israel's populace is united in believing that some Jewish settlement is justified, even necessary for security purposes; yet

---

[17]Attention should be drawn to the following examples. Five universities were opened by Israel (previously forbidden by Jordan) and from 1967 to 1988 the number of pupils studying in elementary and high school grew from 222,166 to 496,181; in those years the number of teachers rose from 7,377 to 17,374 and the number of schools from 997 to 1,560. As for medical services, infant mortality has dropped from 86 to 24 per thousand.

there is a division between those who believe that no compromise is possible (and that it is necessary to eliminate the possibility of realizing the national aspirations of Palestinians) and a very large minority who question the rightness of many such settlements. Caught between a rock and a hard place, Arab Palestinians have experienced increasing frustration.

7) Responding to the *Intifada*

In December 1987 there began the Arab Palestinian national uprising, known today as the *Intifada*. Since then this has spread to almost every Arab village in the administered territories, also affecting many Arab Israeli villages and radically altering the nature of relations between Arab Palestinians and Israeli Jews.

There is no doubt that support for the *Intifada* is widespread, although time has given reason to doubt how willingly that support is being given. Many shops have been forced to close by the *Shabab* (militant Arab youth) against the wishes of the owners and an almost unbelievable number of Arab have died at the hand of their own people.[18] Abu Iyad, one of the more prominent PLO leaders, expressed his concern that this trend will lead to a rule of tyranny in any future Palestinian state. Several Christian Palestinians have also expressed concern over the probable fate of non-Muslims in an independent Palestine: in every Arab country, with the notable exception of Jordan, Christian minorities frequently find themselves at a severe disadvantage. On occasions it appears as if the real war is being waged between the PLO and the ultra-fundamentalist Muslim *Hamas*, each seeking to gain control of the Palestinian national movement.

Of course, not all the violence has been directed inward. Seven hundred and ten (about half) of the attacks in 1989 were directed against Israelis. The *Intifada* has worked marvels in creating an international climate more approximate to Arab Palestinian hopes, and it has served to raise the level of self-recrimination in Israel itself. That is as much as it can hope to achieve. This is a war of attrition. It will be won by the side that can maintain itself longest. While the

---

[18]In the first half of 1989, 670 attacks were perpetuated by Arabs against Arabs, of whom 136 were killed and 245 were injured: see the undated publication by the Israel Ministry of Foreign Affairs, *The Intifada Against the Arabs*.

economic price Israel is called upon to pay is not small, it is within Israel's capacity. The most painful price imposed upon Israel is the loss of national confidence and sense of moral dignity due to the choice between either yielding to the Palestinians or suppressing and controlling the *Intifada*. Arab Palestinians have learnt how to use Israel's moral sensitivities, even if they do not share them.

Though the conduct of the Israeli army in the West Bank cannot be praised unreservedly, no military government anywhere in the world has faced such a situation with more sincere efforts to contain the uprising without loss of life. There are many unacceptable humiliations to which Arab Palestinians are exposed in the course of Israel's administration and many atrocities committed by Arabs. These should all be corrected. Yet this writer's deepest concern is for the process of de-humanization that is taking place in the hearts of both peoples.

8) Israel and the PLO

Israelis naturally are concerned by the practices of the Palestinian Liberation Organisation (PLO) which emerged in the late 1960s and claims to be the chief voice of the Palestinian people. Such anxiety amongst Israelis was not helped by the PLO's siding with Saddam Hussein in the Gulf War, an act which effectively discredited this organization once again. Moreover, the PLO's National Covenant (adopted in 1968 as its official platform, and never subsequently revoked) speaks of the necessity for 'armed struggle' for the 'liberation of Palestine' which will 'liquidate the Zionist and imperialist presence'.[19] In the light of such statements it is not surprising that many in Israel are reticent to negotiate with the PLO or its representatives.[20]

---

[19] See especially Articles 9 and 22.

[20] It is important to note the religious background of such Palestinian sentiments. The myth that claims that Jews lived in Arab lands with freedom and dignity for many hundreds of years cannot be substantiated. Non-Muslims were tolerated in Muslim countries only if they accepted the often humiliating status implied by the *Dhimma* system (see above ch. 5, n.2). For example, Non-Muslims had to pass Muslims on 'Satan's side' (the left), they were always to give way to Muslims and never to come into physical contact with them: see R.R. and H.J. Ruether, *op. cit.*, 32. For further evidence of Muslim religious attitudes towards Israel, see some of the strong statements in *The*

Palestinian spokesmen assure the West that their intention is to live peaceably alongside Israel, yet they repeatedly assure their own people that such a concession would merely be temporary, and that their 'real goal' is 'the total destruction of the Zionist state. Moreover, the PLO (although not itself freely voted into office by the population it claims to represent) also promises a 'secular, democratic state' in place of Israel, but does such a state exist anywhere in the Arab world, and would the PLO be able to create it? If the PLO (or any other influential Palestinian organisation) could convince Israelis of their sincere willingness to live alongside Israel, an overwhelming majority in Israel would insist upon immediate negotiations with the PLO and reasonable compromises, the right wing element in Israel notwithstanding.

Why then is Israel wrong when it follows the declared example of the British Government in 1938, which stated in a Policy Paper concerning Palestine that:

His Majesty's Government must reserve the right to refuse to deliberate with those leaders whom they regard as responsible for the campaign of assassination and violence?

Which set of the PLO statements are to be believed? Does the PLO really enjoy the support it claims to have among Arab Palestinians? Will the PLO be able to impose the will of the majority upon the many splinter groups which are still allowed to operate under the PLO aegis in spite of their consistent disavowal of a compromise? How can we trust the PLO's overtures so long as its National Covenant is not altered?

V. Jerusalem: Hope for the Future

The above has sought to highlight the relevant biblical data and the nature of the historical circumstances into which the biblical Word must be spoken. What is God saying through the scriptures today? Can we find some guidelines for this increasingly pressing problem of Jerusalem and the land?

We will need to remember first that, biblically, Jerusalem and the land can scarcely be distinguished: as

---

Proceedings of the Fourth Conference of the Academy of Islamic Research (El Azhar University, Cairo, Sept. 1968) 34-5, in which Muslim theologians discussed Muslim attitudes to the Arab-Israeli conflict.

already noted, Jerusalem is often used in the scriptures as a synonym for the people of the land.[21] A vision for the future of Jerusalem must, from this perspective, be related to one's vision for the whole of the land.

Secondly, politics is indeed 'the art of the possible'. Divine standards of justice are indeed relevant and vital—setting the goal to which we aspire—yet realism is required as well. Absolute justice is within the reach of God alone and is a state of affairs which awaits the final divine act leading to the restoration of all things. Such justice is part of our confident hope, and as such it governs our choices here and now, but we recognise the fact that it is yet a matter for the future.

The person who seeks absolute justice is evading practical decisions. I do not seek pure justice, nor the settling of historical accounts, but rather possible life, no more than imperfect and tolerable, causing as little injustice as possible.[22]

The biblical principles outlined above suggest the following general conclusions as God's will for both parties in the conflict:-

1) Israelis and Arab Palestinians will answer to God for the way they seek either to gain or retain the land. Sin will expose them to his wrath and to expulsion from the land which they so long to inhabit.

2) God's justice requires that both parties take serious account of the needs, desires and hopes of the other. Mercy, not legalistic pedantry, is called for; grace rather than territorial measurements is the issue at stake. Selfishness, private as well as national, leads to divine judgement. The biblical principle must surely be:

do nothing out of selfish interest or vain conceit, but in humility consider others better than yourselves. Each of you should look not only to your own interests, but also to the interests of others' (Phil. 2:3-4).

3) Land is as important now as it has ever been. Any suggestion that territorial attachments have been superseded by the Gospel fails to take into account the incarnational

---

[21]See above section II.
[22]David Grossman, *The Yellow Wind* (Eng. transl., London, Pan Books 1988) 1.

element of the Gospel; it also fails to do justice to the cultural and historical dimensions of God's workings on earth.

Israel cannot be understood in terms of an abstract, mystical and isolated relationship to God. It can only be understood in relation to the glory of its inheritance, the land of Canaan. This land, and Israel's intense attachment to it, did not threaten communion with Yahweh; it is precisely the visible manifestation of that communion. The land is the fulfilment of the promise. This is the essential meaning of the land for the Israelites in the light of God's glory.[23]

4) The city of Jerusalem is important today. It serves as a major focus in God's gracious undertakings with Israel. It is the crux of God's promises to the nation, the part representing the whole.

5) If Jerusalem and the land are important, they yet belong to God. Human attachment should never be so exclusive as to rule out the practical outworkings of God's ultimate ownership. Moreover, justice is more important than ownership of land.

6) Israel's relations to the land are biblical, not simply historical. The land is therefore somehow integrally related to Israel's calling for the blessing of the world.

These six general principles suggest that a solution to the present dilemma must be one of territorial compromise, a compromise that will take into account the needs and legitimate desires of both sides. This is by no means impossible, since the exclusivist Arab nationalism, which formerly saw no room at all in the Middle East for a Jewish state, has perhaps now given way to a realistic acceptance that Israel, like it or not, is going to stay.

Yet if a compromise solution is to be sought, what might this be? A fully independent Palestinian state on the West Bank and Gaza is hardly viable. With no raw materials, largely uncultivatable land, few water resources and a population ill-equipped for either democracy or modern industrial exploits, how could such a state subsist? Some kind of federative relat-

---

[23] G.C. Berkouwer, *The Return of Christ* (Eng. transl., Grand Rapids, Eerdmans 1972) 226ff.; this then affects our Christian expectation of a 'new earth', which 'is never a strange and futuristic fantasy, but a mystery that penetrates into this existence'.

ionship with another Arab state (most probably Jordan?) ought to be preferred by the Arab Palestinians themselves.

Such a solution would involve some sacrifice on the part of both parties. Will it be possible for the varied Palestinian viewpoints to be united peaceably towards such a goal? Will the PLO be interested in democracy, or will it see the process as but one step nearer the final annihilation of the Jewish state? Will Israelis see the moral imperatives laid upon them by God, or will some of them continue to sacrifice other people's interests with little remorse, so long as they can satisfy their own selfish desires? Many actions taken by Israeli soldiers, by the Government and by the Army are totally unacceptable and will expose the nation to the indignation of God. The process of moral degeneration, mutual dehumanisation and growing anger can do neither of our peoples any good.

What about Jerusalem? As far as Israel is concerned, any compromise formulated will have to include a true and full Israeli sovereignty over Jerusalem, while according Muslims and Christian some kind of special status. The possibilities are many: extra-territorial rights such as those of an embassy, special religious status, or some kind of joint oversight. The human mind can be very inventive when the task in hand will ultimately further its own interests.

Obviously, no single sweep of a human hand can resolve this conflict. Yet it is capable of resolution if our nations are willing to bridge the abyss of hate and suspicion which now separates our two peoples in a step-by-step process laid out with a view to psychological disengagement. Each step must be contingent upon the successful completion of the former and include real guarantees of its success. Present negotiations between Israel, its neighbours and the Arab Palestinians hold great promise—if conducted wisely. Both sides should make concessions which could help create a more positive atmosphere in which they could negotiate.

Let the PLO demonstrate its moral, uncoerced control of the Arab Palestinian population by calling for a cessation of violence rather than its escalation. Let Israel respond by removing its military forces from Palestinian cities and villages. Let the PLO alter its National Covenant, recognize Israel's right to exist and avow peace with the Jewish state. Let

Israel declare its willingness to arrive at some kind of political and territorial compromise. Let the Arab nations declare their prior acceptance of whatever resolution is achieved between Israel and the Arab Palestinians. Let guarantees be given to non-Muslim Palestinians, so that they are safeguarded from a fate similar to that of their brethren in Lebanon. Finally, let it be understood that, whatever be the nature of this new political entity, it is unlikely to enjoy full political independence —if ever—until more of the Middle East problems are successfully worked out. Jews and Arabs alike are subject to God's judgement. So we must hasten to bring an end to the present horrible state of affairs lest the Day overtake us in our sins.

As far as Jewish Christians are concerned, they naturally rejoice with their people as Jerusalem is rebuilt, its ancient sites excavated and its beauties are once again celebrated throughout the world. As the capital and Israel's largest city, Jerusalem has taken on much more than historical importance to most Israelis, Jewish or Jewish-Christian.

Whatever else one might say about the restoration of Jerusalem to Jewish hands, it is impossible to forget that God had promised to bless the people by restoring the city to them. Whether the present stage of world history is part of the fulfillment of that promise no one should state with certainty, any more than one should deny it. If the present restoration of Jerusalem to Israel is a fulfillment of biblical promise, it is also a harbinger of the promised day when Israel will turn to God in Christ and find in him its salvation.

What happens to Jerusalem is considered to be in a very substantial way the fate of the people a a whole. For that reason, Jewish Christians hope that the city will remain in Jewish hands, that the number of Jewish Christians living in the city will continue to grow, and that Jews and Arabs will find in the city a common faith in God's only Son.

Yet our hope, as already noted, is not to be informed exclusively by biblical data—at least not insofar as we are to deal with more than ultimate perfections; historical realities must be allowed an important role in the formulation of our hopes.

Nor may we limit our hopes to merely spiritual matters. As Israel's prophets so eloquently taught us, political and social justice are also important. Whatever God intends to do in the future—present, imminent, or distant—is to be achieved by himself. On no account may we sin in order to help promote those ends which we perceive to be God's ultimate purpose. Nor may we work without taking into account that, however dear a certain thought may be to us, we may be mistaken. We recognize that Jerusalem is special not only to the Jewish people. It is considered holy by Muslims and Christians all over the world, and inhabited by a large Arab minority. So we further recognise our duty to graft our hope into the real world.

Jerusalem does not have to be a dividing-point; it can become the hub of promised blessing. The contenders must be willing to heed each other, take each other's claims into account and respect each other's rights. Is that not what the prophets ultimately promise—that Jerusalem will become the geographic focal point to which 'all nations' will turn (Isa. 2:2)? Note carefully, however, the root cause of such a unity: the God of Israel will be recognized as the God of all the world, and the nations will turn to Jerusalem in order to learn to walk in his ways. If this is to be fulfilled, none of the protagonists involved can expect their absolute claims to be fulfilled without inflicting an injustice on the other. Some kind of compromise must be reached.

Under the present historical circumstances, that is surely the biblical hope for Jerusalem. Until it is achieved, Jewish-Christians will continue to speak of Christ in the city to all its inhabitants and pray for the day 'when the earth will be covered with the knowledge of the Lord as the waters cover the sea' (Hab. 2:14). They will also labour for that form of political justice which will do the least harm to either side, while according to each the maximum of gracious justice that is humanly possible.

POSTSCRIPT
(June 1994)

We are clearly at an important juncture in the history of the Middle East. The signing of the Declaration of Principles in September 1993, by Israel and the PLO fits in well with the hopes expressed above for future peace between Palestinians and Israelis. A large segment of Israeli society believes that it owes a moral debt to the Palestinian people, and will support them in the formation and maintenance of (what, in the course of time, is likely to become) the Arab Palestinian state.

Evidently, the hard facts of reality have begun to make an impression on the minds of both Palestinian and Israeli leaders. It has become obvious that neither side is able to overcome the other—Israel, because of its moral scruples, and the Palestinians, because of their relative military and political weakness. It can only be hoped that this dose of realism will continue to guide the leaders' thinking and, in due course, affect that of the two peoples as a whole. There is now little likelihood of the Arab-Israeli conflict being solved by military means.

Nor does the continuance of the conflict at any level serve the true interests of either people. The western Middle East is too small an area for Palestinians and Israelis to carry on in the same absurd manner they have done for the last fifty years or so. Limited water and mineral resources, the small number of available ports, the absence of naturally-defensible borders—these and many other factors all point to the advantages which both sides could reap if they were to cooperate with each other. It is in their mutual self-interest to lay down their arms and work together for a peaceful Middle East.

The present stage of negotiations gives much ground for hope. Yet no resolution of conflict is possible without sacrifice; both sides inevitably make extreme demands upon each other. Goodwill is currently the most needed commodity in the Middle East, yet at the moment there is little of it to be seen on either side . Extremists, both Israeli and Palestinian, have been allowed to play too large a role in the process, to the detriment of both sides. Such extremists may well prevent the peace-process from continuing to its potential welcome outcome.

Palestinian Extremism

Palestinian extremism is, not, at root, religious. It is the child of a deep-rooted frustration and of hopelessness. Gaza is the most densely-populated area of the world and, since 1948, its inhabitants have been subject to military rule—first by the Egyptians and then by the Israelis. Squalid refugee camps, economic decline and political oppression have all nurtured the frustration upon which religious fundamentalism breeds.[1]

Now there is a glimmer of hope. The Palestinians have won an opportunity to determine their own future. Supported by generous world aid and the prosperity of many Palestinians abroad, economic despair can give way to economic enterprise and growth, and a democratic political process can be born. Political independence and stability is now possible. They have won a great day of opportunity.

Such opportunity will fast become an opportunity lost if Palestinian extremists act in such a way as to lose the goodwill of the people of Israel. Not only would this make further Israeli concessions unlikely; it would also rob them of the many Israeli resources, both human and financial, which are greatly needed for the fledgling Palestinian political entity. If Palestine is to export its produce to Europe it will need access to Israeli ports, and it is impossible to travel between Gaza and the West Bank without Israel's continued goodwill.

Hopefully, these and other hard facts of reality will continue to influence the Palestinians. Self-interest is better served by peace than by conflict. Success will undermine most of the opposition and nurture a more open stance toward Israel.

Yet there are also serious threats to the peace process. One of these is the corruption infecting many echelons of the PLO; this not only weakens the internal moral fibre of the organisation, but also its moral appeal among Palestinians. PLO officials have done little with their available resources to establish a grassroots framework among Arab Palestinians.

Secondly, there is the threat of Palestinian extremism in the form of *Hamas*. During the 1980's, Israel successfully

---

[1]Criticism has been made (above p. 144) of my view that Palestinian nationalism only came into being in the aftermath of 1948 (p. 166). I am restudying the issue, and am open to the possibility that this view is incorrect. If it is, I offer my sincere apologies to my Palestinian friends—and enemies. However, this does not affect my overall argument.

distanced the PLO leadership from the majority of Palestinians under Israeli authority, hoping that such a separation would result in the West Bank and Gaza Palestinians supporting a peace process. Instead, an extreme fundamentalist element, most notably represented by *Hamas*, stepped into the vacuum.

Hamas is respected among the Palestinians for the high standards of its members' morality, religious and otherwise. It has established medical clinics, kindergartens and schools. Its terrorist arm has achieved marked successes and its 'martyrs' have evoked widespread admiration among Palestinians. There is a real possibility that *Hamas* will ultimately replace the PLO. If so, the prospects for the peace process are not encouraging.

Israeli Extremism

Israeli political fundamentalism is more directly the child of a nationalism fuelled by insecurity—an insecurity, it must be remembered, that is the painful result of history. Yet the vast majority of the 120,000 or so Israelis now living in Gaza and the West Bank were lured to settle there by the previous government's cheap housing loans. Many have already expressed their willingness to leave (with suitable monetary compensation).

The remaining 20,000-30,000 are idealists who are likely to do everything possible to make life in the Palestinian autonomy unbearable for both Jews and Arabs, and whose removal from their homes will involve an excruciating experience for the fragile Israeli democracy. The evacuation of Yamit (when Sinai was returned to Egypt) was but a painful rehearsal of what is likely to be involved in the evacuation of many settlements on the West Bank and in Gaza. Those of us who witnessed such events will never forget the trauma. Regrettably, it is the Israeli settlers themselves who are most likely to render their evacuation necessary—if they have not already done so. A different attitude might have secured their ongoing presence on the West Bank, even if limited in comparison with the present. Paradoxically, the settlers are doing everything in their power to ensure that their own aspirations are unlikely to be fulfilled.

The Jewish State is thus likely to face in the very near future one of its greatest challenges and to risk an irreparable rent in the fibre of its national existence. Some right-wing politicians have called for widespread civil disobedience at the first indication of evacuation from the 'land of the fathers'. They have enjoyed the support of religious parties in the Knesset and of important rabbinical authorities. Extremists among the settlers have threatened a 'bloodbath', yet few rabbis and fewer still right-wing politicians have spoken out against such statements. Instead, they have fanned the embers of resistance with descriptions of the inevitable ongoing conflict and terror.

Arab Palestinians can do much to address these phobias—more (sadly) than most Palestinian leaders seem willing to do at the present. Israel's firm and unequivocal denunciation of the massacre at Hebron was commendable. Yasser Arafat's silence in the face of continued terror is as indefensible as it is self-defeating.

The citizens of Israel, including the settlers, will have to make a painful choice: land and the division of the nation, or unity and the division of the land. Most Israelis will probably prefer the latter. They will choose democracy instead of a fear-driven, religiously-motivated nationalism that will destroy many of the young State's magnificent achievements and create a society in which few Israelis will choose to live. Yet the choice will not be made without extremely painful national trauma.

The Next Stage: towards Jerusalem

The Gaza-Jericho agreement is but a first step toward the resolution of the Arab-Israeli conflict. Will both sides now make it work, thereby making that final resolution possible?

Both are torn between hope and distrust, anger and realism. Regrettably, leaders on both sides have done very little to persuade their respective peoples of the wisdom or necessity of the interim agreement they have achieved. Nor have they shown the courage and magnanimity that could help this agreement work. Instead, they have engaged in petty symbolism and mutual recrimination that harbours little promise for the future. The leaders should act courageously, setting personal examples that can stir their respective peoples away from despair and toward more substantial efforts to make this process succeed. Goodwill can do a great deal more than mere formalities.

Inevitably, Jerusalem will be a major obstacle on the way to final agreement. Both sides have a deeply-entrenched attachment to the city, especially its eastern side. Provided the interim period becomes an opportunity for building relationships, a resolution over Jerusalem is not impossible. Various forms of shared sovereignty can be devised, with the exclusive sovereignty of each side assured over those sections of the city which are most important to them. Some such options have probably not yet even been conceived. For the present it is probably unwise even to raise options for possible solutions. If anything, they will be the product of the circumstances which prevail when the final stages of the conflict are resolved.

Internationalisation, however, would be unacceptable to both because it leaves no room for the exercise of national sovereignty. Mere access for religious or political purposes is a similarly flawed proposal. Yet solutions which currently seem impossible could turn into possibilities, if relations between Palestinians and Israelis develop in any desirable direction. The stark realities of the western Middle East seem to indicate that self-interest will ultimately prevail, to the good of all concerned.

Conclusion

Territorial compromise is not a religious transgression. The Bible shows that Israel seldom held the whole of the territory promised; nor is there any indication in Scripture that Israel is now called upon to take hold of it, or that it may do so regardless of the moral implications involved. With respect to territories, Israel's duty toward God is primarily a moral one. Should the Lord of history wish to grant Israel the possession of more territory than the peace accords allow, he can turn events in such a way that this will be done in spite of Israel's generosity. The divine promises cannot and should not serve as the basis for a political platform. God is not in need of human aid to accomplish his purposes.

Israel's moral and religious duty is not to insist upon its right to the land but upon its obligation to love and honour the Palestinians—just as the Palestinians must honour Israelis. Selfishness is never a wise guide toward moral duty. Nor can it be in God's sight an acceptable grounds for national policy.

Jesus had the right to glory, yet he did not cling to his privileges (Phil. 2:6-8). He stripped himself of glory and humbled himself to the utmost degree for the love of belligerent and unworthy men. By so doing he secured the only way of salvation for sinful men. He also set us an example to follow. I can wish my people nothing better than to be like Jesus.

CHAPTER 8

JERUSALEM AND THE CHURCH'S CHALLENGE

Peter Walker

I. Introduction

Different ways of approaching the scriptures in relation to this question of Jerusalem and its significance have emerged in previous chapters; but what does this mean for the Church resident in Jerusalem? Is there any one viewpoint of those so far expressed which has particular currency among the Christian people who daily live in the midst of Jerusalem's complexities? On the other hand, are there any approaches which are theoretically convincing, but practically untenable? What are the differing theological approaches to Jerusalem which are held by Christians resident in the city today, and how does the indigenous Church see its task in the light of these?

The 'indigenous Church' is a simplified term for what in reality is a very complex mixture of various Christian congregations living and worshipping in both 'East' and 'West' Jerusalem. In this chapter it will thus be necessary first to give a brief overview of these different churches and their concerns, before proceeding to describe their varying theological approaches to Jerusalem; in so doing four different understandings of Jerusalem will emerge, some compatible, some mutually contradictory. Finally, a brief re-examination of the early chapters of Acts will prepare the way for a concluding reflection on the Church's continuing mission in the city today.

II. The Jerusalem Church Today and its Concerns

It can safely be said that nowhere else in the world can such a bewildering variety of Christian communities be found within so few miles of each other. Inevitably, because of the undeniable place in Christian history which Jerusalem has as the city in which the Gospel message was both accomplished and then first proclaimed, the place where the New Testament 'Church' came into being, vast numbers of Christian denominations have found it attractive and compelling to maintain within Jerusalem a representative Christian congregation. This process, which can especially be seen in the last 150 years with the arrival of various Western Christian groupings, can also be observed among those ancient Christian communities which have been in Jerusalem for centuries. It is not simply a practical issue of wishing to have in Jerusalem a 'branch office' which can welcome any pilgrims who visit, making them feel 'at home'; for somehow the presence within Jerusalem of such a congregation lends a certain authenticity and credence to the claim of any denomination to be a true church of Christ; without such a presence, on the other hand, a denomination might well feel more vulnerable concerning its apostolic credentials.

As a result, there are within Jerusalem not only the historic Christian denominations (Eastern Orthodox, Oriental Orthodox, Eastern-rite Catholics, Latin-rite Catholics) but also the Anglicans and various Protestant churches (Lutheran, Baptist, Presbyterian, Reformed, and others such as the International Alliance Church, the Nazarenes, Mennonites, Pentecostals, Assemblies of God etc), not forgetting the growing number of Messianic-Jewish (or Hebrew-Christian) congregations.[1] Anglicans and Protestants, however, constitute perhaps only five percent of the total Christian population.

In the light of this multi-faceted situation, one possible task for the Jerusalem Church is clearly to strive together for a greater unity and working co-operation. Since one divine purpose, according to Ephesians 1:10, is to 'unite all things in Christ', any manifestation of disunity speaks more of the conquest of evil and the apparent victory of those 'powers' opposed to God's will.[2] Such an 'ecumenical' goal (which in other parts of the world might by some be felt to be of lesser importance than, say, the task of evangelism) is by no means unimportant in a city where the Christian Church is observed closely by both Jewish and Muslim neighbours and where all

---

[1] In preparation of sections II and III, the author visited Jerusalem, meeting various Christian leaders in the city and inviting responses to a questionnaire examining their respective attitudes towards Jerusalem and the Church's mission. Those approached included Greek Orthodox, Armenians, Latin Catholics, Greek Catholics, Anglicans, various members of the United Council of Christians in Israel (UCCI), the International Christian Embassy and members of both Messianic congregations and Evangelical Arab churches. Written responses were gratefully received from perhaps a third of these.
[2] *Cf.* above, p. 65.

too often the very real lack of unity between Christians has been painfully evident in the past. Such disunity naturally has a very negative effect on any Christian witness.

Recent years have given cause for some encouragement on this score as the historic churches have been able to issue joint pronouncements on issues of practical concern to them all, whilst the various Evangelical groupings come together under the auspices of the United Christian Council of Israel (UCCI). Excluded from these, however, are the various Christian Zionist organizations, such as is the International Christian Embassy in Jerusalem (ICEJ) and 'Bridges for Peace', whose theology is one from which the other churches (to varying degrees) wish to distance themselves.

A comprehensive survey of the churches in Jerusalem (as indeed for the whole of Middle East) can be found in Horner's helpful volume, which includes estimates of the size of the various Christian communities in Israel (within its pre-1967 borders) and 'East' Jerusalem/West Bank.[3] Whilst most denominations are augmented by some sizeable ex-patriate communities, the majority are peopled by indigenous Arabs or Jewish-Christians. This is especially the case for the Eastern Orthodox (though its clergy remain, on the whole, Greek), the Greek Catholics, the Latin Catholics and the Anglicans—a fact which these churches are increasingly at pains to point out to those visiting the country, who might otherwise be unaware of the existence of Christian Palestinian Arabs.[4]

One of the chief concerns of such Christian Arabs is that in recent years there has been a steady emigration from among them. In 1947 Christian Arabs of all confessions would have numbered approximately 45,000, whereas by 1979 this had fallen to perhaps 10,000, and they continue to leave, chiefly

---

[3] N.A. Horner, *A Guide to Christian Churches in the Middle East* (Elkhart, Indiana, Mission Focus Publications 1989) esp. 9, 58, 66, 79, 84, 107 and 112. Perhaps the most authoritative guide (though not so readily available) is that found in the 1986 volume of *Perspectives*, published by the Middle East Council of Churches; this was drawn up with the full co-operation of the local churches. See also C. Amos, *A Many-coloured Mosaic* (London, CMS 1988).
[4] The importance of introducing visitors to the local Christian Palestinians has been especially emphasized by *Living Stones*, an ecumenical trust founded recently for this purpose by one of the conference speakers, Dr Michael Prior.

through wishing to escape from living as second-class citizens under Israeli rule.[5] Archbishop George Carey, when visiting the Anglican community in 1992 for the 150th anniversary of the Anglican Bishopric in Jerusalem, commented on the danger of Jerusalem becoming in Christian terms an 'empty theme park', a museum of Christian history rather than a centre for a living Christian community. Such words are not exaggerated, though the perspective is evidently from the Arab side alone: Messianic believers would wish to draw attention to the marked increase in their numbers in recent years.[6] This points to the volatile situation of the Church in Jerusalem and how the relative ratios between Jewish and Gentile believers might change dramatically in the coming years, opening up a whole new episode in the Church's history in Jerusalem. Meanwhile it leaves some Arab Christian communities with a natural sense that 'survival' is perhaps their chief task, other considerations becoming quite secondary in comparison.

The current situation therefore lends itself to a natural concentration amongst Christians on the twin purposes of ensuring their basic 'survival' and fostering unity with the other Christian minorities within Jerusalem.[7] But what about evangelism? Is this not an essential part of the Church's mission? More particularly in Jerusalem, if many Christians are tempted to emigrate, does this not mean that the Churches will need to consider again the importance of evangelism if they are to avoid disappearing altogether? Christians living far removed from the unique pressures on Christians in Jerusalem need to exercise caution here as they ask what might be perceived as an awkward, though necessary question. For the Christian churches find themselves 'caught in the middle' between two overwhelming majorities, Jews and Muslims, amongst whom evangelism has throughout history proved especially difficult. On the one side, the Israeli parliament ('Knesset') passed legislation in 1977 prohibiting enticements to

---

[5] See Horner, *op. cit.*, 84f.
[6] *E.g.* David Dolan and Joseph Shulam in their responses; according to one source there are now seven Messianic congregations in Jerusalem, one of which meets on Anglican premises in Christ Church.
[7] Christian leaders in Jerusalem list several other problems which face them to differing degrees. These include: shortage of finance and appropriate buildings; a lack of indigenous, trained leadership; and how best to cope with the numbers of visitors and expatriates.

change religious affiliation (interpreted by many as an 'anti-missionary' law), whilst, on the other, the Palestinian Muslims seldom convert to Christian faith, not least in today's climate because they judge many Christians, for either political or theological reasons, to be clear supporters of Israel. Such pressures on both sides frequently result, therefore, in evangelism being given a very low priority in Christian mission, if indeed it features at all; any evangelistic work (and it does exist, amongst both Jews and Arabs) is necessarily 'low-key'.

This 'downplay' of evangelism can be seen amongst Christians on both sides of the Jewish/Arab divide. On the one hand, many Christians supportive of Israel, eager to show solidarity with the Jewish nation in the wake of many centuries of 'Christian' anti-Semitism, espouse theologies which deny the need for Jewish evangelism, no doubt in some instances seeing such activity as in a strange sense a continuance of this anti-Semitic tendency.[8] This may lead amongst some Christian Zionists to a 'two-covenant' theology, in which Christians are to respect and deem the 'Old Testament' covenant with the Jewish people as being equally 'salvific' for the Jewish people, as the 'New Testament' covenant is for Gentiles, thus rendering any Christian evangelism unnecessary and indeed contrary to God's will. Alternatively, it may be linked into some eschatological interpretation, whereby God himself will bring the Jewish people to faith in Jesus, their Messiah, at a time of his own choosing, and seemingly unaided by human assistance. One wonders what any of the first (all Jewish) disciples would have made of either of these two positions.

On the other hand, amongst Arab Christians and those who work alongside them, the natural tendency is for the various churches to adopt a non-proclamatory model of evangelism (appealing, no doubt, for an 'incarnational' approach) and to put their energies into other projects which witness in their own way to the truth of Christ. Much social work is done, for example, showing in important ways the love of Christ in situations often of extreme need.[9] Meanwhile the prophetic

---

[8]For the presentation of this view, see above, ch. 5 (v).
[9]For example, the Greek Catholic community is responsible for a housing project, several health centres, five youth centres and three schools; examples could no doubt be multiplied from each of the

ministry of appealing for 'peace and justice' for all is clearly timely and relevant, giving Christians the opportunity to be seen as agents of unity and reconciliation, rather than as the proponents of a third, potentially divisive creed. This latter emphasis has naturally been heard even more loudly in recent years, as the tensions of the *Intifada* have become manifest.[10]

III. Visions of Jerusalem

Naturally, different parts of the Scriptures are drawn upon in order to legitimate these different perceptions of the Church's task in this city. This is, of course, not unique to Jerusalem. Throughout the world the same process of 'biblical authorisation' occurs whenever Christians seek to explain their particular emphases in mission or ministry. The biblical theme of 'liberation' has priority for some, the prophetic theme of 'justice' for others; some find their motivation from God's vulnerable love shown in the act of the Incarnation, others in the redemptive challenge to repentance and faith issued through the Cross.

All these theological inspirations (and many others besides) are present in Jerusalem in the same way as anywhere else. In Jerusalem, however, such sources of theological inspiration are inevitably supplemented by (or become attached to) particular theological convictions concerning the significance of Jerusalem within God's purposes. For example, Christians emphasizing God's desire for unity amongst his people might in other contexts have appealed to such verses as 1 Corinthians 12:13 ('for by the one Spirit we were all baptized into one body') or Galatians 3:28 ('all one in Christ Jesus'); in Jerusalem, however, they might well be tempted to cite one translation of Psalm 122:3 ('Jerusalem is a city which is at unity with itself') and assert that this remains a prime divine purpose for the continuing city of Jerusalem today, that it should be the place

---

churches. For many (including Evangelicals), such 'relief work' is an essential part of the Gospel message.

[10]It is well represented, from different angles, in chs. 6 and 7 above. See also *e.g.* M. Prior, '*Living Stones*: Christians in the Holy Land', in *Doctrine and Life*, 42.3 (March 1992). Archdeacon Rafiq Farah draws attention to the importance of Jesus' programme of 'freedom for the oppressed' (Luke 4:18).

which manifests (despite all its profound difficulties) the unifying purpose and power of God.

Our task now is to explore this question further and to uncover, where possible, the theological vision of Jerusalem which undergirds each of the different understandings of the Church's task in Jerusalem. How do these different Christian communities understand God's present purpose for Jerusalem? What biblical texts incite them to action? Each of the authors in chapters 5 to 7 concluded with their 'hope for Jerusalem', expressing views which no doubt correspond to those of significant numbers of Christians living and working in Jerusalem. Our task now is to discover if there are any other visions of Jerusalem, and with all of them to press more deeply the question: what precisely is that vision and which particular scriptures can be appealed to for its justification?

To ask the often unexpressed but basic theological question on this issue: what precisely is God's will for Jerusalem? What place does it have in his purposes, and what is he doing to accomplish those purposes? Already in chapters 5 to 7 there have been at least three differing visions of Jerusalem. Is Jerusalem to be the renewed capital of his chosen people, the Jews? Alternatively, is it to be the place where members of all the three great monotheistic faith-communities can show to the world that they can live together in peace and harmony with justice for all? Then again, could it be God's will that instead Jerusalem be the place where increasing numbers of people come to personal faith in Jesus, the Jewish Messiah, the only Son of God? Are these visions compatible? Are there other approaches? What scriptures underlie them?

1) Jerusalem, city of the past

The first theological vision of Jerusalem might be termed the *supersessionist*. Adherents of this view, whilst acknowledging the central place of Jerusalem within the Old Testament purposes of God, would interpret the words of Jesus and the rest of the New Testament in such a way as to call into question whether Jerusalem continues to have any special enduring place within God's purposes in the time subsequent to the coming of Christ. In varying ways this is the conclusion reached by each of the authors in chapters 1 to 4.[11] It is a view which wishes to question severely the apparently more 'straightforward' reading of the biblical texts (especially in the Old Testament, but also in the New) which speak of God's special involvement with this earthly city, and to argue that the essential thrust of the New Testament (which must be taken as normative for all Christian thinking) is one which speaks clearly of God's decisive and completed judgement upon the city and his concern now for the universal spread of the Gospel away from its previously narrow confines in the land of Palestine.

Whilst Jesus clearly taught that he had come 'not to abolish, but to fulfil' the Old Covenant (Matt. 5:17) a case can be made for seeing Jerusalem as one of those aspect of the Old Covenant which had been intended to point towards Jesus and were therefore 'fulfilled' and outmoded by his coming. Key texts for the defence of such a position would include Jesus' several warnings of judgement upon the city (not least in the Apocalyptic Discourse), his prophecy concerning 'true worshippers' worshipping 'neither on this mount nor in Jerusalem' (John 4:21), the emphasis in the Epistles on the New or Heavenly Jerusalem (Gal. 4: 26, Heb. 12:22, Rev. 3:12, 21:2), the missionary mandate to the disciples in Acts 1:6-8 not to be concerned with the 'restoration of Israel' but to be Jesus' witness 'to the ends of the earth', the whole message of Hebrews that Christ is the one who fulfills all that the Temple (and therefore Jerusalem) had stood for, and the general lack of concern with the physical Jerusalem in theological terms throughout the New Testament.

Such a position seeks, perhaps above all, to give adequate consideration to the whole issue of the Fall of Jerusalem in AD 70, taking Jesus' words seriously concerning divine judgement, and interpreting them to mean that the significance of Jerusalem in strictly theological terms is now a thing of the past. Jerusalem therefore may retain a vital role as witnessing to the historic basis of the Christian faith and the emergence of the Christian Church, but God's purpose for Jerusalem is now no different than his will and purpose for any human city.

---

[11]For the important New Testament argumentation of this view, see ch. 3 above.

It would be incorrect to infer from the proponents of such a view that they deny God has *any* purpose for Jerusalem. For they would counter that God has a purposive will for every human institution, which will can be discerned from reflection on other parts of the Scripture. Jerusalem, they would argue, cannot be deemed to have any extra or different role within God's purposes, simply because in the Old Testament period it clearly *did* have such a unique role, for the New Testament revelation brings that to an end; however, once this important point is grasped, there would be nothing inconsistent in looking prayerfully at the current situation in Jerusalem and reflecting on what God's unique will for this city might be, given its unique historical and contemporary realities (for example, that it is 'holy' to three religions, or that it is a place where the Jewish/Arab division might be healed in Christ). As such this view can be combined as a foundational element with some of the other 'visions of Jerusalem' to be examined below, denying to them only any suggestion that Jerusalem is somehow qualitatively different.

However, it needs to be said that such a view is not easily maintained by those resident in Jerusalem. Neither of the two authors in this volume who live in the Holy Land would subscribe straightforwardly to this view; as such it might be deemed the merely 'academic' position of Western theologians who are conveniently detached from the Jerusalem situation, with all its potency, poignancy and pain. For there seems to be something about Jerusalem, hard to define maybe, which stubbornly refuses to be thus dismissed; it is hard when contemplating the unique beauty and history of the city from the Mount of Olives to dismiss from one's mind the thought that somehow this city *is* different, that it is special in some way, perhaps even strategic within the divine scheme of things. Is this a spiritual reality to be recognised and conceded, or is it a temptation to be resisted? Jerusalem is so very alluring, and beckons us to give her a special place in our hearts and in our minds; are we to indulge her whim or not?

2) Jerusalem, city of the Incarnation

A second theological vision of Jerusalem may be termed the *incarnational* approach. Proponents of this view would base their understanding of Jerusalem's uniqueness, not on her role in the Old Testament period, but on the fact that the city 'played host' to the great events of the New Testament, most notably the Incarnation of God the Son, but also including under this heading his Death, Resurrection and Ascension. Theologically speaking, a case might well be made that in fact this incarnational emphasis is in fact an Old Testament theme as well, since what did Jerusalem and especially the Temple come to symbolise but the presence of God *dwelling* amongst his people?[12] In this way, a golden thread might be extracted from the Scriptures, whereby Jerusalem is seen to point to God's desire to meet with his creation, and, though that meeting-place according to the New Testament is now Jesus himself, it is perhaps not inappropriate to think of Jerusalem too as continuing to have a part to play in this process.

Be that as it may, Christians who emphasize this incarnational understanding are wishing to say that the city which witnessed such unique events can never thereafter be treated simply on a par with any other city. God has here acted decisively and dramatically both to reveal himself and to save mankind.[13] Jerusalem must therefore not only be accorded a special place in our human affections, prayers and responsibilities, but also acknowledged as retaining particular significance within God's purposes. What therefore happens in Jerusalem is of special concern to God himself.

Such an understanding is not based as such on any particular verses from the Bible, but is rather a reflection on the whole message of the New Testament concerning the Incarnation, that 'God was in Christ' (2. Cor. 5:19) and that the 'Word became flesh and dwelt among us' (John 1:14). This emphasis would be found (even if in different ways) in all the 'historic' churches within Jerusalem. Why is Jerusalem special to them, what is the mysterious truth which underpins all their liturgical celebrations and ministry to pilgrims? It is that this city was uniquely visited by none other than Jesus, the Son of God. It is this attitude no doubt that fires the imagination too of a vast majority of those who, whilst not resident in Jeru-

---

[12]*Cf.* above p. 62.
[13]To this day, therefore, following the interpretation of Psa. 74:12 offered by Cyril in the fourth century, Eastern Christians think of Jerusalem as the 'navel' (ὀμφάλος) of the earth: see Lutfi Laham, *Jerusalem—the Holy City* (Jerusalem, 1991) 2.

salem, visit it as pilgrims in one form or another: Jerusalem, the 'city of Incarnation', the place where once He walked.

Those inclined to a supersessionist view of Jerusalem might rightly question whether this 'specialness' is merely in the 'eyes of the beholder' or whether it is truly an elemental part within God's current purposes for the city. Does what happened in the time of Jesus determine God's attitude now, or is this emphasis merely a reflection of Jerusalem's great historical role and the benefit which we as mortals derive from such historical associations?

Moreover, is it fair to emphasize the Incarnation as a theological truth to the detriment of a focus on Christ's Death and his redemptive work, a focus which might alter one's consequent understanding of Jerusalem. The 'city of the Incarnation' indeed rings positively, as does the 'city of the Resurrection', but what does it do for the specialness of Jerusalem in the present to refer to it (equally truthfully) as the 'city of the crucifixion', the place where Jesus was not welcomed but rejected?

Such an emphasis on the Cross indeed might modify this incarnational approach in several helpful ways. First, it would alert adherents of this view that the Christian Gospel is not simply about Incarnation, but also about Redemption, and that therefore the Christian task is not simply one of loving identification but also one of clear proclamation, calling people repentantly to meet their Crucified Redeemer. Christian mission is not to be identified simply with passive 'presence'; yes, Christians need to be incarnationally present, yet they also need to be prophetically outspoken. This presents the Church with a challenge which needs to be heard in Jerusalem as much as (if not more so than) anywhere else. It is wrong to take to oneself the comfort of the Incarnation without equally taking on board the challenge of our Redemption.

Secondly, an emphasis on the Cross might give us a window of understanding into an experience that is frequently noted by Christians in Jerusalem: namely that there is here a special sense of 'spiritual warfare'. Such language may seem unfamiliar to some, or unnecessarily 'supernatural', but we are reminded in the Scriptures that our dealings are 'not with flesh and blood, but with the principalities, powers and world rulers of this present darkness' (Eph. 6:12); in Paul's theology, moreover, the Cross of Jesus was (at one level of causation) the work of the 'rulers of this age' (1 Cor. 2:8), though eventually it was the place where Christ 'disarmed' them and 'triumphed over them' (Col. 2:15). Such verses would make legitimate the conclusion that Jerusalem was at the time of the crucifixion the scene of the most significant 'spiritual battle' of all time, the place where the powers of darkness revealed their worst, but were decisively defeated. If this be accepted, then some would suggest that it is not impossible for the repercussions and resonances of such an event still to reverberate through the city today. Whilst the power and goodness of Christ may be celebrated in Jerusalem, it is not hypothetically impossible that Jerusalem could also be a place where evil too holds sway, where the battle between good and evil is particularly heightened, even if the ultimate victory for Christ is assured through that historic Resurrection.

Whatever be made of this final point, it is clear that an emphasis on the Incarnation, however natural and appropriate for Christians when considering Jerusalem, is not necessarily straightforward. On further examination it serves only to reveal some of the complexities of the Incarnation itself and of the continuing city of Jerusalem.

3) Jerusalem, a city restored

A third theological vision of Jerusalem might be termed the *restorationist* approach. Unlike the incarnational emphasis which tends to focus on the past, this restorationist approach sees Jerusalem's significance as lying especially in the imminent future. Moreover, whereas the above incarnational understanding would generally be characteristic of Christians living in 'East' Jerusalem, this restorationist perspective would be the more natural approach of those living in, or closely associated with 'West' Jerusalem. This is very much the modern, new city, the part of the city inhabited by the Jewish people, built with all the attendant excitement of the Jewish people being restored to their 'capital' Jerusalem after nearly 2,000 years of comparative absence. Some Jewish Zionists with religious convictions might undergird this event with eschatological hopes of the Return of the Jewish Messiah, others with the contention that in the restoration of the Jewish people to this city God has, as it were, 'returned to his permanent address'.¹⁴

Christians surrounded by such sentiment, and wishing to empathize with this strong Jewish sense of restoration naturally approach Jerusalem, even as Christians, within a similar framework. They would repudiate any 'replacement theology' (which sees the Church as the 'New Israel') and a supersessionist approach to Jerusalem; instead they would be inclined to endorse Jewish understandings of the special significance of Jerusalem within God's eternal purposes: just as this was the centre of the Jewish nation from the time of David through to AD 70, so now it is appropriately the centre of a revived Jewish nation in the land today; inasmuch as this was the place which, according to so many verses within the Old Testament, God had especially chosen as a 'dwelling-place for his name' and where his people might meet with him in special ways, so today it is a place of special significance in God's purposes, and a place of potential spiritual blessing. This is indeed the 'Zion' so beloved of the Psalmist:

> You will arise and have compassion on Zion,
> for it is time to show favour on her;
> the appointed time has come...
> For the Lord will rebuild Zion
> and appear in his glory (Psa. 102:13, 16).

Moreover, any Jewish eschatological thinking, arising from such verses or other Messianic texts, would be endorsed by many Christian restorationists, though with the vital Christian distinction, that the Messiah to be expected is Jesus returning. Their prayer is that God will reveal himself in Jesus to Zion and thereby to the world at large; in this way Jerusalem will once again prove to be the 'epicentre' of God's purposes.

For obvious reasons, such a vision is based almost exclusively on the Hebrew Bible, the Christian's Old Testament; the whole stance is one designed to be as affirmative as possible of Jewish hopes and aspirations, both political and religious. The distinctively 'Christian' aspect is then added to this Jewish foundation in a variety of ways. Some would espouse an avowedly two-covenant approach, whereby such

---

¹⁴See *e.g.* R. Jonathan Blass in *The Jerusalem Report* (23 April, 1992), 34.

Jewish aspirations (so long as they are true to Judaism's essential ideals) can be affirmed without remainder: God is, as it were, working with two different modes of salvation (one for the Gentiles focused on Christ and the 'New Covenant', the other for the Jews, focused on 'Old Covenant' entities such as the Torah and presumably Jerusalem). As a result God has no higher purpose in restoring the Jews to Jerusalem, than that they should be assured of his promises fulfilled towards them and of their being able to worship him once more 'in the land' according to Torah.

Views of this kind are seen above in chapter 5 and are fairly common amongst people sympathetic with Christian Zionism. However, they would be keenly rejected by many others who yet remain distinctly sympathetic to the Jewish restoration to Jerusalem. These latter Christians (who would include the majority of Messianic Jews and those working in the field of Jewish evangelism) would see the return of the Jewish people to the Land as but a stage within God's continuing dealings with the Jewish people, a prelude to the time when their hearts will be turned to faith in Jesus, their Messiah. Whether they understand this 'return' to be a direct fulfillment of Old Testament prophecy or maintain a more open mind, they are united in the prayer that the Jewish people should turn to Christ; any physical return to the Land without this ensuing 'spiritual return' to the Lord (as revealed in Jesus) would be contrary to all their deepest hopes and prayers. They long for the spiritual restoration of Israel, not just the physical. As a result, though keenly aware that such a 'spiritual restoration' must be the work of God, they work to this end, being active (if discreet) in the work of evangelism amongst Jews and in the building-up of Messianic congregations, which they see as the 'vanguard' of God's work in bringing the Jews to faith in Yeshua, their Messiah. They would tend to distance themselves from those who, by contrast, relying on a particular brand of eschatology, believe it is acceptable in the interim for Christians simply to identify supportively with Israel, leaving their 'conversion' as such in the hands of God alone. Whilst they might be of the opinion that such 'pre-evangelistic' identification with Israel might eventually soften Jewish attitudes towards the Christian Church and its Gospel, they would deem it essentially wrong to emphasize eschatology to the detriment of evangelism.

For all such Christian 'restorationists', however, Jerusalem's significance is based first and foremost on the Old Testament revelation.[15] Whilst New Testament themes can be introduced as well in different measures,[16] the underlying bedrock of this approach is that God's purposes today towards Jerusalem are in direct continuity with those revealed within the Old Testament. As such this approach stands in marked contrast both to the incarnational one (which can be in danger of ignoring the Old Testament altogether) and to the supersessionist one which notes these Old Testament themes but interprets the New Testament in such a way as to see them as now superseded in Christ. We are thus presented with three visions of Jerusalem which, whilst all labelled 'Christian' and indeed 'biblical', stand in almost total contradiction of one another.

4) Jerusalem, city of unity

It is hardly surprising, therefore, since the city itself evokes such divergent responses in those people who seek to interpret its theological significance, that Jerusalem all too often brings forth from the Christian Church a clear manifestation of its evident disunity. In the light of this all-too-evident state of affairs, it is perhaps ironic that the fourth and final vision of Jerusalem espoused by Christians is that the city should be a place of *unity*. This unifying purpose would probably be endorsed by the vast majority of Christians in Jerusalem, and indeed can be superimposed on any of the three foundational perspectives outlined above. Yet again, however, it can take different forms.

As noted above, given both the vast array of different Christian communities resident in Jerusalem and their comparative smallness in the face of the Muslim and Jewish majorities, such an urge towards unity amongst Christians is under-

---

[15] In addition to those Old Testament texts already discussed above in chs. 2 and 5, Christians in Jerusalem tend to emphasize passages such as Jer. 31, Joel 2 and Ezek. 36.

[16] The most common would be Luke 21:24 ('Jerusalem will be trampled on by the Gentiles until the times of the Gentiles are fulfilled') and Rom. 11:26 ('all Israel will be saved'), interpreted in the manner which is countered above (pp. 65-7).

standable; yet there remain many reasons from history as to why the path towards such unity and co-operation can be long and hard. Despite these great difficulties, however, the prayers of many would be for a fulfillment in Jerusalem of Christ's prayer, made to his Father in that self-same city, 'that they may be one' so that the 'world may know that you sent me' (John 17:21, 23; *cf.* 13.34). Looked at positively, Jerusalem, presents the Church with a unique opportunity for the different Christian traditions to recognise and accept one another, not minimizing their differences, but beginning the task of mutual understanding and the relinquishing of prejudice. Here East can meet West.

More poignantly still, here in a special way Jew can meet Gentile. This ancient division between Jew and Gentile, felt so keenly in the generations before the coming of Jesus and never subsequently healed, is, of course, heightened in Jerusalem today through contemporary politics into a tension between Israeli and Palestinian. The lines are hard-drawn between them. Yet for many this situation presents an exciting challenge to the power of the Gospel. With the emergence of Messianic congregations (where Christians from Jewish background can still endorse their Jewish roots and not find them dismissed in a predominantly Gentile culture) a situation pertains once again which is in some ways evocative of the New Testament era. Given the present political realities, it is by no means easy for Jewish and Arab Christians to worship together;[17] yet Paul's vision in Ephesians 2 (based itself on a reflection concerning the Temple in Jerusalem and how Gentiles were not to trespass beyond the 'Court of the Gentiles' through the dividing wall) remains a powerful focus for Christian prayer in Jerusalem:

Christ himself is our peace, who has made the two one and has destroyed the barrier, the dividing wall of hostility. . .His purpose was to create in himself one new man out of the two, thus making peace, and in this one body to reconcile both of them to God through the cross, by which he put to death their hostility. . .Through the Gospel the Gentiles are heirs together with Israel, members together in the promise in Christ Jesus (Eph. 2:14-16; 3:6).

---

[17] At the 'Baptist village' (Petah Tikva), for example, there were occasional conferences for both Jewish and Arab believers before the *Intifada*, but not since.

An organisation called 'Musalaha' has recently been formed to help implement this Pauline vision and to enable Jewish and Arab Christians to meet together.[18] To those who have this heart for reconciliation, Jerusalem can therefore come to be seen as the key to unity—the place where God will at last heal this ancient division between Jew and Gentile, with potentially dramatic results not only for the Holy Land, but also for the rest of Christendom.

Yet obviously it is far from easy. This is not simply because of the many hurts inflicted between Israelis and Palestinians to which Christians themselves are far from immune and which need to be overcome for meaningful fellowship; there is also inevitably the fact that such *rapprochements* would easily be misconstrued politically by their fellow nationals on either side. For Jewish-Christians this is compounded by their awareness that, in the eyes of their fellow Israelis, the Church is inherently Gentile and 'conversion' is seen as tantamount to a denial of one's jewishness. They are therefore eager not to give the wrong impression or to be over-compromising in a Gentile direction.[19] Meanwhile, Arab Christians are naturally sensitive to the fears of Muslim Palestinians that Arab Christians are tacitly on the side of Israel. Yet the Pauline vision of a true 'unity in Christ', transcending ethnic divisions, abides as a lasting vision for Jerusalem: could this not be God's deepest desire for Jerusalem—that those who know him through his Son should reveal to the watching and waiting world that unity and peace which 'the world cannot give' (John 14:27) but which comes alone through Christ?

Yet Christians remain a tiny minority. For the above vision to become reality, Christians would need to work hard not only at the task of increased unity amongst themselves, but presumably at the even harder task of outreach to others. It is at this point, faced with the enormity of the Jewish and Muslim majorities on either side, that some Christians are naturally tempted to opt for a seemingly more feasible vision for

---

[18] This organisation was founded by one of the conference speakers, Salim J. Munayer, a lecturer at Bethlehem Bible College. 'Musalaha' is an Arabic word which stands for 'forgiveness and reconciliation'.
[19] This is seen, of course, even more clearly in the response of Messianic believers to the 'institutional' churches in Jerusalem.

Jerusalem: the unity that is God's will must instead be seen as residing, not among Christians alone, but among all the faiths represented in Jerusalem; in particular, Jerusalem has the unique opportunity of showing to the world how the three great monotheistic faiths (Judaism, Christianity and Islam) can co-exist peaceably alongside one another.

Such a vision of inter-faith unity again might entail different things to different people. Most Christians perhaps would endorse this at a political and social level, asserting that political or social discrimination between people on religious grounds is incompatible with the Christian revelation. They would thus advocate Jerusalem being recognised as the 'spiritual capital' of all the three religions, perhaps suggesting as a political consequence that the city should be given a special, 'international' status. The Catholic Patriarchs of the Eastern Churches, for example, pronounced in 1991:

> We must develop an original formula which allows every believer—Christian, Jew, and Muslim—to feel at home in this Holy City on the same and equal rights with the others without distinction, without predominance of one party above the others. In that way, this Holy City, instead of being the city of conflict, of division, of dispute and inter-religious fighting, can be the city of peace, of meeting, of brotherhood for all her inhabitants and a sign of hope for the whole world.[20]

Many would endorse this as a practical vision but would question whether this could be accepted as a strictly theological vision: for, if freedom of religion needs to be preserved in this way as a practical principle, this should in no way detract from the theological conviction that Christ alone is the 'Way, Truth and Life' (John 14:6), and that God's purpose therefore remains to bring people to a recognition of his Son and to 'bring all things. . .under one head, even Christ' (Eph. 1:10). Others would reject this 'theological particularism' and argue that this unifying vision of Jerusalem needs to be based on a genuinely

---

[20] Cited by Archbishop Dr Lutfi Laham (Greek Catholic Church in Jerusalem) in his letter *Jerusalem—the Holy City* (7 Nov. 1991). He argues there that, because Jerusalem is holy to all three religions, no exclusive sovereign control should be exercised over Jerusalem: 'I call upon them not to debase this holy city, making of it a political capital like all the capitals of the earth. Believers of the world, save Jerusalem, make of it the city of the Spirit'.

theological universalism of some kind, whereby Jerusalem would reveal how all faiths indeed can be seen to lead in their own way to God.[21]

This latter vision is naturally tempting for those confronted with the exceptional stresses of the Jerusalem situation, yet one wonders if it can genuinely claim to be an orthodox Christian option. As with Christian Zionism, there is the sense that such a route collapses too easily the necessary tension that Christians inevitably must experience of accepting Christ's unique claims upon their own lives, yet finding those claims ignored or dismissed by the majority. The apostle Paul, for example, knowing that people could be 'zealous for God' but that their zeal was not 'based on knowledge' of Christ (Rom. 10:2), experienced 'unceasing anguish' in his heart for his fellow Jews (Rom. 9:2), and asserted that God 'desired all men to be saved' (1 Tim. 2:4). Are we seeking to avoid this pain? Is this not what all Christians are called to, not least those who live in Jerusalem? Was not Paul's anguish a precious gift from God, reflecting the pain in the very Father-heart of God caused by the unbelief of mankind and the suffering of his people?

If so, then perhaps our vision of Jerusalem should be informed again, and in yet deeper ways, by the example of Jesus who revealed this divine anguish so clearly as he came in sight of the Jerusalem of his day:

As he approached Jerusalem and saw the city, he wept over it and said: 'If you, even you, had only known on this day what would bring you peace—but now it is hidden from your eyes. The days will come when your enemies. . .will not leave one stone on another, because you did not recognise the time of God's coming to you' (Luke 19:41-44).

Christ's own vision of the Jewish Jerusalem of his day, must still be in some way foundational for any Christian vision of Jerusalem, albeit two thousand years later. Whatever be made

---

[21]Space forbids a full discussion of this important, contemporary issue concerning inter-faith dialogue and worship: for a defence of 'particularism', see *One God, One Lord: Christianity in a World of Religious Pluralism*, edd., A.D. Clarke and B.W. Winter (Grand Rapids, Baker; Carlisle, Paternoster 1992, 2nd ed.); see also the Anglican discussions in G. Carey, *The Gate of Glory* (London, Hodder & Stoughton, revd. ed., 1992) ch. 13.

of those more positive approaches to the city (represented by those who focus on Christ's incarnation, the city's restoration, or its potential for unity) this theme of anguish must remain: Jerusalem had been the place of the divine 'name', the 'city of God', but it was ignorant of God's coming and ultimately rejected him. In what ways and for what reasons, we may ask, would Christ's attitude to the city be different now?

IV. The Book of Acts: an Apostolic Precedent

The Book of Acts is not an easy work to apply to any contemporary situation. Its capacity to give us genuine guidelines for the Church's task today would be questioned by many: dispensationalists, for example, would not see it as normative for the Church in the post-apostolic period, whilst recent critical scholarship would raise questions as to its historical reliability or its theological relevance; its theology to many would appear either 'primitive' or else highly 'revisionist', presenting a Utopian ideal never realised in practice. These important and legitimate questions cannot be discussed here, though some of them will be treated in the sequel to this volume.[22]

It is probably for these reasons that the Book of Acts seems seldom to be given a 'high profile' by Christians in Jerusalem today. Even so, with its description of the life and witness of the Early Church in Jerusalem, it remains a biblical text which is far from irrelevant for the modern Church in Jerusalem as it seeks to continue the Christian witness in that same city. Indeed, its very 'simplicity' and straightforwardness may be instead the source of its power and relevance, as it challenges the Christian Church, in Jerusalem as anywhere else, to a renewed conviction of the essence of the Christian Gospel. A brief overview of the themes of its early chapters (especially chs. 1-4) would therefore be appropriate as we conclude this enquiry into the various biblical texts which may inspire the theological vision of the Church in Jerusalem today.

In doing so, one is only too well aware that the atmosphere today in Jerusalem is indeed highly charged and the situation indeed far more complex than that which we

---

[22]See the sequel to this volume: *The Book of Acts in its First-century Setting* (Grand Rapids, Eerdmans; Carlisle, Paternoster, 1993).

encounter in Luke's presentation of the first century; moreover, the pressures brought to bear upon the Church today are enormous and the future always uncertain. Nevertheless, the example of the apostles as recounted in these chapters may serve as a timely reminder of the apostolic message and come as an incentive to a renewed faith in God's power made available in difficult circumstances. Some might wish to go further and suggest that these early chapters in Acts are the place where one can see most clearly the purposes of the risen and exalted Christ for Jerusalem and his Church in that city.

Three themes of particular relevance to our present concerns can be detected within these chapters.

1) Jesus the Messiah—rejected but raised

It need scarcely be said, but a reading of Acts 1-4 alerts one afresh to the centrality of Jesus' Resurrection; this is the message with which these chapters throb. The message about Jesus' life is not forgotten (1:22; 2:22), but the whole significance of that important episode now comes into focus because of this startling and frankly unexpected reality: the Jesus who was crucified and laid in a tomb is no longer dead, but 'God raised him up, having loosed the pangs of death' (2:24). This theme becomes the unmoveable centre of Peter's preaching and the unshakable foundation of his new boldness. Although we are familiar with this, Peter's example challenges us immediately to ask ourselves: is the Resurrection of Jesus a central theme in our Church life, do we sufficiently proclaim with real faith the reality of the Risen Christ, and could it be that our lack of boldness so often in the Christian enterprise stems from a failure truly to take this message to heart?

Yet Peter's courage is seen in a deeper way. For this was no simple and comforting message of 'new life', or of God's ability to bring good out of evil conforming to a pattern in our lives of resurrection through death, true though these thoughts be. What was it that 'cut his hearers to the heart' (2:37)? Partly, no doubt, it was because Peter spoke unashamedly of a brute historical fact;[23] yet more than that, it was because he consistently pointed out that this was the very same

---

[23] Note Peter's implicit challenge to his audience to investigate the tomb for themselves (2:29).

Jesus whom they (or their contemporaries) had effectively rejected and caused to be crucified:

this Jesus. . .*you crucified* and killed by the hands of lawless men' (2:23); let all the house of Israel therefore know assuredly that God has made him both Lord and Christ, this Jesus whom *you crucified* (2:36).

The essence of Peter's message can then be found in three important verses of his speech before the Jewish authorities, as recounted in ch. 4:

Be it known to you all, and to all the people of Israel, that by the name of Jesus Christ of Nazareth, *whom you crucified, whom God raised from the dead*, by him this man is standing before you well. This is the stone which was *rejected* by you builders, but which has become the head of the corner. And there is salvation in no one else, for there is no other name under heaven given among men by which we must be saved (4:10-12).

The power of Peter's message is therefore seen not simply in his proclamation of a historical Resurrection (remarkable in itself), but in his declaration that the One whom God had chosen to raise from the dead was the One whom mankind had, by contrast, chosen to reject. Drawing on imagery from the Psalms that Jesus had used of himself causing similar offence (Psa. 118:22-23, in Mark 12:10-11), Peter dared to speak of Jesus as the 'stone rejected by men but in God's sight chosen and precious' (his wording later in 1 Pet. 2:4).

The Resurrection is therefore the divine vindication of Jesus and all that he stood for, but it is also (and herein lies the rub) a declaration of God's divine opposition to all who are opposed to Jesus. God declares himself, in the Resurrection of Jesus, to be totally behind Jesus, fully endorsing his claims, and challenges people henceforth to be sure that they too side with Jesus as their 'Lord and Messiah'. This message challenges people in every age to consider as the most important issue of all: in God's sight, would I be considered amongst those who have accepted Jesus, or amongst those who have rejected him?

The simplicity of Peter's message is indeed alarming. Yet it is a straightforward challenge, rooted in the essence of the Christian Gospel and evident in its first proclamation, which we must respond to with honesty. A true embracing of this challenge would rekindle and inspire the mission of the Church in many places, yet it has particular repercussions in

Jerusalem today. For it alerts the Church which bears Christ's name in that place to the fact that this awesome challenge is an integral part of its essential message. The glories of the Resurrection cannot be celebrated in that city without an acceptance of its obvious consequences; the 'comforting' corollaries of the Resurrection cannot be highlighted to the exclusion of those which are more challenging and 'confronting'. In Jerusalem, as anywhere else, many deny Jesus as the Messiah, many deny him as the Son of God, but the Resurrection declares that, notwithstanding such opinions, this Jesus, though rejected by men, has indeed been vindicated by God as both 'Lord and Messiah' (2:36). The Resurrection is a declaration in advance of the pattern of God's future judgement, but in the mercy of God opportunity is given to 'repent' (2:38). People in Jerusalem, then and now, together with people 'from every nation under heaven' (2:5) are invited to 'change sides' and to give their allegiance to Christ.

Peter's message is indeed a challenge to all. In today's Jerusalem, of course, with its Jewish and Muslim majorities, it would be particularly significant in its consequences. His uncompromising statement that 'there is salvation in no one else' (4:12) might, being but a single verse, be deemed by many as an insufficient authority for the necessity of evangelism to all; yet, seen in the light of the Resurrection of Jesus, the rejected but raised Messiah, it has a logic and power of its own. Christ's charge to his disciples was that they were to be his witnesses 'in Jerusalem...and to the ends of the earth' (1:8), a commission which, despite their small numbers, they set about obeying without drawing up a list of exceptions.

Above all, any application of Peter's theology in Jerusalem today would need special care in view of the fact that Christians rightly wish to step back from the anti-Semitic charge made in times past that the Jewish people are to be seen as Christ's crucifiers. However, it has been argued above that a careful and proper reading of the New Testament 'cuts off at the root' such anti-Semitism.[24] Moreover, as just noted, Peter's own language subsequently of Christ being 'rejected' ὑπὸ ἀνθρώπων (1 Pet. 2:4) would seem to suggest that already at that time it was understood that Christ was 'rejected' not simply by those who happened to play a part in the events

---

[24] Above, pp. 74f.

leading to his crucifixion, but also by all those who subsequently had heard the message of Christ but not responded to it. The message about Christ being rejected can therefore legitimately be 'universalized' and applied to us all; Christ was rejected 'by mankind'. No particular stigma attaches to the Jewish people; the charge stands against us all.

Moreover, there might be some validity in seeing this message of Jesus 'rejected but raised' as having important consequences for Jerusalem itself as a city. For as hinted at previously, the fact that Christ's crucifixion and Resurrection occurred just outside the city of Jerusalem does not necessarily redound to Jerusalem's glory.[25] On the contrary, God's vindication of Jesus is seen to be a deliberate divine reversal of Jerusalem's treatment of Jesus. As such the Resurrection could then be interpreted as a declaration of God's judgement upon Jerusalem, a judgement which then was realised in AD 70.[26] Again this would suggest that the positive connotations of the Resurrection for Jerusalem cannot be accepted without the negative ones as well.

Yet is this message in the early chapters of Acts simply one of challenge to the Christian Church? No, the message of Jesus, the Messiah rejected but raised, also includes great encouragement. For it holds forth the promise to those who currently are being mistreated and marginalised because of their commitment to Christ, who perhaps feel that they are being 'rejected' as was Christ himself, that they are yet on the 'resurrection' side. As Paul said in a different context, 'if we are united with him in a death like his, we shall certainly be united with him in a resurrection like his' (Rom. 6:5). The Christian Church can so easily be discouraged, and the prevailing pressures in today's Jerusalem would often make understandable any such feelings amongst its members. In this situation the message of Jesus' Resurrection brings new hope and indeed, as for Peter, a new courage to 'take the side of Christ' in witness and service. The daunting challenge of Christ's commission to be his 'witnesses in Jerusalem' remains unaltered, but the confidence in God's resurrection power is given to sustain.

---

[25] Above, p. 86.
[26] For the suggestion of such a connection, see above pp. 63-4.

2) The Holy Spirit: source of power and unity

Christ's commission was given not just with Resurrection-hope, but also with the promise of the Holy Spirit: 'you will receive power when the Holy Spirit comes on you' (Acts 1:8). As for all Christians, it may be that the experience of this divine power is in some way proportionate to the preparedness to step out as Christ's witnesses: no witness, no power.

In the Jerusalem context of today, however, it should be noted that the power of the Holy Spirit is given, not simply for the important task of witness (already sufficiently stressed above), but also as that power which can bring unity in the face of deep diversity.

Since the Gospel is for all people without exception, its challenge must be taken to those living in both 'Judaea and Samaria' (1:8), to those who at that time were divided between themselves by deep racial enmity, something still experienced in the Holy Land today between Jews and Arabs. Yet, once the Gospel is received, how can such enmities be laid aside? The answer is given in the event of Pentecost, an event which reveals the power of the Holy Spirit to overcome the ethnic divisions between people and nations.[27] A new unity, indeed a new humanity, was now possible through the reconciling work of Christ on the Cross and the indwelling power of the Spirit.

In much of our earlier discussion, the theme had emerged of the Jerusalem Church having a special opportunity to reveal again the unity of Christ's Church. Here in the first pages of Acts there is a reminder that such unity is the gift of the Holy Spirit, and can only come about as people are open to his working. Just as those first Christians 'waited' for this gift and 'devoted themselves to prayer' (1:4, 14), so too now it is appropriate, even though we live in the Age when the Spirit has been given, for us all, and especially when in Jerusalem, to pray earnestly for this gift, without which all attempts at

---

[27] Some would interpret Acts 2 as a theological reversal of the breakdown of human communication symbolised in the tower of Babel (Gen. 11:1-9). Yet, even if this was not in Luke's mind, the incentive towards unity is seen in Acts, not only in the 'shared life' of the believers (2:44ff.) but also in the importance attached to the apostolic 'council' called to overcome the emerging disunity between Jewish and Gentile Christians (15:1-35).

Christian unity or witness will be impaired. A divided world needs so much to experience this unifying gift of God's Spirit.

3) Jerusalem: source of the Gospel, scene of opposition

Finally, the Book of Acts (despite its being criticized for its idealism) forbids us to look at Jerusalem idealistically. Jerusalem, for all it physical beauties and historical uniqueness, for all the biblical events with which it is associated, is seen in these pages to be a place where the Good News of Christ is met with unveiled opposition.

Christ's experience of being 'rejected' is matched too by his disciples. For all their experience of the Resurrection, they know too the pain of the Cross. For all the powerful blessings of Pentecost, the Church is thereafter prone to persecution and partial exile. Though it was surely necessary for the Gospel of Christ to be first proclaimed in this city (ensuring that the Christian Church could see itself as 'authentic Judaism' and not inherently 'marginal' or sectarian from the beginning),[28] the message of Acts as a whole is that the dynamism of the Church soon was relocated to other places. Somehow, despite its being the 'city of the Resurrection' and the scene of Pentecost, the Christian Church was evidently going to find it a difficult place in which to survive.[29]

Such a description of the early Church in Jerusalem, of course, need not be prescriptive for all time to come. Yet it does cause us to face reality. It may encourage some to consider whether the place where Jesus was 'rejected' will ever substantially 'change its colours'. Others might deduce in similar vein that perhaps in Jerusalem the Church will ever have this painful experience of sharing in a special sense in the sufferings of Christ, a thought which ought to move all to a greater solidarity with those Christians who are called to live in the complexities of modern-day Jerusalem. Above all it should remove some of the unwarranted idealism concerning

---

[28] See *e.g.* F.F. Bruce, 'Paul and Jerusalem', *Tyndale Bulletin* 19 (1968) 3-25.

[29] A reflection on the history of the Church in Jerusalem throughout the first century prompted John Wilkinson to conclude in *Jerusalem as Jesus knew it* (London, 1978) 176: the story of 'Christianity in Jerusalem makes depressing reading'; how could it be that 'in Jerusalem of all places in the world, Christianity could be so small and weak?'; see also my *HPHC*, 9.

Jerusalem. Jerusalem is a city, faced with all the issues faced by other cities and many more peculiar to itself, and the Church which witnesses there will inevitably be caught up in those issues. The Church's task in Jerusalem will always be complex.

This brief review of Acts 1-4 has provided a useful insight into the Church's difficult task of following Christ in this city. The themes of witness, unity and suffering emerge most strongly. How these then inter-relate with the 'theological visions' of Jerusalem (outlined in III) is more complex: the vision of Christian unity is encouraged, but not that interfaith unity which denies the uniqueness of Christ; the vision of the incarnation's significance is confirmed in a qualified way, inasmuch as the Church must continue in the steps of her Master, but it is seen that this is inextricably entwined with the themes of bold witness and patient suffering.

As for the irreconcilable visions of the supersessionist and the restorationist, the evidence in these early chapters of Acts supports neither view conclusively: the apostles were working within an eschatological framework, being encouraged to expect the return of Christ from heaven (1:11) and evidently seeing themselves as living in the 'last days' prophesied by Joel (Joel 2:28 in Acts 2:17). Such language of the 'last days' occurs throughout the New Testament (*e.g.* 1 Tim. 4:1, 2 Tim. 3:1 etc.) and is understood by many to reflect the conviction that all the Christian dispensation subsequent to Christ is to be deemed as the 'last days'.[30] Questions would then be raised of eschatological frameworks which suggest that particular events in and around Jerusalem today might be associated with the 'last days' in some other sense.

On the other hand, Peter speaks in Acts 3:21 of Christ remaining in heaven 'until the time for establishing all that God spoke by the mouth of his holy prophets from of old'. Are the contemporary events in Jerusalem the fulfillment of those ancient prophecies, a harbinger of Christ's return, or does the New Testament teach (as argued above in ch. 3) that the prophecies concerning Jerusalem and the Land have now been fulfilled in the coming of Jesus?

Any conclusion would depend on an interpretation of that crucial passage in Acts 1:6 (already discussed twice) when the disciples ask Jesus, 'Will you at this time restore the

---

[30] See O. Cullmann, *Christ and Time* (London, 1951).

kingdom to Israel?' and Jesus replies enigmatically, 'It is not for you to know times or seasons'. Does Jesus' reply indicate a forward reference to our own twentieth century, or does his immediate commissioning of the disciples 'to the end of the earth' suggest instead a radical revision of their understanding of 'restoration', with Israel being 'restored' precisely when at last it serves the function of being a 'light to the world' and a 'blessing to all nations'?[31]

V. Conclusions

The above chapters indicate the divergent views that exist concerning Jerusalem, its Christian significance and the appropriate mission of the Church in Jerusalem.

On this latter issue the different approaches can be reduced in essence to two. On the one hand, there is the *evangelistic* approach, drawn from a consideration of such biblical material as we have considered in Acts; this needs to be understood in quite a broad sense as the approach which is concerned that the *evangel* of Christ be central to the Church's purpose and that, where possible, it should be proclaimed with a view that people should come to faith in him and be incorporated into the Christian community. On the other hand, there are those approaches which focus more on *identification*, believing the Church's witness is best implemented by showing solidarity with those outside the Christian community.

At first glance, given the complexities and sensitivities of the Jerusalem situation, the identification model would appear to be the preferred option. Yet, paradoxically, it is precisely the presence of the Jewish and Muslim majorities in the city which reveals an apparent weakness in this approach; for, pushed to extremes, it can lead to mutually conflicting results. On the Arab side, Christian identification may find expression, not only in appropriate social concern, but also at the present time in the Christian conviction, shared with Palestinian Muslims, of the need to speak out politically and to work for justice for those in the region deemed to be 'under occupation'. On the Israeli side, by contrast, a commitment to Christian identification would result in the stance of those Christian Zionists who show essential solidarity with the

---

[31] On this passage, see above pp. 12 and 68.

Jewish people and the political state of Israel. In other words, an over-identification with either side can lead to the Christian community being politically both for and against the State of Israel at one and the same time. While this may give the Church a unique opportunity to act as a 'bridge-builder' and an agent of peace and reconciliation, the Church can find itself over-stretched with its members upholding mutually contradictory viewpoints.

In seeking theological legitimation for their respective commitments to identification, those on the Arab side appeal to the Incarnation for their method and the *ethics* of the Old Testament for their message, whilst those on the Israeli side appeal to an eschatological theology of restoration and an outworking of Old Testament *prophecy*. Appeal is made to the same Bible, but irreconcilable convictions are the apparent result. Many pro-Palestinian Christians see themselves as having almost nothing in common with pro-Israeli Christian Zionists, yet strangely their viewpoints stem from a similar source, namely this principle of identification. The same can be said for those who, with a liberal theological basis, work for inter-faith unity: despite wishing it otherwise, their views turn out to have some unexpected parallels with Christian Zionism.

Seen in this light, the evangelistic approach offers a healthy corrective, re-alerting the Church to its primary function of proclaiming a spiritual message and not simply following a political programme.[32] It acts as a reminder that the principle of identification can be taken too far, and that it is in Christ alone that ultimate spiritual unity will be found. Such an emphasis does not dismiss the value of the practical need for incarnational and supportive identification with those to whom the Church ministers; for in Jerusalem, for many historical reasons, there is an inescapable need to heal the hurts of the past, to disavow the stereotypes of the Church which have inflicted injury in time gone by, and to show in loving deed the truth and love of Christ. The visions of sensitive evangelism and loving identification are therefore not incompatible but complementary. Problems only emerge

---

[32] The former Dean of St George's, Jerusalem, has expressed elsewhere the pressing need for Christians in Jerusalem to emphasize again the refreshing themes of 'grace and forgiveness', not simply 'peace and justice' (*Yes*, CMS, 1992).

when identification ceases to be means to an end, and becomes an end in itself. As a result, the prayer of the first disciples, when facing opposition in Jerusalem to their message, might be re-echoed for Jerusalem Christians today: 'Grant to your servants to speak your word with boldness' (Acts 4:29).

This evangelistic emphasis seeks to preserve the distinctiveness of the Christian message. The contemporary climate is one in which in many quarters Christians are tempted to believe, paradoxically, that it is distinctively Christian to surrender that which is distinctively Christian. St Paul indeed spoke of the need to be 'all things to all men', but his stated purpose was 'to save some' (1 Cor. 9.22). In concluding the conference, it was observed that in our deliberations we had perhaps allowed ourselves to lose the necessary focus on Christ himself, crucified but risen, and that this needed to be preserved as the centre of the essential Christian message— yes, even in Jerusalem. Unavoidably the Cross and Resurrection are distinctive and therefore potentially divisive, but without them there is a danger not only that the Church's message and activities become too closely identified with a sub-Christian agenda, but also that we lose the very source of unity and reconciliation which alone they can bring.

Pray for the peace of Jerusalem!

EPILOGUE

Colin Chapman

The writer of this Epilogue has the advantage over most of the contributors of having watched (on television) the signing of the Peace Agreement between Israel and the PLO (on September 13th, 1993) and the transfer of power to Palestinians in Jericho on May 12th and in Gaza on May 18th, 1994.

At this moment in time, there is still a certain sense of exhilaration and anticipation in some circles, although it is impossible to share the easy optimism of those who seem to think that the end of the conflict is in sight. On the other hand, it may be wise to resist the temptation to complete cynicism and despair, for the agreement does indeed represent such a remarkable breakthrough. It can scarcely be compared to the breaking down of the Berlin Wall or the holding of the first democratic elections in South Africa. Yet limited and fragile as it is, it represents an incredible paradigm shift on the part of modern Israelis and Palestinians, and offers the only possible hope for some kind of peaceful resolution.

It is not appropriate for a mere spectator to try to tell the two sides how to put their houses in order and how to face their partners across the negotiating table. But a postscript to these eight essays can at least attempt to tie together some of the loose ends and highlight some of the questions which must remain on the agenda for those who are concerned for Jerusalem—not only for its 'past and present', but also for its future.

1. What is actually happening in Jerusalem today?

If this seems an unnecessarily provocative question with which to begin, Peter Walker's study of Christian attitudes to Jerusalem in the fourth century provides a strong argument for beginning with the present context: 'Theological thinking can rarely, if ever, be done in a vacuum; a theologian's context invariably results in certain theological thrusts receiving greater emphasis than others' (p. 87). 'In our own day, we must ask, what are the chief influences upon us from our own circumstances?' (p. 90).

Na'im Ateek sees evidence of a deliberate Israeli government policy of 'judaizing' Jerusalem through building settlements, purchasing Palestinian property in the Old City and through other activities designed 'to create new facts on the ground' (p. 147, 152). If this is indeed what is happening in and around Jerusalem, it is easy to understand why the Palestinians are so afraid that by the time the Israelis *are* willing to discuss the future of Jerusalem, even more new facts will have been created to strengthen their hold on the city. While the scholars continue to reflect and debate, the politicians, it seems, simply get on with the task of appropriating land, planting trees and making new roads.

In this situation one longs to hear the voices of contemporary Elijahs pointing the prophetic finger at the Ahabs who may be stealing much more than the equivalent of Naboth's vineyard. Perhaps, therefore, it will be the journalists, the television crews and the human rights groups who will have a more vital role in unmasking what is actually happening under our noses than the theologians and historians.

2. Is there any future for Christianity in Jerusalem?

Peter Walker has drawn attention to the very real fear in the minds of many that there may not be a Christian community worth speaking of in Jerusalem by the year 2000 AD. Even if the stones of the Holy Sepulchre and other sites in Jerusalem are still there for the constant stream of tourists and pilgrims, there may not be many 'living stones' with whom visiting Christians can worship and pray.

If Palestinian Christians are to resist the temptation to emigrate to Europe, North America or Australia, they will need urgent help with housing, education and employment. They will need to be assured by fellow Palestinians that if ever a Palestinian state comes into being, it will not be a state based exclusively on a religious creed (namely Islam), thereby mirroring the Israeli state (based on Judaism) and causing them to become second-class citizens.

But who is going to speak for the Christian communities? Can they draw closer together in order to speak with one voice? Does the recent Vatican recognition of Israel (December 1993) suggest that the Vatican would now like to be in a position to speak for all Christians in Palestine? And how can Christians round the world say something and actually do something on behalf of the Palestinian churches?

Meanwhile there is equally great pressure (though of a completely different kind) upon the various Jewish Christian congregations. Although they make up a tiny fraction of the Christian population in and around Jerusalem, they sometimes receive a greater support from the Western Church. Yet they have dilemmas as to how to relate to their Jewish roots and to their Jewish neighbours. The recent episodes in which Jewish people known to be Messianic believers have been debarred from taking up residence in Israel is but one expression of the way government authorities view their presence in the country.

Once again we are dealing here with vital questions that arises out of the present context. Perhaps we scholars are wasting our time if our writings do not contribute to changes of attitude and practical strategies to ensure that Christian communities remain rooted in and around Jerusalem.

3. How should Christians think about Jerusalem today?

If Christians are to formulate a 'theology of Jerusalem' that is appropriate for the present situation they will need both to reflect on the strengths and weaknesses of previous theologies of Jerusalem (discussed in chapter 4) and also to wrestle with the contemporary questions explained so fully in chapter 8.

Any theology put forward as a result of this reflection will have to satisfy the following criteria:

1) It will have to take seriously the political issues concerning the status of Jerusalem. Political problems require political solutions, and any solutions will have to be both realistic and impartial.

2) While recognising whatever common ground there is between Jews, Christians and Muslims, it must point to a vision of Jerusalem which is distinctively Christian, but which refuses to make exclusive and possessive claims to the city.

3) It must be able to give indigenous Christians good reasons for wanting to stay rooted where they are—inspite of all the problems they face.

4) It must explain why the city of Jerusalem continues to have a significance to Christians all over the world, and why they want to be assured of continuing access to its 'holy places'.

If Christians today cannot come forward with a clear vision, and if they suggest that Jerusalem has *no* special significance for Christians and for Christianity, they will appear to have nothing to offer as an alternative to the more absolutist claims of Jews and Muslims.

4. Can Jerusalem be shared by two peoples and by three faiths?

Margaret Brearley and Baruch Maoz have explained what Jerusalem has meant within Judaism through the centuries, and Na'im Ateek has similarly explained the special place of Jerusalem in Islam. This background is vital if we are to understand the special reasons why Jews and Muslims feel it is so vital that they have political control of the city today. Christians have long since recognised that the Crusades ruled out the exclusive political claims of Christians on the city once and for all. Fortunately that particular brand of Christian Zionism is totally dead.

The vital question that remains, therefore, is whether Israeli Jews and Muslim Palestinians will continue to put forward claims which demand exclusive sovereignty. Maoz says that 'Jewish Christians hope that the city will remain in Jewish hands' (p. 176). But he recognises the need for compromise on *both* sides when he goes on to say: 'none of the protagonists involved can expect their absolute claims to be fulfilled without inflicting injustice on the other. Some kind of compromise must be reached' (p. 177; *cf.* also p. 182). One hopes that more Jews and Muslims of all persuasions will admit publicly the need for compromise and accommodation, and recognise what Ateek sees as the 'innate inclusivity' of Jerusalem (p. 147).

Jerusalem would then have, in Peter Walker's words, 'the unique opportunity of showing to the world how the three great monotheistic faiths (Judaism, Christianity and Islam) can co-exist peaceably alongside one another' (p. 200). If Jews believe that the Land ultimately belongs to Yahweh (Lev. 25:23), if Muslims believe that 'sovereignty belongs to God' (Qur'an, 64.1; *cf.* 3.26, 22.56) and if Christians (whether Arab or Jewish) believe that the kingdom of God which began to come in Jesus is no longer associated with any one land or with any one people (Acts 1:6-8), the theologians of all three faiths must surely be willing to give the politicians the freedom to work out practical options. It can hardly be beyond the wit of human kind

CHAPMAN: Epilogue

to work out some political formula for Jerusalem which (a) refuses to allow to any one faith or any one people exclusive and absolute rights over the city, (b) encourages each party to respect the claims and theologies of the other parties, and (c) allows free access to people of all races and faiths to the places they regard as 'holy'.

5. Is the polarisation between Zionists and non-Zionists inevitable?

The Zionist case has been powerfully expressed in the papers by Margaret Brearley and Baruch Maoz. But, as Brearley points out, 'the contrary view appears to predominate' (p. 120). Does this reflect the prejudices of the editor and the organisers of the different conferences? Or does it suggest that the weight of evangelical scholarship today (at least in the UK) tends to support the non-Zionist position?

If Christian Zionists are to come forward with the 'detailed exposition of the biblical and the logical basis for Christian Zionism' for which Brearley pleads, they cannot afford simply to rehearse well-tried arguments, but will have to engage with the biblical case presented here by Chris Wright, Gordon McConville and Tom Wright. Is it too much to hope that a sharpening of the agenda through reflection on the urgent current concerns in Jerusalem will move the discussion away from abstract debate between different schools of eschatology and reveal unexpected areas of convergence? Or are the Zionist and non-Zionist positions doomed to move further and further apart, each labelling the other as heretical?

6. Where is the witness to Jesus in Christian concern for Jerusalem?

All the writers have been wrestling with the question of how we are to show our 'natural concern for the city in a way that is truly Christian' (p. 97). But where is the distinctive witness to *Jesus* in the way Christians show their concern for this city?

Attention was drawn in two of the chapters (3 and 8) to the fact that it is what Jesus of Nazareth says about Jerusalem, and what happened to him in that city that needs to determine Christian attitudes: 'Christ's own vision of the Jewish Jerusalem of his day must still be in some way foundational for any Christian vision of Jerusalem, albeit two thousand years later'

(Walker, p. 201). This focus on Jesus will not, unfortunately, be welcomed by all, for 'unavoidably the Cross and Resurrection are distinctive and therefore potentially divisive' (p. 212). Yet the Cross and Resurrection must be central for they are the basis for the distinctively Christian themes of forgiveness in the midst of suffering, and of new life emerging in the midst of death; they are the ultimate basis for the hope that good will triumph over evil.

Christians can hardly claim any monopoly in calling for 'peace with justice'. Yet they may have a distinctive contribution to make if they are able to follow the example of Jesus in renouncing hatred and revenge and seeking forgiveness and reconciliation. A tantalisingly brief footnote (p. 211) hints that the call for 'grace and forgiveness' could be one special contribution from Christians to the task of peace-making. The person whose comment is quoted, Peter Crooks (the former Dean of St George's Cathedral in Jerusalem) has spoken with great feeling of the visit of Desmond Tutu to Jerusalem in December 1991 and of the incomprehension on the faces of his Jewish listeners when he spoke of ways in which he and others had responded to abuse and violence during the years of apartheid. If Christians have made such a significant contribution to the recent breakthrough in South Africa, could they, even as a tiny minority, make a similar contribution in the equally intractable conflict in Israel/Palestine?

Tom Wright sees some of the potential for a genuinely Christian witness in this context when he writes: 'It might be a sign that the Easter which is celebrated in the church of the Holy Sepulchre is also good news for those who wait at the foot of the Western wall, and for that matter those, too, who worship on its Eastern side' (p. 77).

7. How are we to pray for Jerusalem?

Perhaps the way Christians *pray* for Jerusalem and its peoples (plural) will at the end of the day be the most searching test of the way they think about Jerusalem. Will their prayers 'for the peace of Jerusalem' (Ps. 122:6) include a passionate plea for justice for *all* the communities living in and around Jerusalem, including those *other* parties for which they have little natural sympathy? Will they pray for the survival of a living Christian community in the city, and even perhaps dare to pray for this community to grow? Are they able to echo Paul's prayer for all people and especially for the Jewish people 'that they may be saved' (Rom. 10:1), and to join in with his exuberant doxology over 'the wisdom and knowledge of God' (Rom. 11:33)?

The stakes at the moment are very, very high. We can all only hope and pray that an awareness of the very unique opportunities and dangers that face Jerusalem at the present time will enable Jews and Arabs, Christians and Muslims and all the watching world to recognise 'the things that make for peace'—and to do so *before* we have to be told, 'but now they are hid from your eyes' (Lk. 19:42).

INDEX OF AUTHORS

Amos, C.	185	Dronke, P.	106
Anderson, G.W.	25	Dubois, M.	120
Anderson, J.	112	Dumbrell, W.J.	49
Ateek, N.	133, 150, 165	Dunn, J.D.G.	8, 11, 14, 18,
Atiyah, E.	99	Duvernoy, C.	108, 112, 120
Avi-Yonah, M.	88	Eckardt, A. & R.	113, 120
Avineri, S.	114	Efrati, N.	102, 105-6, 113, 116
Bahat, D.	22	Epp, F.	146
Baker, W.W.	132	Epstein, I.	104
Bamberger, B.	115	Farmer, W.R.	60
Barker, M.	71	Ferrar, W.J.	83
Barnes, T.D.	82, 90, 92	Fisher, S.N.	99
Barth, M.	120	Flannery, E.H.	122
Bavinck, J.H.	2,	Foakes-Jackson, F.J.	82
Beegle, D.M.	132	France, R.T.	10, 13, 15
Belkin, S.	103	Frankel, W.	119
Ben Arieh, Y.	115	Fretheim, T.	2
Berg, S.B.	47	Gager, J.	120, 122
Berkouwer, G.C.	174	Gilbert, M.	100, 118, 119
Betz, O.	12	Goldingay, J.	19, 21
Blass, J.	195	Goldschmidt, A.	99
Blauw, J.	2	Goodman, M.	54
Borg, M.J.	59	Gordon, R.P.	29
Brearley, M	119, 123	Gowan, D.E.	53
Bright, J.	23, 24, 25	Grayzel, S.	115
Bromiley, G.W.	160	Green, J.	19
Bruce, F.F.	14, 19, 210	Grossman, D.	173
Caird, G.B.	9, 60	Hafarhi, A.	106
Carey, G.	201	Hahn, F.	9, 15
Carmesund, U.	151	Hanson, J.S.	54
Chadwick, H.	84	Hanson, P.D.	46
Chapman, C.	19, 39	Hanson, R.P.C.	92
Chesnut, G.F.	81	Hasson, O.	127
Childs, B.S.	31, 36	Hawthorne, G.F.	12
Clements, R.E.	27, 30, 33	Hengel, M.	54
Clines, D.J.A.	45	Herzl, T.	117
Cohen, A.	103, 113	Heschel, A.	iii, 106
Comay, M.	165	Hitti, P.K.	126
Coote, R.B.	126	Hooker, M.	19
Cragg, K.	128	Horner, N.A.	185-6
Craigie, P.C.	32	Horsley, R.A.	54
Crombie, K.	108	Hultgren, A.J.	16
Cross, F.M.	30	Hunt, E.D.	88
Cruise O'Brien, C.	119	Ice, T.	153
Cullman, O.	209	Jeremias, J.	9
Davis, M.	108	Johnson, P.	115
Davis, W.D.	137, 154	Join-Lambert, M.	99
Day, J.	28	Kamleh, T.	127
De Bethune, C.	106	Kirk, J.A.	19
Drake, H.A.	84	Knibb, M.A.	53

Kvarme, O.C.M.	19	Ruether, R.R. & H.J.	166, 171
Laham, L.	192, 200	Runciman, S.	100
Lambert, L.	107	Sanders, E.P.	8, 9, 11, 15, 56
Laqueur, W.	114, 117	Schechter, S.	104
Lee, S.	83	Schwartz, D.R.	68
Levine, L.I.	82, 89	Scott, J.M.	54
Lindsay, H.	153	Shaid, I.	128
Littell, F.	120	Sharif, R.	108, 109, 111
Malachy, Y.	108	Shepherd, N.	108
Mansfield, P.	99, 119	Sigal, P.	104
McConville, J.G.	2, 4, 6, 46	Silver, A.H.	103
Meyer, B.F.	8, 9, 10, 57	Telfer, W.	81
Mosley, L.	112	Theissen, G.	8
Motyer, S.	17	Thompson, W.M.	112
Moule, C.F.D.	12	Torrance, D.W.	19
Mowinckel, S.	32	Trachtenberg, J.	122
Munck, J.	16	Trimingham, J.S.	128, 130
Neill, S.C.	56	Tsafrir, Y.	88
Nicholson, E.W.	27, 28	Tuchman, B.	108
Noth, M.	45	Van Buren, P.	113, 120
Ollenburger, B.C.	4	Von Rad, G.	1, 27, 36, 47
Ord, D.R.	126	Walker, J.B.	160
Parkes, J.	113, 120	Walker, P.W.L.	82, 84-90, 139, 208
Pawlikowski, J.	120	Waltke, B.K.	19
Payne, D.	23	Weinfield, M.	30
Peters, J.	156	Weiser, A.	32
Plöger, O.	46	Wenham, G.J.	30
Poliakov, L.	122	Werblowsky, R.J.Z.	102
Pragai, M.J.	108, 111	Westermann, C.	36
Price, R.	153	Wilkinson, J.	81, 84, 208
Prince, D.	39	Williams, G.H.	91
Prior, M.	188	Williamson, H.G.M.	44, 45
Pritchard, J.B.	24	Wilson, G.H.	32
Prittie, T.	119	Wilson, M.R.	19
Richards, K.H.	63	Wiseman, D.J.	24
Riches, R.	19	Witherington III, B.	10, 11, 15, 17
Ridder, R.R.	2	Wright, C.	5, 7, 13
Rodinson, M.	119	Wright, N.T.	4, 12, 17-8, 53, 56, 61, 63, 66-7, 72
Rogerson, J.	22		
Rowland, C.	8, 9, 11	Yaari, A.	117
Rowley, H.H.	1	Ye'or, B.	100
Rubenstein, A.	105	Yoder, J.	137
Rubin, Z.	89	Zeitlin, I.M.	8
Rudin, A.J.	19	Zimmerli, W.	43

INDEX OF SCRIPTURE REFERENCES

Genesis		6:11-13	157	17:8	121
1-11	1	10	1	22:2	126
1:26-7	156	11:1-9	207	22:18	158
2:7	156	12	1	**Exodus**	
2:10-14	42	12:1-3	26	19-34	25
3:17-18	157	14:17-24	32	19:5-6	26, 102
3:23-4	157	14:18	126	19:18	26
4:11-12	157	15:18	158	24:3-8	26

25:21f	25, 40	2-3	23	2	27, 35
28:36	102	6:7f	40	2:6	26
34:6	103	8-12	29	22:27	2
Leviticus		8:7	29	24:1	133, 158
2:24-5	158	**2 Samuel**		37:11	11
18:19,24-5	157	6	25	46	27, 32
19:2	104	5:6-10	22	46:4	42
19:22	157	7	26, 41	46:7	27
19:29	157	7:1	22	47:8ff	2
20:22	133	7:5-7	27, 29	48	27
23:22	158	7:12-17	5, 26, 35	48:2	27
25:23	133, 158 216	20:1f	23	48:13	iii
26	157, 161	24	29	50	25
Numbers		**1 Kings**		50:2,3	26
6:27	121	2:2-4	26	51:18	121
12	27	3:16-28	145	68	25
20:12	157	8:27	30	72:17-20	2, 31
32-34	158	12:16	23	73	31
Deuteronomy		19:18	2	73-89	31
4-5	37	25	31	74	31
4:25-6	133	**2 Kings**		74:12	192
6:10-13	157	18:14f	24	76	27, 32
7:7	157	19:20	33	78:68ff	27
9:4-6	157	19:35-7	23	79	31
10:5	25	21:1-9	24, 30	84	27
12	30	22f	38	86:9	2
12:5	29	25	24	87	2
12:10	22, 26	**1 Chronicles**		87:2-4	30, 104
12:14	29	16:29	102	89	31
14:23	121	23:13	5	89:1-37	32
15:17	132	**2 Chronicles**		90	32
16:2,6,11	121	6:32-3	103	90:1	32
17:14-20	29	7:14	45	91	32
24:19-22	51	36	45	91:1,2,4,9	32
26:2	121	36:18-22	24, 44	93	32
28	121, 133	**Ezra**		95:3	133
30:3-4	15, 121	1	24, 31, 44, 45	96:5	133
31:9	25	1:1	24, 44	96-99	32
32:43	162	1:11	44	97	133
33:5	29	2:1	44	100	27
Joshua		3:10-13	45	101	31
8:29	64	4:1	44	102:13-22	2, 8, 104, 195
10:26f	64	6	24	103	31
15:63	22	9	45	107:3	15
18:1	25	**Nehemiah**		108-110	31,32
22	23	1	24	110:1f	26
23:15-16	133	1-6	24	118:22-23	196
Judges		9	45	118:28	124
1:21	22	9:36f	53	119	33
18:31	25	12:43	27	122	27
20	23	**Psalms**		122:3	180
1 Samuel		1	33	122:6	121, 212, 218
1:3	25			124	31
1:22	132			131	31
				132	26

Indices

132:7,13	36	40-55	34, 35, 36	60:9-62:12	124
132:13	26, 104	40-66	35	60:10-14	8
137:5-6	159	40:1	34	60:17-20	36
138-145	31	40:2	35, 36, 45	61	10
147:2	113	41	107	62:1,6f,11	35
Isaiah		41:27	35	63:16-19	36
1:10-17	149	42:6	2, 63, 158	64:10	36
1:26-7	85, 124	43	12, 107	64:13f	36
2:1-4	34, 36, 50	43-46	34	65:17	36
2:2	177	43:1f	35	65:18	85, 124
2:3	iv, 4, 66	43:5f	15	66:1	36
4:5f	33	43:6	113	66:10	124
5:16	154	43:15	35	66:13	35
6	33	43:16f	35	66:18-24	8, 36
6:9-13	34	43:18f	35	66:19ff	7
7	33,34	43:22-4	36	**Jeremiah**	
7:9b	34	44:3-4	134	2:7	133
7:11-13	161	44:5	2	4:31	37
8:18	33	44:26-8	35	6:2,23	37
9:6f	4	45	12	7:1-15	37, 154
10	2	45:20ff	7	7:4,5-7,12-15	iii, 37
10:12	33	45:22ff	2	7:12	30
10:24	159	46:1f	34	8:19	37
11:1-5	4	46:13	159	12:15	162
11:1-9	2	47:1-4	34	14:13	161
11:11	114	48:3-5	36	15:5	i
12	2	49	121	16	7
12:5f	33	49:3	36	16:18	133
13	61	49:5f	8, 16	16:19	2
13:10	62	49:6	2, 14	17:9-15	162
14:1	121	49:12	15	19	121
14:32	33	49:14	35	21:7	61
19:19-25	2	51-56	121	22	38
24	7	51:3	104	22:15	38
24:23	33	51:4f	4	22:30	38
25	2	51:5	160	23:1-6	4
26:9	7	51:17	35	23:7-8	135
27:6	114	52:1f	35	23:22	161
27:9	66	52:3	61	24	38
27:12-13	114	52:7-11	35, 61	25:ff	7
30:19	33	52:11f	62	25:12	24
31:4f,9	33, 38	52:12-53:12	36	25:12-14	38
34	7	53	10	26:1-6	37
34:4	62	54:10	121	29:1,4,16,20,31	44
35	7	55:1,3,6	35	29:10	24, 38, 44
35:8	102	56-66	34, 36	30-33	3, 4, 7, 38-9, 121
37	34	56:1-8	8	31	66, 197
37:33-38	33	56:7	63	31:31-4	38
37:21-39:8	33	57:1	36	31:33	4, 40
38f	34	58	36	31:34	66
38:1	34	58:6f	36	31:35-7	121
38:2-6	34	59:15-20	76	31:38-40	39
39	34	59:20f	35, 66	32:6-15	39
39:5-7	34	60-62	36	32:36-41	39
40	46	60:1	85		

32:39-41	4, 40	48:35	42, 50	16:14	59
32:42-4	157	**Daniel**		19:28	11
33:9	39	1:1-7	44	21:5	11
33:12-26	39	2	61	21:43	15
33:17f	6	7	10, 61-2	22:1-4	15
33:23-6	157	7:13	14, 62	27:53	86
35:19	6	9	46	**Mark**	
37:11-15	38	**Hosea**		1:5	86
41	46	1:10	15	3:7-8	130
50-1	61	2:23	15	3:33,35	58
50:4f	4	6:1-2	12	8:31	12
51:6,45	62	10:8	63	11:17	15, 62, 76
51:26	62	**Joel**		11:23	62
51:46	62	2	197	12:10-11	196
52	24	2:28	209	13	60
Ezekiel		3	7	13:2	62
1:1	44	3:17	102	13:7f	62
3:11,15	44	**Amos**		13:10	115
6:2	41	9	7	13:14-17	62
8-11	40	9:11f	16	13:24	62
10:18	40	9:12	2	13:26	62
11:2	40	**Habakkuk**		13:27	15, 62
11:16	40	2:14	177	14:24	11
11:16-21	43	**Zephaniah**		15:38	137
11:19f	41	3:9ff	7	**Luke**	
17:22-4	41	**Micah**		1:16f	13
20:32	41	2:1-2	153	1:32f	13
20:40	41	2-3	7	1:68ff	13
20:41b,42	41	4	7	2:29-32	13
34:1-24	4	4:1-4	34	2:36-38	13
34:14	41	4:2f	66	3:8	2
34:23f	41, 43	**Haggai**		4:16-21	10
36	4, 158, 197	2:6ff	2, 18	4:25-7	15
36:22-38	49	**Zechariah**		12:32	11
36:24,33-38	41	1-8	46	13	59
36:40-48	49	2:6	15, 62	13:34-5	59
37:15ff	4	2:10-13	2	13-21	60
37:22-26	41	2:11	2	14:18	180
38f	42, 43	8:20-23	2	16:17	121
38:8	42	9-13	10	17:21	138
39:2,4	41	9:9ff	8, 11	17:37	60
39:17-20	42	14:16ff	7	18:31-33	12
39:25-39	4	**Malachi**		19:9	58
39:28a	42	1:11	2	19:41-4	138, 201, 219
40-48	42, 43, 50	**Matthew**		21	59
41-48	41	1:21	13	21:23f	61
43:1-5	4, 40	5:5	11	21:24	197
43:7-9	42	5:17-20	121, 159, 190	23:27-31	63
44:3	43	8:11f	15	23:31	63
47	50	8:12	15	24	11
47:1-12	4, 42	10:6	16	**John**	
47:15-20	42	12:43-5	60	1:14	192
47:21-3	135			2:19	137
48:9	42			3:16	138
48:8-22	42			4:21	190

Indices

8:33-44	3	8:1-4	19	3	138
14:6	200	8:9	70	3:4-6	8,
13:34	198	8:19-21	157	3:6	8, 198
14:27	199	9-11	3, 17, 73-4	3:15	ii
17:21,23	198	9:2	201	6:12	193

Acts

1	13	9:6-10:21	3, 73	**Philippians**	
1:1-8	12	9:6ff	17, 66	2:6-8	182
1:7	163	9:24f	15	3	74
1:6-8	68, 190, 205, 207, 209, 216	9:30	66	3:20	69
		10	75	**Colossians**	
1:8	68	10:1	219	2:15	194
1:11	209	10:2	201	3:1-2	92
1-4	203, 207, 209	10:13	66	**1 Thessalonians**	
1:14	207	11	75	2:16	64
1:22	203	11:15	159	**2 Thessalonians**	
2:5	205	11:25-8	17, 65	2:1-2	64
2:26-21	14	11:26	65, 197	**1 Timothy**	
2:17	209	11:26b-27	66	2:4	201
2:22	203	11:27b	67	4:1	209
2:23	204	11:28-9	159	**2 Timothy**	
2:24	203	11:33-6	67, 219	2:13	164
2:29	203	**1 Corinthians**		3:1	209
2:29-36	14	2:8	194	**1 Peter**	
2:36	204-5	3:16	70, 137	1:4	19
2:37	203	6:19	70	2:4	204-5
2:38	205	9:22	212	**Hebrews**	
2:44	207	12:13	188	3:12-4:11	18
3:1	72	15:4	12	4:14	18
3:18-26	14	**2 Corinthians**		6:13-20	18
3:21	209	1:20	73	7	32
4:10-12	204-5	3	69, 74	8:1	18
4:29	212	5:19	192	8:5	18
5:29-32	14	**Galatians**		8:13	70
7:56	14	2:19-21	68, 74	10:19	18
11:15-18	16	3	17, 67	10:21	18
13:32ff	14	3:10	54	11:16	70
13:47	14	3:10-14	68	12	73
15	16	3:26-9	138	12:18	70
15:1-35	207	3:28	188	12:22	18, 69-70, 92, 190
15:12-18	16	4	17, 66, 69		
16:3	121	4:16	68	12:26-8	18, 71
21:26	121	4:21-31	17	13:10	18, 70
28:20, 23, 28-31	14	4:25ff	69	13:12-14	19, 70
		4:25-6	68	**Revelation**	
Romans		4:26	190	3:12	190
1-4	74	4:26-7	92	21:2	69, 190
2:28	3, 17	4:29	69		
3:1-3	121	6:16	66		
3:26	162	**Ephesians**			
4	66, 70	1:10	184, 200		
4:5	162	2	17		
4:13	67	2:11-22	8		
5-8	67	2:14-16	198		
6:5	206	2:19	123		
8	72				